See The Theatre of Revolt
(Brustein) pp 87–134

[Strindberg at F. Th]

31. 1. 27   The Stronger   Practice
12. 6. 27   Miss Julie   T.G.
19. 11. 28   The Spook Sonata (Ox. P)
29. 4. 29   Intoxination   Crossley
25. 10. 31   Gustav Vasa   T.G.

(2000)

Strindberg and the Five Senses

Strindberg and the Five Senses

Studies in <u>Strindberg's Chamber Plays</u>

$\left(2000 \right)$

$\boxed{230}$

HANS-GÖRAN EKMAN

Dr Ekman considers Strindberg's four *Chamber Plays* of 1907: *Storm*, *The Burned House*, *The Ghost Sonata* and *The Pelican*, the works which have gained most interest internationally. For the first time, these works are stud ied in relation to Strindberg's lifelong obsession with the five senses, and t fact that impressions from a stage can only be seen and heard. This brough Strindberg to disregard the senses in favour of wisdom and an inner vision; and it is for this position that the *Chamber Plays* were written.

AUTHOR: Dr Ekman is Assistant Professor of Literature at Uppsala Universit He is a member of the Editorial Board of Strindberg's *Collected Works* and *Strindberg's Letters*, and is a former Vice President of the Strindberg Societ

THE ATHLONE PRESS
LONDON AND NEW BRUNSWICK, NJ

First published in 2000 by
THE ATHLONE PRESS
1 Park Drive, London NW11 7SG
and New Brunswick, New Jersey

British Library Cataloguing in Publication Data
*A catalogue record for this book is available
from the British Library*

ISBN 0 485 11552 2 HB

Library of Congress Cataloging-in-Publication Data
Ekman, Hans-Göran, 1943–
Strindberg and the five senses: studies in Strindberg's chamber plays/
Hans-Göran Ekman.
    p. cm.
Includes bibliographical references and index.
ISBN 0–485–11552–2 (alk. paper)
    1. Strindberg, August, 1849–1912—Criticism and interpretation. 2.
Strindberg, August, 1849–1912. Spèksonaten. 3. Senses and sensation in
literature. I. Title.

PT9817.S45 E46 2000
839.72′6—dc21

                                                                00–057621

Distributed in The United States, Canada and South America by
Transaction Publishers
390 Campus Drive
Somerset, New Jersey 08873

Typeset by RefineCatch Limited, Bungay, Suffolk
Printed in Great Britain by
Cambridge University Press

Contents

List of Illustrations

Acknowledgements

For permission to reproduce photographs, drawings and paintings, I would like to thank the following: Photograph Beata Bergström, Kungliga biblioteket, Stockholm, Photograph Lasse Lindkvist, Musée national de Céramique, Sèvres, Musée national de Moyen Age – Thermes et hôtel de Cluny, Paris, Nationalmuseum, Stockholm, Stockholms Stadsmuseum, Strindbergsmuseet Blå Tornet, Stockholm.

Preface

The so-called chamber plays of August Strindberg (1849–1912), of which *The Ghost Sonata* is the most challenging example, belong to those works by Strindberg that have reached beyond the borders of his native country and played an important role in the development of modern international drama. A great deal has been written about these plays but until now scholars have neglected to see them as the dramatic sequence they actually constitute. The fact that most scholarly discussions of Strindberg's chamber plays still consists of isolated initiatives has stimulated me to make an attempt at a more cohesive analysis.

A long overture precedes the rise of the curtain for the first chamber play, *Storm*, on page 64, but it seemed to me necessary to provide such a background in order to set Strindberg's ideas about the deceptiveness of the senses – what he calls the world of illusions – in relief.

After the opening chapter, the chamber plays are dealt with in chronological order, applying a similar analytical model to all of them. Even though I consider the dramas to be a cohesive unit, I have sought to present them in such a way that each analysis might be read separately.

In my view, an analysis of the dialogue affords only a partial view of Strindberg's dramas; more than most playwrights he creates a physical drama, which means that his stage directions should be read as carefully as the dialogue. In my earlier work *Klädernas magi* (*Strindberg and the Magic of Clothes*, 1991) I stressed the importance of costume in the plays. In the present volume I deal with different kinds of sensory impression, both those that affect the characters on stage and those that reach beyond the proscenium to the audience. These sensory impressions are often exposed to disturbances of various kinds and are especially interesting precisely for that reason.

This book, which was first published in Sweden in 1997, is now presented to an English readership thanks to a generous grant from

The Swedish Council for Research in the Humanities and Social Sciences (HSFR). I wish to thank Mikael Steene warmly for having assumed the difficult task of translating my text into English. I also want to thank Michael Robinson for reading and commenting on the manuscript before publication. Margareta Cherry has helped me with the correspondence and Sten-Ove Bergwall with the disks.

A note on Strindberg's own text is appropriate. In order to make my presentation as clear as possible, it has been necessary to make new translations of all quotations from Strindberg's texts. To use existing translations when available would have resulted in a chorus of voices, which it was important to avoid.

I would mention, however, that the chamber plays and certain other Strindberg texts referred to in this volume do exist in excellent modern translations. Eivor Martinus has published *The Chamber Plays* (Absolute Classics, 1991); Inga-Stina Ewbank has translated *Three Chamber Plays* (Alumnus, 1997); and Michael Robinson's *Miss Julie and Other Plays* (Oxford University Press, 1998) includes a translation of *The Ghost Sonata*. It should also be mentioned that many of Strindberg's essays, among them the important 'Deranged Sensations', are included in Robinson's English edition of Strindberg's *Selected Essays* (Cambridge, 1996).

The glossaries included in the national Swedish edition of Strindberg's Collected Works have also been useful as guidelines in this translation.

Page references in parenthesis in the text refer to Strindberg's Swedish text in the critical edition of his *Samlade Verk* (SV) which commenced publication in 1981 with Lars Dahlbäck as general editor. In isolated cases I have had to use the older edition of Strindberg's *Samlade Skrifter* (SS), 1912–19, edited by John Landquist.

References to Strindberg's Letters are identified only by date. The Swedish originals are to be found in the twenty volumes of *August Strindbergs Brev*, which began publication in 1948, edited by Torsten Eklund. In 1989 the editorship was taken over by Björn Meidal.

Hans-Göran Ekman
Uppsala

Introduction

It is well known that during his so-called Inferno crisis in Paris during the 1890s Strindberg was interested in Delacroix's painting *Jacob luttant avec l'ange* (Jacob Wrestling with the Angel) in the church of Saint-Sulpice in the Latin Quarter. In the section of his autobiographical fiction *Legends* which takes its name from the painting, Strindberg describes the strength he derives from it (SS 28:329). In the same text he also describes a visit to the church of Saint-Germain l'Auxerrois on the Right Bank of the Seine where he becomes attached to a picture of a smiling angel above a font of holy water where he claims to have received a vision of a very much milder kind of religious feeling than that depicted in the Delacroix painting.

It is unclear whether Strindberg ever visited the Musée de Cluny next to the Sorbonne in the area between these two churches. Since the early 1880s the museum's greatest attraction had been six medieval tapestries called *La Dame à la licorne* (The Lady and the Unicorn) which provide allegorical representations of the five senses and – in the last tapestry – the overcoming of the senses.[1]

If Strindberg saw *Jacob luttant avec l'ange* as an illustration of his own present crisis, and the smiling angel as a hint of a milder religion, a latter-day observer cannot help but conclude that the tapestries *La Dame à la licorne* might actually be said to anticipate the dénouement of this crisis. A not inconsiderable aspect of Strindberg's conversion has to do with a turning away from a sensuous affirmation of life to a certain denial of the world of the senses. Some years into the new century he would label the world experienced only with the senses 'the world of illusions' (*villornas värld*). A desire to overcome such a material and deceptive world becomes a central feature in his production during the new century. Such a perspective certainly leaves its mark on the chamber plays he wrote in 1907.

In this context it is worth mentioning yet another work of art in the Paris area which illustrates the same theme: the porcelain vase

La coupe des sens (The Vessel of the Senses), decorated by Evariste Fragonard, in the Musée National de la Céramique at Sèvres, which was opened in 1823. This vase, which is the most important item in the museum's collection, illustrates the five senses from different aspects in a number of juxtaposed panels. Thus, pictures representing both noise and silence illustrate hearing; in the same manner, scent and foul smells are depicted side by side. Sight is illustrated through sensations of both light and colour. Touch and taste are limited to a single aspect. But in addition to these nine panels, a tenth one displays the most interesting illustration, which the artist has entitled 'Les illusions des sens'.[2]

There is no evidence that Strindberg showed an interest in either *La Dame à la licorne* or *La coupe des sens*, but it deserves mentioning that these famous pieces of art existed in his surroundings, and it is a fact that in *The Dance of Death* (1900) he subsequently includes the stage directions for a silent scene in which the protagonist systematically takes his leave of one sense after the other.

On other occasions, too, it came naturally to Strindberg to think in terms of the 'five senses'. Thus, in the essay 'Woman's Inferiority to Man' (1890), he describes how, in his opinion, the nature and quality of Woman's five senses are inferior to Man's,[3] and in an entry in his *Occult Diary* for 31 October 1898, he reports having come upon a playing card – 'the five of spades' – which he immediately associates with 'death' on account of its colour and through the number 'five' with the five senses, thus combining to represent the death of the senses.[4] Moreover, as late as 3 October 1911, in a letter to the writer and diplomat Birger Mörner, Strindberg offered a surprisingly powerful definition of realism: 'there is form also, colour and shading, perceived and understood by the "healthy five" (realism!)'.

Strindberg's path to the concept of 'the world of illusions' is not a straight one, but it serves to trace his passage from his naturalist period through the snags and snares of the Inferno crisis to those elements of a personally perceived symbolism and the proto-expressionism apparent in the dramas he wrote during the first decade of this century A moral-religious wrestling with feelings of guilt certainly comprise the core of Strindberg's crisis, but these feelings are connected with what is most concrete to him: his tormented senses.

★

The purpose of this study is to describe the development of this 'philosophy' or cluster of ideas which Strindberg himself calls 'the world of illusions', and thus to contribute to the interpretation of the four chamber plays in particular.

The tenor of Strindberg's ideas is hardly unambiguous. The first time the concept is mentioned in any kind of detail is in the novel *Black Banners* (*Svarta fanor*) (manuscript 1904, published 1907).[5] When Max declares that the age in which we are living is 'the world of illusions' (SV 57:139), he is referring to Plato, who he takes to argue that our ideas regarding matter are real, but 'matter itself is only schematic shadow pictures, subjective conceptions of the real pictures' (139). Similarly, he also refers to Schopenhauer on similar grounds: 'Schopenhauer has said it best: that matter lacks reality.'

This philosophical reasoning is combined naturally in the novel with a commentary on morality. Thus, attached to the idea of 'the world of illusions' is the notion that people consciously cheat each other, and that life is thus a tangled web of lies: 'Lies in teaching and life, lies in relationships, in friendship and love, in law, administration, management, politics and religion' (139). Strindberg likewise designates such things as 'illusions'. Besides these 'illusions' from the philosophical and moral spheres, Strindberg also includes in the idea of 'the world of illusions' the sensory notion, motivated physiologically rather than philosophically, of the human senses as inadequate or misleading instruments.

In reality it becomes difficult to uphold this attempt to differen tiate between different types of 'illusions'. Thus, in Strindberg's world people often cheat each other not solely by lying but also by manipulating each other's senses. This latter idea I perceive as very specific to Strindberg. It is expressed above all in the world of the chamber plays, but it also problematizes, to a varying degree, his own activities as a dramatist. As such he risks becoming precisely someone who 'alters the vision' of an audience. 'To think an audience allows its vision to be altered', he writes, in a letter to Harriet Bosse on 14 April 1906, only a few months before he returns to writing for the theatre with his chamber plays.

★

With the chamber plays Strindberg captures the quintessence of his experiences from the Inferno crisis during the 1890s and the

following years. This is done in a compressed form – the chamber
play format – using partially new and expanded dramaturgical tools.
The plays were written during the course of only half a year – from
January to June 1907 – and despite certain formal differences
between them, they are thematically very tightly interlinked. One
of my intentions here is to show how much of a thematic pattern
is already established in *Storm* and then undergoes what I call
a 'demonization', i.e. attains a progressively more destructive
character in the subsequent chamber plays.

*

The development towards what will become Strindberg's dramaturgy in the chamber plays begins with the author's departure from
a naturalist *Weltanschauung*. I have found it necessary to describe this
development, although only in general terms. In doing so, I employ
a variety of sources, including both literary and scientific texts as
well as letters and diaries.

The summer of 1888 offers a natural starting point. This is when
a process begins that is characterized by reflections on Strindberg's
part as to in which domain a person's sensibility and imagination
may best be realized. He first exemplifies this in the long short story
The Romantic Sexton on Rånö and then in the novel *By the Open Sea*.
The main character in the former is richly endowed with imagination – in which he takes great joy – whereas the protagonist of the
second work strives to discipline his senses through scientific activity, with tragic consequences. In an almost prophetic manner
Strindberg has anticipated his own coming crisis through the predicament of his central character, the Inspector of Fisheries, Axel
Borg. However, Strindberg does not succumb like Axel Borg, but
recovers by structuring a new universe that is partially concealed
from mankind and out of reach of our senses.[6] The limitations
of the senses are no longer identified with Strindberg's personal
shortcomings but are inherent in earthly life itself.

After this survey, which takes the form of a general analysis using
a certain established perspective, I move on to discuss some of the
post-Inferno dramas and, in particular, the chamber plays against
the background of the emerging philosophy of the world of
illusions, as this becomes increasingly entrenched.

I read these plays as dramatic texts intended to be transposed to the stage. It is only in performance that the essential meaning of these texts is realized. Therefore it is necessary, in the course of any analysis, to attempt to realize the author's intentions on the inner stage, which is the reader's – something that may at times be easier than in a real theatre with its built-in, tangible sluggishness.[7]

In my view, 'the five senses' model is also a useful instrument for the analysis of Strindberg's dramatic texts. Strindberg aims at an obviously *physical* theatre. To a great extent, his drama builds upon the way in which the protagonists react to the external world with all of their senses; therefore his dramas are more physical than intellectual. The following analyses often focus on how the senses function in the *dramatis personae*. A considerable amount of his dialogue in fact consists by the speakers commenting upon precisely such matters.

What has been said up until now concerns the so-called 'internal communications system', i.e. the relationship between the *dramatis personae* on stage.[8] However, a drama does not come alive until it also becomes a part of an 'external communications system', in other words, reaches an audience. Strindberg always writes with an audience in mind, but here something interesting occurs, especially where the chamber plays are concerned. Strindberg does not seem to consider the limitations of this external communications system when his plays incorporate important elements of taste and smell. The theatre lacks the necessary 'channels' to convey such sensory sensations directly. As Manfred Pfister remarks, in a book, *Das Drama* (1977), from which I sometimes borrow terminology and definitions: 'Dramatic texts have the potential to activate all channels of the human senses. Over the centuries, of course, dramatic productions have been restricted almost exclusively to texts employing acoustic and visual codes alone. Exceptions to this are more recent developments such as happenings from ritualist theatre, which also experiment with haptic (physical contact between actors and audience), olfactory and even gustatory effects.'[9]

The situation can be illustrated with a shortened version of Pfister's diagram outlining the channels of communication between stage and audience:[10]

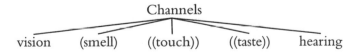

Channels

vision (smell) ((touch)) ((taste)) hearing

In this communication model, 'smell' is placed within parenthesis and 'touch' and 'taste' between double parenthesis since, according to Pfister, a drama communicates almost entirely via vision and hearing.[11]

It is a truism that Strindberg himself experienced his surroundings intensely on the private level, and with all his senses. To a large degree this was also the case when the chamber plays were written, as his diary makes plain. His Inferno period ten years previously had been a torture to these same senses, and, of course, he consequently includes such experiences in his texts. Between the dramatist himself and reality there are five channels, but when the theatre text becomes a performance to be conveyed to an audience, only two channels are available. Sensations of smell, taste and touch must be re-coded to words, mime and gesture, whereby the channels of vision and hearing risk becoming overloaded. This in turn means that certain elements in the plays may be difficult to understand.

1
The World of the Senses

I know at heart every vagary of my senses
Strindberg, 'Sensations détraquées'

Sensuous joy

It is not difficult to find early prose works by Strindberg that convey
a sense of pleasure at sensuous reality and offer precise descriptions
of different types of sensory experience. In the article 'How I found
Sehlstedt' which he contributed to the Stockholm daily *Dagens
Nyheter* on 2 July 1874, Strindberg describes an August morning at
Dalarö on the Baltic coast with marked sensuous concreteness. The
sun is working its way 'out of a bundle of broken van Dyck-brown
clouds' (SV 2:42), the customs officials are snoring, a tub of butter
stands forgotten in the sunshine, the innkeeper inspects his cucum-
bers and takes a nip at the breakfast table, the tar begins to smell in
the ship joints. The account appeals to several senses at one and the
same time, and the sum total of these impressions is a saturated
description of how sensual it can be to wake up on a summer
morning in the Stockholm archipelago.

The opening of *The Red Room*, written five years later, is also
brimming with sensuous observations – and not just of how the
sunbeams illuminate the windows of the Customs House or the
Lidingö woods, for the scene is also enriched by descriptions of
scents and sounds. Here Strindberg depicts the coming of spring:
the maid performs the ritual act of tearing off the winter padding
from the interior windows and lets out the smells of winter: 'a
dreadful odour of frying fat, beer spill, spruce twigs and sawdust
rushed out and was carried far away by the wind' (SV 6:8). Below
the Mosebacke Terrace the newly awakened city 'rumbles', steam
winches 'spin', iron rods 'rattle', the lock keeper's horns 'whistle',
the seagulls 'screech', and signals and rifle shots are heard from
Skeppsholmen and Södermalmstorg. And at seven o'clock the
sound of at least four of Stockholm's church bells is to be heard.
The scene comes alive not just through vividly rendered visual

impressions but also through descriptions of penetrating sensations of sound, scent and light.

The narrator in the autobiographical novel *A Madman's Defence* (1887) finds himself in the same vicinity, and here too the author underscores how the opening of a window can change the living conditions of those residing in the house.[1] In Strindberg's world people live cooped up and shut off from healthy sensory impressions in the winter, a season when they spend their time interpreting sounds from other apartments and are often tormented by smells and flavours in a claustrophobic atmosphere. But in *A Madman's Defence* it is still summer:

> Everything was there, side by side, laid out for inspection against the navy blue canvas of a Nordic sky. The noise of wagons, of whistles, clocks and winches; and the smell of machine oil, newly salted herring, leather and colonial goods were blended with the scent of lilacs, and refreshed by the eastern breeze that comes in from the sea and has been cooled off on its way by the pack ice in the Baltic.
>
> I had turned my back on my books and stuck my head out of the window to bathe with my five senses when the guard filed past, playing the march from *Faust*.[2]

This depiction, too, at the start of a novel concerned with a love affair, is heightened by the author's method of combining different sensory impressions. The view from the palace window is described in concrete detail, at the same time as the reader receives an image of the narrator as a person who would rather 'bathe' with his senses than read books.

All these passages describe people who enjoy their senses in an uncomplicated way. Later on in Strindberg's writings, the world of senses and sensations becomes more complex.

Miss Julie *and 'The Secrets of the Flowers'*

In the theatre it is more difficult to communicate certain types of sensory impressions. But this did not keep Strindberg from endowing the servant Jean, in the naturalistic drama *Miss Julie*, with a fine sense of smell and a well-developed taste, as well as a hypersensitivity to his physical surroundings. This is demonstrated as early as the first scene when Jean smells the food (SV 27:120) that Kristin is cooking, checks whether the plate is warm enough and reacts with pain when Kristin pulls his hair. He also tastes the wine and warms the glass with his hands when he finds it too cool. The next moment he reacts with disdain at the foul-smelling concoction that is being prepared to help Julie's pure-bred bitch abort the pup she has conceived with the gatekeeper's mutt. Jean has barely tasted the wine before he shows off by identifying Miss Julie's perfume.

The opening of *Miss Julie* is rich in references to the senses. They may be interpreted either as an indication that Jean really possesses these senses or else that he has adopted certain manners in order to play the part of an aristocrat. In the preface which was, of course, written after the play, Strindberg seems to maintain that Jean has taught himself to be a 'gentleman', though not without having an innate gift for the role: 'He has had an easy time learning, finely developed senses (smell, taste, vision) and a sense of beauty' (107). However, there may be another side to the possession of such well-developed senses, for Jean is oversensitive to the *sight* of the count's gloves and at the *sound* of the bell that serves as an extension of the Count in his room upstairs: 'I only need to see his gloves lying on a chair to feel small – I only need to hear the bell up there to rear like a frightened horse' (150).

In the summer and autumn of 1888 Strindberg also became interested in the functioning of the senses on a pseudo-scientific level. Two months after completing *Miss Julie* he wrote the essay 'The Secrets of the Flowers'. The essay purported to discuss the colours of various flowers. However it evolved – via musings on the relationship between colour and taste – into a theory on the nature of the senses. Strindberg advances a hypothesis that all senses are in reality tactile senses. Thereby he develops a mechanical model that may seem appropriate to a naturalist:[3]

> Now, if we were to advance the hypothesis that the senses are only tactile senses . . . that we apprehend the density of solid objects, etc. with our sense of touch; the consistency of solid and liquid bodies with our taste; of bodies of steam and gas objects with our smell; movements of the air with our hearing, and movements of ether with our sight, then we have made the senses similar in nature and only quantitatively separate (SV 29:217).

For the time being 'sensibility' for Strindberg is something purely physical and the following section from 'The Secrets of the Flowers' may be read as a commentary on Jean's performance as a connoisseur of wine:

> The fine wine taster who thinks he can taste the quality of a wine is in part the victim of a delusion. What he calls the bouquet touches only his sense of smell, but the level of tannic acid contracts the tongue's taste buds and the tongue acts merely as a sensory organ. It is not unlikely that if driven to it, a wine taster would be able to train his fingertips to such a high degree of sensitivity that they would be able to discern bitterness, saltiness and tartness. For we know how the magician, by filing his fingertips on pumice and then grating away the skin with potassium may develop such a sensitivity that he *feels* with his fingers which card he has beneath his hands.

This is Strindberg's physiological stance on the senses in the summer of 1888. In the future he himself would subject it to debate.

By the Open Sea

A change has already taken place in the novel *By the Open Sea*, of which the first two chapters were completed in May 1889 and novel as a whole in June 1890. Strindberg describes the senses of his main character, Axel Borg, as quite refined and part of a constitutional make-up:

> He even heard by the tempo of the squalls when danger was near, he felt in his right eardrum when the wind pressed harder and threatened to drive the water higher, it was as if he had used his delicate senses to improvise nautical and meteorological instruments, to which wires were openly connected from the large battery of his brain (SV 31:12).

Axel Borg's aspiration is not – as in Jean's case in *Miss Julie* or in the example of the magician in 'The Secrets of the Flowers' – to enrich his own senses but rather, to shield them from too strong impressions, in part, at least, out of a sense of self-preservation: 'But when he was travelling and forced by necessity, he could so to speak shut down all the wires connecting his sensory tools with his perception and harden himself against every unpleasant sensation' (45). These latter sensations are described as so fine that Borg could even sense someone's smell on an old newspaper. He could also discipline his sense of taste: 'Endowed with an overly sensitive sense of taste, he had, through disciplined practice, acquired the ability to repress unpleasant sensations. Therefore he swallowed the drink without blinking' (23).

Thus, Borg hardly delights in his senses; rather they threaten his peace of mind. Incoming impressions are sorted or censored. After a poetic description of the 'music' of a long-tailed duck comes the sober reflection:

> The observer did not enjoy the great spectacle with the obscure and hence disquieting sensations of a poet's dreamy imagination; rather it was with the calm gaze of a scientist, an awakened thinker that he surveyed the connections in this seeming disorder (34).

This sober approach is repeated in another section of the novel where the roar of the sea is first described as a 'symphony of sound', after which Borg delivers an analysis of the origin of the individual sounds. When it is pointed out to him that this scientific description might destroy his experience of nature, he replies:

> That is to make nature intimate! I derive peace of mind from knowing that, and I am thus liberated from the poet's half-hidden fear of the unknown, which is nothing more than memories from the poetic age of the savage when one sought explanations but was unable to find them in a hurry and therefore, out of need, created fables of mermaids and giants (95).

Thus Borg's struggle to subsume everything under his intellect can be seen as an act of exorcism by a hypersensitive and chaotic person who tries to keep chaos and the madness he fears at bay. Strindberg had previously treated a similar problem in the drama *The Father* (1887), where scientific research acts as the Captain's escape into an orderly world.

In order to describe Borg's hypersensitivity, his exceptional associative ability and his increasing sense of confusion, Strindberg uses a device that is unusual for him: synesthesia. As Karl Åke Kärnell has noted, Strindberg had already shown an interest in the subject in 'The Secrets of the Flowers' when he tells of a painter he had met in Germany, who was considered insane because 'his senses of sight and hearing amused themselves by changing roles with each other, so that the man who was a musician wanted to translate into colour what he played' (SV 29:218).[4]

Pointing out that in general synesthesia does not play a major part in Strindberg's prose, Kärnell locates the reasons for this in the author's passion for fact and exactness:

> Sensory analogies have a synthesising function rather than an analytical one; they are suggestive rather than directly graphic and often serve as linguistic expressions for a lyrical absorption in tones or colour . . . . Strindberg's attitude to the shifting abundance of impressions of colour and sound in his surroundings is the direct opposite: he has the naturalist's ambition to cultivate his sensory impressions and to analyse them as closely as possible.[5]

Kärnell's remarks are striking. However, one might add that it is strange that the use of sensory analogies is so rare in Strindberg, since he possessed a considerable talent for thinking by analogy, something which was deep-seated in him and soon became his dominant method in all his forays into science, whether chemistry, linguistics or some other subject. But apparently synesthetic phenomena simply did not appear in a spontaneous and natural way to him, as they do to certain individuals. Another explanation for their rarity in Strindberg's writing may have been his fear of synthesthesia because it tends to dissolve an established and disciplined order between the five senses.[6]

Kärnell concludes, however, that in *By the Open Sea* Strindberg uses sensory analogies, which are otherwise rare in his writing.[7] As Kärnell also points out, one reason for this might be Strindberg's concern to depict Borg as over-refined, like Huysmans's Des Esseintes in *A rebours*. However, there is a good deal of evidence that Strindberg eventually came to associate synesthetic arrangements with madness. One illustration of this might be a carefully arranged sensory analogy in *By the Open Sea* which appears to be constructed in order to emphasize the refinement of the perceiver's senses; yet madness is not far away. The sight some women and their gestures are translated into music and take hold of Borg's entire being:

> The same modulations that a series of harmonious tones created on the eardrum and transplanted to the nervous system, the same mild vibrations were now created by the eye and rang through the white strings that stretched from the shell of his cranium

through the resonating wall of his chest, thus transplanting the vibrations through the whole foundation of his soul (69).[8]

Like his treatment of other sensory impressions in the novel the originality of Strindberg's attitude towards synesthesic phenomena often lies not in his description of objects but rather in his accounts of the way the different senses function. A naturalist of Zola's type describes a corner of reality seen through a temperament. Strindberg's foremost interest seems to be neither reality nor temperament but the functioning of the senses at the very moment of perception.

The sense that is studied in greatest detail in the novel is sight. In a frequently quoted passage Borg conjures up an Italian landscape with a marble villa and stone pines in the middle of the barren Swedish archipelago. The intention is firstly to give the superstitious inhabitants a sensation only then to unmask this as a simple optical illusion, constructed by someone with superior knowledge in optics and meteorology. However, the experiment runs amok; through an optical hoax a large moon appears in the middle of the day, and everything begins to resemble a floating graveyard. This is the most elaborate example in Strindberg's prose of an 'illusion'.

The inhabitants of the archipelago prefer illusion to the truth – this is the moral of the episode – and it is significant that the words 'optical vision' are used at different times as synonyms for 'misunderstandings'. Characteristically for Strindberg, an important theme 'infects' the language. Thus Borg's demonstration of the illusion infects a reference to John Stuart Mill's view of women as based on 'an illusion, *second sight*' (in English in the original, 133). Another example talks of Borg as 'the victim of such an optical illusion that his listeners understood what he said. He had spoken to a wall and taken his echo for the voice of the other!' (172). For once, the meaning in a Strindberg text is unclear for linguistic reasons, perhaps because Strindberg is confusing the senses and their visual associations. What the sentence is probably meant to imply is that Borg has falsely imagined that his listeners have understood what he said. To speak of an 'optical illusion' in such a context is far-fetched, and the context does not become any clearer when the next sentence refers to the more adequate sense of hearing. The linguistically clumsy finish to the paragraph can perhaps be explained with the assumption that the author intended to internalize these perceptions in Borg, who is on the verge of a breakdown. But the fact remains that they are expressed by an omniscient author who seems to have placed himself, to a large degree, in the predicament of his central character.

Judging by *By the Open Sea*, Strindberg rejected the ability to create illusions as simplistic, at least for the present; he now saw the imagination as a quality endemic to demagogues and charlatans. His own solution to such a belief, which is a precarious one for a creative writer, would be to find a way that would allow him to use both exact realistic observations *and* the imagination.

'Swedish Nature'

After *By the Open Sea* was completed in June 1890 Strindberg set out on a journey through the Swedish provinces that he had long planned and which was undertaken in order to collect material for a work about Sweden's nature and people. In reality it became two journeys. The first included Uppland, Dalarna and Skåne, while a second one northward, begun in August 1891, was completed in Sundsvall on one of the first days in October.

The project is mentioned in a letter as early as 1885 and during the planning stage, it had a popular focus. In a letter dated 31 May 1887 Strindberg speaks vaguely of a 'Swedish Pick-Wick – or a trip in Sweden (fun) or both or something more'. However, no such trip would materialize until the autumn of 1890, when the new editor-in-chief of *Dagens Nyheter*, Fredrik Vult von Steijern, managed, with the aid of several patrons, to scrape together the necessary capital. By then the focus of the work had changed in a more scientific direction.

In 1886 Strindberg had undertaken a field trip similar to the one now planned, when he had embarked on a journey through the provinces of France to collect material for his sociological study *Among French Peasants*. However, the Swedish project centred above all on botany and geology. Strindberg wrote to Vult von Steiern on 17 August 1890:

A physio-geographical description of the land, depicted in an awesome survey from Skåne to Lapland, following the geological formations and the latitudinal [distribution of] vegetation from the North European continental climate to the arctic climate, and only seeking the particular physiognomy of the landscape as it expresses itself in its oceans, lakes, rivers, mountains, forests and marshes irrespective of any administrative or judicial divisions – this, in short, is what I have in mind.

After Strindberg abandoned the original popular approach, he aimed for a time at a work that was more in the tradition of Linnaeus, and would treat both 'Sweden's nature and [its] people'. However, on 23 September he wrote to Vult von Steijern that, for economic reasons, he had 'left the *People* and took on *Nature*, on a large scale!'

Strindberg's focus of interest recalls that of Borg in his recent novel *By the Open Sea*, but Strindberg, the traveller, is more robust than his fictional character, and derives a sensuous joy from his travels. This inspired mood continues after his return home from his journey as he sits down to write what was now intended as a lecture for the Swedish Academy of Sciences, but which he never had the occasion to deliver. Instead, 'Swedish Nature' was published as an essay in the annual, *Svea*, in 1886.

During the journey Strindberg kept a diary. Three notebooks – to which he later referred when writing – have been preserved intact and tell of his experiences at the time.[9] On the third day of the journey Strindberg is in Rånäs, in central Uppland, and notes: 'Tall fir forest with lake behind. Birch meadow and grassy knolls. Beautiful. More smiling than Roslagen. Exquisitely beautiful'. Two days later he is in northern Uppland and registers an auditory impression: 'cowbells, jays, steam hammers, singing, vespers ringing'. It is beautiful here too: 'The wonderful lake with the reeds at Dannemora. Morning mist'.[10]

It is of interest that during this journey Strindberg was briefly the guest of Hjalmar Öhrvall, now Professor of Physics in Uppsala, and engaged primarily in research on sensory physiology.[11] One may hazard a guess that when the two friends met that September, Strindberg quizzed him about a subject that, from his travel journals, had come increasingly to occupy him.

On 20 September Strindberg is in Mora and notes in his journal: 'The starling sings from birch top. High asps; huge willows; Birch trees as white and straight as on Falun promenade! Tall lilacs'. A note concerning 'excellent asparagus' suggests that Strindberg had tasted this vegetable, and that as a traveller he was not merely an observer but took sensuous pleasure in many of his experiences.

However, Strindberg the traveller is above all matter-of-fact. For the most part his journals include the names of plants and geographic notations, sometimes with small drawings. But occasionally – especially in the early stages of the journey – this matter-of-factness is replaced by sensuous outbursts of the kind quoted above. However, the auditory impressions noted in the journals are limited to what has been cited above, and on no occasion does Strindberg note a sense of smell in spite of the number of plants listed. Nor does he add any of these later on when writing up his journey for publication; in this respect he differs from Linnaeus who, for example in his *Skånska Resa* (Scanian Journey), is relatively liberal with descriptions of scents.[12]

The strangest note in the travel journal is to be found in the second notebook. Under the heading 'About Eye Sight' Strindberg refers at length and with several drawings to an experiment he performed at the Stenstorp Inn in Västergötland on 23 October 1890 while waiting for a train. Holding a magnifying glass in front of a burning candle he finds that at a certain distance the flame appears to be upside down in the glass, but when he moves it closer to his eye, it appears right side up again. Strindberg notes that 'extensive and exact inquiries' are required with recourse to photography in order to explain how this change occurs. Apparently he thinks that such experiments will help explain another mystery, for he adds: 'The goal is to explain why, in general, the eye sees pictures right side up while they are reversed on the retina'.

The example leads Strindberg to a further reflection on the possibility that children up to a certain age see things upside down; accordingly, he tries to interpret a drawing of a wine glass which his own children had made, and which he now draws from memory. However, the drawing that appears in Strindberg's journal makes it more likely that his misunderstanding was simply due to the fact that his children were incapable of reproducing the proportions between foot and glass correctly.

The experiment might appear mere whimsy but it probably has a more serious side. Strindberg frequently allows himself to doubt established truths where sight is concerned; it is a problem he continuously returns to in several articles during the 1890s as well as later on in the *Blue Books*. Doubting established truths rather than his own inventiveness is really the driving force behind his 'scientific' work.

A comparison of Strindberg's notes with the published text of 'Swedish Nature' reveals several things of interest. It could be said that when he freely adds diverse sounds at his writing desk in Djursholm Strindberg is only demonstrating both the delight he takes in nature and his craft as a writer. There is little support in his journal notes for the acoustic impressions found in the manuscript where, for example, Skåne's beech forests are described as follows: 'If the wind is blowing in the tree tops, it is calm down below and the gentle ringing and, at times, rustling and whispering sound of the hard leaves are tuned to a happier note than the thinly tuned Aeolian harps of the melancholy pine trees'. (SV 29:247) His notes under 'beech forest' in the third journal are entirely taken up with Latin plant names. But in the manuscript the same forest is described in quite poetic terms: 'If it is a cold, windy day, one will hear new tones in the beech forest: when the wind races through the leafless tree tops, it whistles as in a frigate's rigging and the frozen trunks creak' (247). It is true that Strindberg embarked on his journey in the autumn – unlike Linnaeus whose journey was undertaken in the spring – but he has either stored these auditory impressions in his memory or composed them later on, when writing.

According to a letter to Vult von Steiern, 'Swedish Nature' was to be characterized by an objective attitude and comprise a 'physio-geographic description'. However, when considering Strindberg's future development, it is interesting to discover in 'Swedish Nature' a tendency similar to that in *By the Open Sea*. Phenomena are carefully observed and noted, but the way Strindberg experiences them changes according to his immediate circumstances. For example, in his description of the mountains of Västergötland he points out that 'If one should happen to get a view of them in the afternoon at dusk, one might at first believe [one is] seeing great mounds of earth, bastions, enormous castle ruins. But in the light of day they will turn out to be table-mountains, consisting of layers of younger types of rock' (253). Significantly, the mountain of Kinnekulle is likened both to a 'mirage' and to an island hovering in the air, rather like the optical illusion Borg creates in *By the Open Sea*, and only then is it described in detail:

Letting your eyes rest on the lowly situated edge of the forest, your glance is drawn involuntarily out into space, captured by a landscape hovering in the distance, which the eyes have trouble focusing on. At first it looks like a very thin and light cloud but shifts form and consistency, like a cloud; it may be taken for a mirage, but at last it solidifies into an island swimming in the air – its shape compressed, stretched-out like a pyramid. And only when the beautiful vision ceases to surprise, do you reflect and realize that this is Kinnekulle – the most beautiful mountain in Västergötland and in all of southern Sweden (253–4).

And again, when Strindberg travels from Vänersborg to Gothenburg in western Sweden, he ponders the colour of the mountains, which he finds impossible to define: 'These mountains, which rise up to the sky in Bohuslän archipelago, take on the most shifting, often magnificent forms, which vary in colour according to the amount of humidity in the air, the position of the sun, the time of year, and so forth' (255).

Reflections of this type are missing in Strindberg's predecessor Linnaeus but are all the more common in another optically interested traveller whom Strindberg himself does not mention: Goethe. In the second part of his biography of Goethe Georg Brandes observes:

In Italy Goethe had thoroughly studied the artistic rendering of light in so far as this reveals different shades according to the non-transparency of the air, thus making objects appear in finely shaded nuances. The air perspective (says Goethe in his *Italian Journey*) actually depends on the important fact that all transparent media (*Mittel*) are to a certain degree murky (*trübe*). Thus the atmosphere is always more or less non-transparent, especially in the South when the pressure is high, the weather dry and the sky clear, and one can observe a very distinct shadowing (*Abstufung*) of objects that are found at a short distance from each other.[13]

Sometimes Strindberg's imagination gets the upper hand in a way that makes him Borg's opposite, given the latter's contempt for the poet who, in his ignorance, restored to 'tales of mermaids and giants' (p. 24). Strindberg, the traveller, finds on the other hand that in Skåne old blackened rushes whisper of 'old dark tales of ghosts and highwaymen, of blood feuds and assassinations' (252). On the same occasion he observes an islet in the bay. The fir trees are blackened by humidity and covered in moss, so they appear like cypress trees, and everything is like 'A floating graveyard on black water'. Once again one is reminded of the optical illusions in *By the Open Sea*.

The text is full of expressions such as 'sometimes the eye wants to see' (260), 'first the eye is confused' (261), 'at closer observation' (261) – expressions that are to be taken literally, and which foreshadow the rich metaphors of sight that characterize several of Strindberg's texts from 1900s. For the present, however, it is sufficient merely to note the author's awareness that observations depend upon changes in external conditions. This is hardly a feature that seems obvious in a documentary account of the Swedish countryside but it is an indication of Strindberg's shift in interest from the observed object *per se* to phenomena that deceive his observing eye.

Antibarbarus

Another aspect of the uses to which the senses are put occurs a few years later when Strindberg moves yet further away from fiction towards science. He exchanges his desk for the laboratory, which is perhaps not so very strange a step for so dedicated a naturalist. However, in Strindberg's case the reason prompting this change was not in order to achieve greater objectivity in his observations but rather to see through such quasi objectivity. During these experiments he would expose his delicate senses to a bombardment of sensations.

In *Antibarbarus* – which Strindberg wrote in Brünn in Mähren during October and November 1893 – he describes a number of chemical experiments which are intended to cast doubt on the established division of the elements in favour of his own monistic theory inspired by the German biologist and philosopher Ernst Haeckel.[14] Here he uses mainly the sense of smell in order to identify chemical substances. Never before had Strindberg lived in a world so filled with intrusive smells as during these chemical experiments, often performed in cramped hotel rooms.

An outside observer – the Finnish writer Adolf Paul – describes the interior of Strindberg's hotel room on Rügen during the summer of 1893: 'Then he spent the entire day standing over his crucibles, even during the worst July heat, usually clad only in his night shirt and slippers, a girdle round his waist and a straw hat on his head. It was hot as hell up there, and it smelled of pitch and sulphur!'[15] In Paul's account of Strindberg's savagely misanthropic moods that summer he remarks interestingly that Strindberg expressed a dislike of food — not primarily because it tasted bad but rather because he found it *falsified* and his sense of taste perverted:

> If he raised a glass of beer to his mouth, the response was immediately: 'horrible, falsified, not fit to drink!' What the German cuisine offered was simply: 'over-cooked swine fodder!' If he tasted fresh fish, then it was only 'sludge fish', fried in 'false butter. The fishermen had trampled on it with their tarred boots, before it landed in the frying pan!'[16]

In the novella *The Cloister* from 1898 Strindberg lets the male protagonist experience 'falsified' food at an inn on Rügen:

> To this was served a type of over-cooked swine fodder, so that you left the table hungry and remained hungry all day long. Everything was falsified, even the beer, and the innkeeper's family had first cooked the meat for themselves; the guests found only gristle and bones — precisely as one feeds dogs (SV 50:65).

Aside from Paul, the company at Rügen included the stone-deaf Finnish author Karl August Tavaststjerna whose impairment, according to Paul, made Strindberg lose his composure.[17] However, during his previous acquaintance with Tavaststjerna in Weimar at the beginning of August 1892, Strindberg had taken advantage of his deafness and flirted with his wife, Gabrielle: '*Neue Liebe!*' he had written to Paul at the time, 'Complete declaration of love in the presence of the male' (7 December 1892).[18] Neither the experience with 'falsified food' nor the company of a deaf person would merit mention here were it not for the fact that in several of the first plays he wrote immediately after the Inferno crisis (e.g. *To Damascus I* and *Advent*), Strindberg utilizes precisely these experiences.

Antibarbarus also contains instances of the way in which Strindberg shifts the focus from the object under scrutiny to the sensory perception itself. Such is the case, for example, during one of his countless experiments with sulphur:

> I place the crucible over the fire and allow the sulphur to melt. It

becomes a golden amber fluid at 115° and only now does it smell, not of sulphur but of turpentine and resin, almost like floor-polish (= wax and turpentine). The temperature rises, the colour moves towards the red end of the spectrum, and orange overtakes the red, so rapidly that the orange fuses with the red and creates the mixed colour of reddish brown at 160°. A condensation, whether chemical or physical, or both, has occurred and now the smell of camphor appears. When I observed this for the first time, I did not trust my perhaps oldest and therefore most developed sense; instead I called my laboratory teacher (SS 27:119).

On another occasion Strindberg is prepared to admit that air contains combustible gas but doubts that this is nitrogen: 'What is nitrogen? How does it make itself known? How does it taste? How does it smell? How does it appear to the eye?' (168). The answer is that nitrogen can only be defined in the negative: 'It has no smell, no taste, no colour' (168). This irritates Strindberg who is now vacillating between doubting what lies beyond his sensory borders and doubting the senses themselves.

During this period Strindberg particularly questions the sense of sight. This can be seen in the so-called 'Fifth Letter' – a kind of sequel to *Antibarbarus* which was, however, never published.[19] According to a title page, the 'Letter' discusses 'The Form of the Earth, and Astronomy', and approaches these subjects via optics. The presentation as a whole apparently sets out to question the eye's ability to 'see correctly'. A second title page contains the following subheadings: 'Thoughts about the Sun, the Moon and the Stars in the World of Illusions'. The expression 'the world of illusions' refers at this stage to an illusory world in a literal sense. According to Strindberg, the phenomena he studied were intended to cast doubt on certain inadequate proofs that the earth is round. He also claimed that the same observations could prove that both the rings of Saturn and Jupiter's moons were illusory.

Strindberg now approaches total scepticism with regard to the reliability of sight: 'Optical phenomena! Where do these begin, and where do they end?' On the first page of the manuscript the eye is called 'defective' and on the last page 'deceptive'. At the expense of the sense of sight, Strindberg launches the idea of 'reflection' or 'an inner sense': 'the inner sense is more reliable than any organ and this organ does not reach the level of deductive power (= Fantasy)'.[20]

Here Strindberg has taken yet another step in his long leave-taking of naturalistic attitudes and ways of thinking.

What is striking, however, is the speculative attitude that characterizes the published portions of *Antibarbarus*. Descriptions of individual experiments are often formulated as questions, with which Strindberg induces the reader to believe that the whole of contemporary chemistry was in fact full of question marks: 'Why does impure carbon bisulphate smell of selenium or rotten black radish and why does selenium, at 700°, smell of "unclean" carbon bisulphate?' (154). He himself offers no answer.

Again and again Strindberg is puzzled by the smells he perceives around him. Probably at no other period of his life did he employ his sense of smell as much, or on such unusual errands. It confirms an interest in olfaction which remains an abiding part of his life, whether he wishes it to or not.

'Sensations détraquées' ('Deranged Sensations')

Strindberg's essay 'Deranged Sensations' from the end of 1894 is of great interest in terms of his wrestling with the complex problem of the reliability of the senses. The symptoms of his impending Inferno crisis, which are anticipated in those elements of paranoia already apparent during the time he spent on Rügen, do not improve but are merely translated to a new geographic and cultural context.

Gunnar Brandell has pointed out that Strindberg's own word in the title – *détraquée* – is stronger than 'confused' (*förvirrad*), which has been the usual Swedish translation: '[*détraqué*] means mentally deranged, half crazy'.[21] Brandell also points out that it was a Parisian fashion at the time to be 'crazy in an ingenious and sensitive manner.'[22] Karl Åke Kärnell also assumes an association with a contemporary literary fashion on Strindberg's part but also mentions that there can be no 'doubt that the experiences themselves are authentic. [. . .] Rather, it is the instruments of reception that have become more refined and sensitive'.[23] It is difficult to regard Strindberg's essay as no more than exhibitionism, a coquettish flirtation with the idea of hypersensitive senses. In my opinion, Strindberg's essay displays the same strategy that he had previously assigned to Borg in *By the Open Sea*. The problem is that his rational explanations tend to become increasingly fantastic, but this is something that Strindberg himself did not realize at the time. 'Deranged Sensations' is clearly far more beholden to authentic experience than literary fashion; least of all is there any indication in the text that Strindberg is seeking to following the footsteps of his French contemporary, Rimbaud, who in a famous letter of 13 May 1871 recommended a 'derangement of all the senses' as a means of reaching the unknown. Despite the fact that his essay is classified as a 'Vivisection', Strindberg does not seek out situations that cause him stress; he simply finds himself in such predicaments and must choose between finding rational explanations for what he has experienced or taking to his heels. A good deal of the confusion conveyed by the text is due to this fact: the author is both vivisector and guinea pig. In addition, a solution to the crisis that has just begun is suggested in passing by Strindberg – a solution that he became interested in, in earnest, two years later.

When one first encounters the 'traveller' *Strindberg* (italic from here on to suggest an authorial persona) in 'Sensations détraquées', he is exhausted after travelling for two days by train. His fatigue is accorded a kind of naturalistic explanation: he has been 'forced to breathe in the carbon dioxide and nitrogen fumes' (SS 27:596)[24] of his fellow travellers as well as coal dust and sulphur from the engine (597).

Rested after the trip *Strindberg* convinces himself in a rational manner that his exhaustion is responsible for certain curious reactions. Diverse optical illusions are explained 'scientifically' as the result of his brain having been shaken up by 'the jolting of the railway carriage' (597). When *Strindberg* is about to approach Louis XIII's pavilion at Versailles he has a strange experience. After walking for what he estimates is three-quarters of an hour, he feels he should have reached the pavilion or, at least, that it should at least appear larger than it had done before. Now, however, it seems that the building recedes as fast as he approaches it. Again he seeks a rational explanation, and once again the cause of his deranged vision is said to be the exhausting trip: 'This disturbance to my sense of vision is a natural result of the strenuous trip' (598).

After a night's sleep *Strindberg* is prepared for a new attempt. It starts out much like the first time, in that he does not feel as if he is getting any nearer to the pavilion. But this time he takes a more rational approach; he not only takes along a watch but also a map, and calculates that after walking for ten minutes he should have only five hundred metres left to the pavilion. He concludes that he day before he had evidently been the victim of an optical illusion:

> the perspective changes as I stride along; at the same time, my angle of vision increases, and this infernal play of invisible lines confuses my mind, where the irradiating rays of the enchanted palace imprint themselves. Once the solution to the problem has been found, I am at ease again (599).

Elsewhere in 'Sensations détraquées', Strindberg writes: 'What a calming effect to be able to explain everything! It takes away the fear of the unknown'. (599) One recalls Borg in *By the Open Sea* who reacted similarly. The statement hardly supports Brandell's conclusion that Strindberg's text is an exhibition in a modish form of craziness.

Strindberg's attempt to cross the great open space of the Place d'Armes is likewise complicated by physical laws: 'The great building attracts me the way large bodies attract small ones' (600). When he suddenly discovers that he is drawn towards the palace, he searches among past experiences for something similar. However, he is forced to ask himself whether some unknown force might not be the cause: 'The learned deny this and maintain that energy is constant' (601). Then he employs a strategy which, on a larger scale, will help him through the full-blown Inferno crisis two years later: he gives the unknown phenomenon a name and is thereby able to establish a relationship to it and create a kind of meaning in chaos: 'I rebel against this blind, brutal power, and in order to be able to fight it more successfully, I personify it, I turn it into a god' (601).

In a fit of agoraphobia *Strindberg* clings to a lamp post[25] but still seeks a 'scientific' explanation for his reaction. He adopts mesmerist models of explanation and imagines that the post acts as a 'fortifying medium of touch', a 'psycho-magnet' which exerts a calming effect on his nerves. But alongside this pseudo-scientific explanation Strindberg gropes for a supernatural explanation – again anticipating the way in which he resolves the later crisis: 'an old habit of mine prompts me to raise my eyes towards this blue formation of gas, through which rays of warmth and light are filtered and which the faithful have rightly called heaven, for there live primeval forces' (602).

What then happens is that the author gives free reign to superstition and fantasy. Fantasy becomes a 'vessel' that helps him from the 'cliff' in the square where he finds himself. With its help *Strindberg* raises himself from the sphere of material reality, which he experiences as a tremendous release:

> What does it matter that, when all is said and done, they are merely shadows, like everything else! Now I am a poet and magician. I choose for myself the sturdiest of these steam ships, I carefully climb aboard . . . Onward . . . Wonderful, the crossing is completed! (602).

It is some considerable time since fantasy had been accorded so strong a position in Strindberg's world. In 'The Fifth Letter' there were intimations of the primacy of fantasy over observation. But when the word 'fantasy' was mentioned, it was within parenthesis.[26]

In 'Deranged Sensations' the author saves himself resolutely with the help of his imagination. The essay 'Des Arts Nouveaux! Où Le Hasard dans la production artistique' ('The New Arts! or the Role of Chance in Artistic Creation') also shows that at this time Strindberg hardly rejects the imagination; in fact he observes that, 'Nothing is as pleasant as setting the imagination in motion.'[27] The remark would seem to correct the picture of an author who has abandoned a life of fantasy and artistic endeavour. It sounds more like the exclamation of an author who is finding it increasingly difficult to write.

In the park at Versailles Strindberg does not only experience visual phenomena. He is also intoxicated by the scent of flowers, and the breeze over the fields which carries waves of perfume (603). When *Strindberg* strolls on the terrace, he finds the ground swaying beneath his feet as if he were on a suspension bridge. Once again it is time for a 'reassuring conclusion'. Below the terrace lies the arched ceiling of the orangerie:

> . . . in exerting a counter-pressure outwards, the arches ought to offer a superabundance of strength, against which the soles of my feet react, so that the impression is transmitted to my nervous system, whose sensitivity is heightened by my physical and mental suffering (603–4).

Strindberg's peculiar perceptions also apply to hearing. He feels that the Marble Garden at Versailles is similar to 'the auditory canal of a

giant ear, the auricle of which is formed by the wings of the building' (604).[28] What follows seems to show that *Strindberg* is himself
aware that his ideas so far oscillate between playfulness and
seriousness:

> Captivated by this new fantasy and happy to have come upon this
> bizarre idea that I am like a flea in a giant's ear, I listen pressed
> against the wall . . . What a surprise! . . . I can hear! I can hear a
> rumbling sea, the wailing of crowds, abandoned hearts whose
> beats pump up an exhausted blood, nerves that break with a tiny
> dull thud, sobs, laughter and sighs!
>
> I ask myself if these are not subjective sensory impressions, if it
> is not myself I hear.
>
> No, I know every vagary of my senses by heart (604–5).

The author refuses to believe that his hearing would trick him. He
recalls having heard a sailor tell how, after three days at sea, he could
still hear the ringing of bells through the concave side of the sails,
which acted like a 'burning mirror'. Here Strindberg offers an
imaginary blend of optics and acoustics.

The first section of 'Deranged Sensations' is dated October 1894.
In the manuscript, the second part of the essay is dated December
1894 and contains, among other things, certain speculations regarding the function of the eye. One day upon waking, *Strindberg* 'sees' a
net of bloody, red threads on the marble stove in his room and tells
himself that it must be his own retina that has been projected there,
enlarged. He believes that he can see projected in the same manner
the blood-vessels of his cornea and the red and white blood cells.
The observation leads him naturally to the conclusion that the eye,
the sense of sight, is not to be trusted. Just as he had wondered at
Versailles if it was not himself he heard, he now asks if it is not
himself that he sees. If so, the senses would be dead-ends rather than
channels of information.

After a series of sensations of this type, it is a relief for *Strindberg* to
leave the city where his senses are continuously exposed to stress.
Out in nature he says he can both think clearly and experience his
senses functioning sensitively but correctly – that is, not as an
over-cultivated modern city dweller but more in the manner of a
primitive savage. His description offers a utopian image of the
unadulterated senses at play:

One beautiful morning before sunrise I enter that wood. Influenced by my surroundings, which I do not want to resist, I feel stripped of my civilised attire. I discard the mask of the citizen who has never acknowledged the so-called social contract; I let my rebellious thoughts roam freely, and I think, think . . . without fear, with no reservations. Then I see with the penetrating vision of the savage, I listen and sniff the air like a redskin! (613).

'Études funèbres' – 'In the Cemetery'

One year later, in autumn 1895, Strindberg finds himself in the middle of his Inferno crisis and writes the essay 'In the Cemetery'. Only a few months later, in February 1896, he will move into the Hôtel Orfila on the rue d'Assas where the crisis peaks in June, provoking a series of sudden departures and flights from place to place.

Strindberg's portrayal of the cemetery of Montparnasse does not fit naturally into an elegiac literary tradition. Rather than depict a funereal mood, the author observes his sensory impressions.[29] Strindberg is in search of a new world view, but philosophical thoughts and a literary approach still do not blend comfortably together. This gives the essay two principal aspects, part experimental data and scientific report, part literary description.

Strindberg achieves an autumnal mood by describing yellowing linden trees and withering roses. A thrush that no longer sings but utters sneering laughs adds an auditory dimension. The air of the cemetery is said to be unhealthy because of unwholesome vapours and *Strindberg* gets a taste of verdigris on his tongue, which he concludes is caused by the souls of dematerialized bodies floating in the air. As if this were not enough, the author collects a sample of this air in a bottle and takes it back with him to his hotel room where he pours a drop of acid on it: 'It swells up, this dead matter, it quivers, begins to come alive, exudes a rotten smell, grows still once more, and dies' (662).

The text of 'In the Cemetery' is dominated by feelings of discomfort: 'the dead exuded sulphurous odours and these unwholesome vapours created a taste of verdigris in my mouth' (664). Flowers too are associated with decay, when the author comes across roses and jasmine on the grave of the poet Théodore de Banville: 'If this was the dead man's wish surely he must have known that a cadaver smells of roses, jasmine and musk?' (666). Even more interesting is the author's reaction to a portrait of a six-year-old child on a small mausoleum. The description of this relief becomes a picture of innocence precisely because the child's sensory organs have not yet had to engage with a repulsive reality. In its purity the child seems related to the savage with which Strindberg had previously identified:

> a tiny nose, slightly flattened at the tip from habitually pressing against a mother's breast; placed there like a pretty ornament, with shell-shaped nostrils above a heart-shaped mouth, not meant for scenting prey or for catching perfumes or bad odours, not yet a real organ (669).

In the essays from the 1890s in which elements of fiction never dominate – even if spontaneous ideas and a certain reverence for the imagination do appear – Strindberg can be observed making his way to a new way of thinking.[30] The first stage in this development becomes a study of his own senses and a stubborn clinging to the idea that he is not experiencing anything unreal. On the other hand, Strindberg admits – not without pride – that his sensibilities are abnormally heightened. From 1896 onwards, this attitude is documented above all in his diary. At the same time, another development is taking place: in his published essays Strindberg argues the opposite, namely that our senses are inadequate. This is a form of double bookkeeping which, in the long run, becomes extremely taxing on his psyche.

In the essays 'On the Action of Light in Photography'[31] and 'A Glimpse into Space', which were published in the journal *L'Initiation* in 1896, Strindberg reveals his doubts as to the reliability of the senses – referring now, as in the 'Fifth Letter', to man's senses in general and not to his own alone. Strindberg's studies in chemistry, optics, and the other sciences led him increasingly to the point of view that no objective knowledge exists; rather, everything is subjective perception: 'Is the sun round because we see it as round? And what is light? Something outside of me or within me, subjective perceptions?' (353). Or differently phrased: 'Where does the self begin and where does it end? Has the eye adapted itself to the sun? Or does the eye create the phenomenon called the sun? (354).

This freely subjective and anxiety-creating point of view accelerated the early course of Strindberg's crisis and makes him fumble for an outlook that can create meaning from chaos. During the Inferno period he reaches a point where the explanations to some of his experiences tend to become all too fantastic. Strindberg is on the verge of madness. What saves him is his positive acknowledgement of a world view where the notion that the senses are insufficient is almost an a priori assumption. Strindberg creates such a world view for himself and accepts an ambiguous world, but a world with an organizing kind of divine power behind it.

The Occult Diary

It is the revealing letters to the theosopher and journalist Torsten Hedlund in the summer of 1896 and the so-called *Occult Diary* that he began keeping in February 1896 which assist in drawing certain conclusions about Strindberg's state of mind and his development towards a new, enabling vision of life. One of the Diary's several title pages bears a motto (possibly written after the fact, when Strindberg had gained new insight) which sums up the outcome of his protracted reflections on the nature of the senses. It is attributed to *The Talmud* and reads: 'If you wish to know the invisible, then observe the visible with an open gaze'. The visible world is described here as a guide to the inner world. With this formula Strindberg can presume the existence of two parallel worlds. Furthermore, by taking up, at this point, the idea of both a pre-existing and an after-world, he makes the present appear altogether less important.

An entry on the Diary's first page contains a reflection on the ability of deaf-mutes to express themselves through sign language and gestures. The entry – consisting of a single line – concerns people who have lost two of their senses. One can guess from where Strindberg derives the observation; it is most probably inspired by his experiences in 1894 when he lived in the Hôtel des Américains on the rue de l'Abbé de l'Epée, opposite the Deaf-Mute Institute.[32] The street bears the name of the eighteenth-century educator of deaf-mutes who developed a sign language and hand alphabet.[33] It can be assumed that Strindberg knew this. He seems to have found the sight of the deaf-mutes as fascinating,[34] and his interest in pantomime during the coming decade may be traced, in part at least, to similar impressions during the Inferno crisis as well as to later experiences.[35] The line about the deaf-mutes in *The Occult*

Diary reads, in all its cryptic simplicity: 'The hand alphabet of the deaf-mute and the man's hands. (gestures)'.

The next line is also an example of how certain Parisian experiences contributed to Strindberg's later dramatic work: 'To construct a mirror that turns the world right-side up, so that we may open our eyes'. The line is followed by a question: 'What is the cylinder-shaped mirror called, which makes deformed figures look right?'

What Strindberg clearly has in mind is a world turned the wrong way for human eyesight, though he exemplifies this only with reference to flowers and butterflies. Man's vision has become 'distorted', but with optical instruments it would be possible to see things 'as they are' is his somewhat paradoxical conclusion. What is so characteristic is that he does not only imply that the world is deformed in a moral sense; he seems to be more than playing with the idea that the human eye really does perceive the world in reverse,[36] and that a mirror would rectify this. It is always difficult to determine when Strindberg's metaphors are only metaphors, but they should probably be taken literally more often than one might believe, or else be regarded as both literal and metaphorical. Moreover, the idea is encountered elsewhere in Strindberg's work, for example in 1901, in a crucial passage in the promotion scene in *A Dream Play* where the stage directions specify the presence of a mirror (SV 46:37). Indra's daughter goes up to it and exclaims: 'Do you know what I see in this mirror here? – The world turned right side up! – Yes, since it is the wrong way round itself!' (SV 46:38, cf. 71).

Other sensory impressions that are noted down and reflected on in *The Occult Diary* prior to the writing of *Inferno*, i.e. 21 November 1896, focus on scents and sounds. It should be noted that such entries do not disappear when the Inferno crisis is over. Quite the contrary, they reappear in the future when Strindberg enters further critical stages in his life or when he is faced with changes of a far-reaching nature.[37]

But let us return to Strindberg's experiences in Paris in the spring of 1896. On 3 May he thinks he hears the song of a cricket in his pillow and notes: 'The sound of the grasshopper in general; for me it has always sounded as if it came from an empty underground hall with a great echo (*ventrolique*). Cf.: The sound of the shell.' The same experience is described in a long, distraught letter to Hedlund on 18 July and is accompanied by a number of almost desperate and

fantastic explanations. Strindberg is terrified that he might be hal-
lucinating. His explanations seem to be aimed at saving his own
sanity – it is no longer a case of exploring the senses as such. And
what he writes has of course nothing directly to do with zoology,
botany or physiology:

> And at times I hear a sound in my pillow, like a cricket. The
> sound a grasshopper makes in the grass has always struck me as
> magical. A kind of ventriloquism, for I have always felt that the
> sound came from an empty underground hall. Supposing that
> grasshoppers have sung in fields of flax, don't you think that
> Nature or the creator can make a phonograph from the plant
> fibres, so that their song echoes in my inner ear, which has been
> trained through suffering, love and prayers to hear more than is
> normal? But this is where 'natural explanations' fall short, and I
> immediately put them aside!

Strindberg thus perceives at last that his explanation is far too fantastic, and he changes the subject. The letter gives a confused
impression – regardless of how one wishes to diagnose Strindberg's
behaviour in psychiatric terms. His reasoning aims at offering a
realistic defence of his experiences; what Strindberg wants to talk
about in his own hysterical way, is that everything he experiences is
real. He does not hallucinate, i.e. he is not insane. The day after this
letter was written he leaves the Hôtel Orfila in panic, the very day
when, according to Johan Cullberg, he is overtaken by a shorter
paranoid psychosis.[38]

Thus the long letter to Torsten Hedlund should be seen as a
distraught letter of defence for the existence of a type of 'inner
reality'. Strindberg now claims that this inner, invisible reality is just
as great a reality as the external one:

> Hallucinations, fantasies, dreams seem to me to possess a high
> degree of reality. If I see my pillow assume human shapes those
> shapes are there, and if anyone says they are only! in my imagin-
> ation, I reply: You say 'only'? – *What my inner eye sees means more
> to me*! And what I see in the pillow, which is made of birds'
> feathers that once were bearers of life, and of flax, which in its
> fibres has borne the power of life, is soul, the power to create
> forms, and it *is* real since I can draw these figures and show them
> to other people. (My italics)

Strindberg has here erased the borderline between fantasy and reality or has expanded the domain of 'reality' to also include such things as dreams and fantasies. In this new world he cannot find his bearings with his senses, a bane for which he later compensates with religious belief. Inner reality becomes the truest reality and obeys the laws of the Creator which sometimes – but not always – are apparent to Strindberg himself. In this way a threatening situation has changed into an enigmatic one.

In its most acute phase, the Inferno crisis appears to be accompanied by different types of sounds that Strindberg interprets as hostile and aimed specifically at him. Most of the sounds that he experiences seem to have a trivial source, but in his overheated brain they are magnified and appear threatening.[39] The observation that birds are building nests in his chimney and their chirping can be heard in his room might seem disturbingly fanciful, yet it could, nevertheless, be quite true. His landlord recalled that when Strindberg's room was cleaned after his flight, he noted that Strindberg had never used his stove, and that a number of dead sparrows had fallen down the chimney.[40]

On one occasion Strindberg is disturbed by the sound of a family arguing and a child crying, even at night, from an adjoining room. And on Sunday, 14 June, he notices that he can hear sounds he should be unable to hear: 'The cuckoo called; it was heard from my room, 60 rue d'Assas; which is impossible'. He also hears the bells of Sacré-Coeur, which he feels ought no to be possible. Obviously, there could be natural and trivial explanations for these sounds too.

Likewise, when he arrives at his in-laws' in Klam in Austria, Strindberg continues to be surrounded by disquieting sounds. Animals scream (on 11 September), he hears a rumbling sound in the attic during the night (19 September), a screaming black crow pursues him (27 September), the wind howls (20 October). When the church bells chime on 1 November, they are interrupted by a howling storm. What these impressions have in common is that they are unpleasant, and that they appear more or less ominous.

On 20 December 1896 Strindberg is in Lund. For the past month he has been in the process of 'constructing' the novel *Inferno*. The experiential concerns focus, to no little extent, on the sensations of sound and smell, which he now interprets in a somewhat less distraught state of mind than during his time in Paris, Ystad and Klam. On Sunday, 1 January, he observes 'Bird song', and when he eats dinner at the pub Åke Hans on 10 February, he hears a violent bang behind him. But he soon gives a rational explanation for such phenomena: 'It turned out to be a workman fixing a door stop'. In the evening he sits with the author and publisher Gustaf af Geijerstam at the same hostelry and hears a pattering sound in the attic. He discusses the sound with Geijerstam who feels that it must be a rat, while Strindberg believes it is a cat. In the course of this conversation Strindberg notes that every now and then the door is jerked to, but he is now inclined to de-dramatize these occurrences. His life has entered a new and calmer phase. What occurs around him now is no longer of a hostile nature, but rather a series of more or less mysterious signs to be deciphered, or indeed, as in these last examples, trivial occurrences that are of no significance, however hard he tries to find one.

On 28 February, Strindberg calmly observes a chaffinch singing in Lund. On Sunday, 21 March, a house sparrow chirps at a quarter part eight in the evening as Strindberg is leaving the Åke Hans pub. 'On arriving home, a dog howled. But in my rooms there was a pleasant fragrance, which sometimes happens, though not often'. The 'but' with which the sentence opens is a sign that Strindberg now allows pleasant experiences to outweigh unpleasant ones. Thus, a week later, when he goes out in the morning, 'the air in the garden smelled of flowers', and on 9 June, while working on the chapter 'Swedenborg' in *Inferno*, he recognizes the scent of flowers in his room.

Swedenborg

The turning point of Strindberg's Inferno crisis occurs in September 1896 when he reads a selection of Swedenborg's writings. These help him to transform unpleasant experiences into mysterious signs and enable him to see his fate as controlled by a higher power. If Strindberg had previously been an unproductive writer, he now assumes the responsibilities of an author who sets out to interpret both his own fate and the world in which he finds himself. Artistically, this means that he can now accept his dreams and what his imagination comes up with as part of reality, thus creating a basis for the dreamlike elements in his later plays.

Strindberg's dependence on Swedenborg has been carefully studied by Gunnar Brandell, Göran Stockenström and Johan

Cullberg. Here I only wish to show how this dependence can be clarified by the particular focus I have chosen for my study.

Swedenborg's teachings about parallel or corresponding worlds suited Strindberg's manner of thinking which was markedly analogical. According to both Gunnar Brandell and Lars Bergquist, however, Strindberg, differed from Swedenborg in seeking these analogies or correspondences on a horizontal plane, by comparing one thing with another.[41] This may be so, but it is equally the case that when faced with terrestrial phenomena, Strindberg pondered over their higher meaning, which makes him a kind of symbolist. His symbols often tell, more or less mysteriously, of a higher order, while in general they are not ambiguous in the sense of 'dissipating' horizontally.

In its basic contours, Emanuel Swedenborg's crisis in the middle of the 1740s is similar to Strindberg's some one hundred and fifty years later. In his gigantic but unfinished work *Regnum Animale*, Swedenborg attempted to explain man's five senses in a mechanistic way. Strindberg tried to do something similar in his essay 'On the Secrets of the Flowers' of 1888. The third part of *Regnum Animale*, which supersedes Swedenborg's famous *Dream Book* of 1743–4, remained unfinished but Swedenborg rewrote a draft, which would become known in the English-speaking world as *The Five Senses*, and which is charecterized by doubts about the ability of the senses to convey a feasible reality.[42]

Strindberg encountered Swedenborg's *Dream Book* in the spring of 1897. He may well have identified with this work and its depiction of a crisis that moves from physical observations to the beholding of a reality beyond the sensory.[43] Sensory experiences in no way ceased to be of interest to Swedenborg after his crisis, and the same holds true for Strindberg who, in this respect, is noticeably influenced by his predecessor and mentor. Thus Swedenborg's method of assigning a moral meaning to various smells is adopted by Strindberg. In the excerpts he made from Swedenborg's works during the Klam period, words like 'faeces' and 'faeces smelling' are often used.[44] In Swedenborg's *Vera Christiana Religio*, which Strindberg had access to in Lund when he was writing *Inferno*,[45] great emphasis is placed on smell as an indicator of moral status. In Swedenborg's hell there is a 'stench-like smell that comes from latrines and from corpses and from dunghills'.[46] In another formulation the smell is likened to 'stinking excrement and the smell of cadavers and rotten urine'.[47] When Strindberg notes in *The Occult Diary* for 9 and 10 September 1896 both the 'smell of rotten urine' and a 'stench of faeces', this suggests that he might already have been inspired by the vivid descriptions of *Vera Christiana Religio* while living with Frida Uhl's family at Klam in Austria.

Such Swedenborgian elements are prominent in the novel *Inferno*. Thus in one Parisian episode in which Strindberg describes himself standing in front of 'an enormous shed that stinks of raw meat and rotten vegetables, especially cabbage' (SV 37:27), this concoction of odours is not to be interpreted as a naturalistic device as in (say) Zola's *Le Ventre de Paris*, to which it bears a superficial resemblance.[48] Rather the passage seems intended to illustrate, in a Swedenborgian manner, the hellishness of existence. Similar passages are common in Strindberg's novel. For instance, when he describes his living-quarters in Austria, he refers to Swedenborg by name and goes on to describe it in Swedenborgian terms as hell:

> It is a country house that smells of dung, purine, sulphate of ammonia and carbon bisulphate. A cacophony of cows, pigs, calves, chickens, turkeys, doves, goes on all day long (219).

Likewise, when depicting autumn Strindberg blends similar impressions of smell and noise:

> The roads are so dirty that one cannot go out; the leaves rot; all of nature stinks, dissolved in putrefaction.
> The autumn slaughtering has begun and all day the shrieks of the victims rise towards the dark sky, and one steps in blood and among the carcasses of animals (253).

In *Inferno*, one of the principal reasons for *Strindberg*'s repeated dramatic departures from different milieux is his inability to cope with night-time noise. Before he arrives at the Hôtel Orfila he lives at a another hotel where he has difficulty sleeping since, in an adjoining room, someone is playing the piano in three different places. In the morning he is woken up by the hammering of nails in two of the adjoining rooms, and when he tries to sleep after breakfast, he is awakened by a loud ruckus in the room above, causing plaster to fall down from the ceiling. In retrospect Strindberg seems inclined to interpret these noises according to the same moral pattern that he had learned from Swedenborg in respect of different odours.[49]

Strindberg derived another practical lesson from his reading of

Swedenborg. When he returns to writing drama after the Inferno crisis, he adopts Swedenborg's idea that after dying people retain their senses and are thus unaware of their true predicament. In *Heaven and Hell* Swedenborg formulates this notion as follows:

> For when man enters the spiritual world or life after death, he is a body just as in this world. To all appearances there is no difference, since he does not feel or see any difference. But his body is spiritual and thus separated or cleansed from earthly matters, and when the spiritual touches and sees the spiritual, it is just as when the natural sees and touches the natural. Therefore when man has become a spirit, he does not know anything other than that he is within his own body, just as he had been on earth, and hence he does not know that he is dead. The human spirit can also rejoice at every external and inner sense at which he rejoiced here on earth. He sees as before, hears and speaks as before, he also has a sense of smell and taste, and when he is touched he perceives it with the same sense of touch as before.[50]

Here Swedenborg presents a possibility that would allow a person in, for example, a drama to both possess his senses and play blind man's buff with a higher being – a dramaturgically very rewarding situation.

Montaigne

During his visit to Frida Uhl's relatives in Dornach in the autumn of 1896 Strindberg's reading was not confined to Swedenborg. Two months later, on 9 November, he makes the following short notation in *The Occult Diary*: 'Read Montaigne which I longed for, it brought happiness'. Naturally, it seems curious that during this difficult period in his life Strindberg could find happiness in reading the French sixteenth-century sceptic; what place had such a writer alongside the spiritual clairvoyant Swedenborg?

An informed guess is that in Montaigne Strindberg found his newly found scepticism *vis-à-vis* the human senses confirmed. In the longest of his essays, 'Apologie de Raimond Sebond', Montaigne expounds on the topic, 'We no longer know what our senses are'.[51] He also advances the idea that man may lack one or several senses: 'My first consideration on the subject of the senses is that I doubt that Man is equipped with all existing natural senses.

[. . .] who knows if we too might not lack one, two or several senses. For if one is lacking, our reason would not discover it.'[52]

Such reflections lead to the conclusion: 'Man cannot get away from the fact that the senses are not sovereign rulers and reliable in every situation'. After all, as Jean Starobinski has pointed out, appearance, 'dissemblance' – what Strindberg would come to call 'illusion' or 'mirage' – is central to Montaigne's thinking where 'All is "betrayal", "farce", "something external" and "make-up"'. According to Starobinski, this is how Montaigne's fundamental experience of life may be described.[53] One essential point of difference, however, is that after describing the illusory nature of the world, Montaigne does not, like Strindberg, fall into almost total pessimism and misanthropy but rather returns to a position where illusion is accepted.[54]

Schumann's 'Aufschwung'

During a particular period of his life, Strindberg was haunted by Schumann's piano piece 'Aufschwung' from his *Fantasiestücke*, Opus 12. According to the musicologist Per Anders Hellquist, '"Aufschwung" seizes hold of the listener with its aggressive driving rhythm and fanfare-like themes.'[55] At the Hôtel Orfila *Strindberg*, the narrator of *Inferno*, is repeatedly disturbed by this music: 'I rear like a war-horse at the trumpet blast; I draw myself up, feel excited, breathe. It is Schumann's call to arms: *Aufschwung*'. This description would seem to have been taken from an entry in Strindberg's diary, dated March 1896: 'Schumann's Aufschwung was heard in the distance.'[56] In the novel the experience is depicted as one of terror for *Strindberg* is convinced that the music emanates from his former pupil 'Popoffsky', who has come to Paris in order to kill him. According to the novel the music continues for a whole month, and is always played between four and five in the afternoon (103). *Strindberg* thus associates Schumann's 'Aufschwung' with a threat to his life. Meanwhile, the novel includes what Strindberg claims is an excerpt from his diary for 2 June: 'Schumann's Aufschwung has ceased, which makes me calm' (111). For some reason Strindberg, the novelist has here disavowed the author of the diary, for on this day the diary in fact contains the following note: 'And Schumann's Aufschwung was played'. One can only speculate as to the reason for this discrepancy; maybe Strindberg the novelist needed a dramatic rhythm and changed the text of the diary for artistic reasons.[57]

With this misquoted passage from the diary, Schumann's music disappears from the novel but not from Strindberg's life. His reaction to it changes, however, and it must be seen as a sign of recovery when on 10 July in Lund, he writes in his diary: 'Soon afterwards I met Herrlin who had bought Schumann's Aufschwung. Brodén played it, and I was cheered up'. The same piece, which had previously filled him with mortal fear, now has the opposite effect.

'Look'

The artistic gain that Strindberg derives from the Inferno crisis consists of an expanded view of reality. After the crisis he becomes increasingly interested in the presence of the invisible, in an abstract as much as a concrete reality. His perception of the outside world becomes both richer and more uncertain.

From the *Occult Diary* it appears that henceforth Strindberg discusses the realistic basis of his experiences with a new sense of reality. Four days after completing *Inferno* (29 June 1897) he notes: 'When I woke up this morning I saw Herrlin', adding: 'This is the first vision I have had'. A little later in the summer, on 10 July, he writes: 'Met Frida on the street in Lund; she was dressed in brown. When I turned my head she disappeared. But there was no gate, no alleyway. Was this a vision?'

The remainder of the diary contains a great many such entries about *seeing* this or that. Often such an entry is prefaced by the word '*saw*'. At times Strindberg places the verb within quotation marks, thus indicating his uncertainty as to the reality of the experience. This happens, for example, on 24 September 1898: 'Nervous. "Saw"'. On 27 July the following year he writes: 'In the morning I "saw" three women dressed in mourning, sitting on my sofa; one looked like my sister Anna'. On 3 January 1900 he notes: 'these colours aroused in me the memory of a pattern in the same colours that I "saw" on my clothes in Heyst sur Mer and which I found again in the pillow I was given by Esther Bülow, and on my sofa in Grünegatan.'

One variation of this phenomenon of *déjà vu* is found in Strindberg's habit of mistaking people he meets for persons he has known in the past. He believes that he sees a certain individual but afterwards realizes that it must be a case of mistaken identity. Such is the case on 23 January 1901, when he writes that he 'saw' Gustaf af Geijerstam in the royal box at the Royal Dramatic Theatre in Stockholm. He adds: 'It obviously wasn't him, but for a few minutes I had a complete illusion that it was.'

From now on, therefore, to *see* for Strindberg means both to observe with one's sense of sight and to *believe to see*, or in some other manner experience the presence of someone or something. This type of response to the world around him will have important consequences when he begins to write for the theatre again.

'Scanian Landscapes with Digressions'

Immediately upon his arrival in Lund in December 1896, Strindberg contacted the newspaper *Malmö-Tidningen*, which was affiliated to *Dagens Nyheter* in Stockholm. He needed money and proposed writing a series of articles about the various types of landscape in Skåne. The result was four articles which were published on 19 and 30 December 1896 and 9 and 21 January 1897.

However, Strindberg did not seem disposed at the time to naturalistic depictions of the kind he had written in *Swedish Nature* in the early 1890s, prior to his mental crisis. In the Malmö articles the liveliest depiction is found at the end of the first piece, but to a great extent it is compiled of passages from Linnaeus's *Skånska resa*:

> And in Herrestad parish near Gytebo he [Linnaeus] found a wine mountain (note!). The stork, the nightingale, the bell frog chattered, sang, chimed in a great mass of light, and on ash trees and privets, Spanish flies were creeping, shining like gold and green forests . . . (SV 29:232).

In the third article it is somewhat surprising for the genre to find an account of a restless night, reminiscent of a number of similar accounts in *Inferno*, which Strindberg was to begin writing a few months later. But the episode has little to do with the Scanian landscape:

> The night has fallen and through the stillness one can hear like heavy sighs, the last gasps of someone drowning. From time to time there is a crackle as if the earth's crust was bursting. When we draw the blinds and look out into the night, only the hazy fog

and starry skies are visible, and from out the mist come sighs and a cracking sound (237).

The article ends with Strindberg's comparison of descriptions of Skåne by A. U. Bååth in the 1870s and Ola Hansson in the 1880s[58] with what he himself sees. Now the source of inspiration appears to be Swedenborg's depiction of hell rather than Linnaeus's botanical Skåne:

> Now the billowing field does not sway, the land is not yellow but rather a disconcerting copper green; the factory with its prison-like buildings and its ugly smokestacks blocks out everything. [. . .] A factory landscape where the scent of clover can't out-smell the ammonium sulphide from the sugar refinery's stinking ditch (240).

The smell of sulphur pursues Strindberg. Not until the fourth and last article does he temporally recapture something of his love of nature in his depiction of Ringsjö's northern shore: 'And when the linden tree flowers, it has the scent of wholesome honey, and that is when it sings, though the singing cannot be heard above the bees' (241). But depictions of nature on any larger scale did not suit Strindberg at this time and in April he abandons a planned sequel. Instead, he sets about writing the novel *Inferno*.

Memories from Paris

When Strindberg wrote *Inferno* he returned in his memory to the critical periods he had experienced in Paris and Austria, and to sounds, smells and visions of a different type than those in Skåne. A draft written on Strindberg's familiar Lessebo manuscript paper with a watermark from 1900 is covered with notes related to the sights and sounds of Paris. The sheet – 9:1,14 – is headed 'Montparnasse' and has the subtitle 'Pantomime'.

The first notes relate to visual memories: 'She walks on the opposite boulevard, waiting for someone who doesn't come.' Strindberg had already used this particular memory in 'Études funèbres' and would return to it in the play *Crimes and Crimes*. A note referred to as 'The mausoleum of a child' refers in all likeli-hood to the one which is also mentioned in 'Études funèbres' (see above, p. 28; the mausoleum is not preserved). Then follow several notes about the *sounds* of Montparnasse:

The trams; noise of wagons. The omnibus horn.
Song with guitar = *Petits pavés*:
Street callers – *Cresson* = The Old Goat:
Locomotive whistles:
The stone mason tapping – – –

This is probably one of the first drafts in which Strindberg gathered this type of sensory impression together for dramatic use. In the future too – as in the draft of the never-completed drama 'The Gold Galleon' (3:22, 62) – one can see how Strindberg plans visual and acoustic effects rather than concentrating on any theme. The draft contains headings such as 'Lighting Effects' and subtitles like: 'Sun:/Moonlight'. Another heading reads 'Sounds', followed by 'Doorbell. – / Pianola. – / Nightingale. – / Children's song. – / Church bells in the distance'. Strindberg is preparing to pursue his new vision, with its emphasis on sensuous impressions, in the type of drama he begins to write around the turn of the century.

2

The Return

This argument has led me to a point where I must
reflect on the senses:
They are the most important reason for our
ignorance and the evidence of it.

Montaigne, *Essays*

To Damascus

Strindberg's post-Inferno dramas are visually and acoustically
richer than his earlier dramas. They often refer to an invisible reality
which manifests itself through visions or sounds, sometimes of an
objective kind (i.e. also perceptible to the audience) and sometimes
of a subjective kind, where the protagonist must verbalize his
'visions' or 'auditory sensations'.

In this context it is helpful to study the first dramatic *exposition*
Strindberg constructed following his return to drama, in the
opening scene, 'At the Street Corner' of *To Damascus I* (1898).

In various ways Strindberg makes the audience aware that the
protagonist of the play, the Stranger (Den Okände), is disorientated
in his relationship to the real world about him. He 'does not know'
why he is standing at the street corner; he knows that he is 'waiting'
but not what he is waiting for (SV 39:15), and nor does he 'know'
why he has left his wife and children. As the scene progresses this
impression of disorientation increases: 'If I only knew why I exist,
why I stand here, where I must go, what I must do' (16). For the
time being, the audience is kept in ignorance of the kind of information that usually forms part of an exposition, which is meant to
place the protagonist in a comprehensible context.

However, the physical surroundings are in no way strange: '*One
sees the side portal of a small Gothic church; a post-office and a café with
chairs outside*' (15). In addition there is an acoustic reference: '*One
hears the tones of a funeral march approaching and then receding.*' The
Stranger finds the music frightening, and conveys this to the Lady

and the audience in the theatre: 'Listen again now, listen to those horrible tones!' (15). On two other occasions when the funeral march is heard, the Stranger reacts in a similar way (17, 20).

Other sounds function in a similar manner. One of the funeral guests imitates a 'death-watch beetle' (31), which is the second allusion to death within a short space of time. The acoustic elements in the first scene of *To Damascus* have an ominous character, and the scene ends in what is acoustically a very frightening way: '*A high-pitched chorus of women's voices, close to a shriek, is heard from within the church*' (38).

This last acoustic element is coupled with a visual change that is also ominous: '*The illuminated stained-glass window suddenly grows dark; the tree above the bench starts to tremble; the funeral guests rise from their places and look up at the sky, as if they saw something unusual and frightening*' (38).

Earlier in the same scene the drama projects a sphere of unreality – again through sound but in terms of the Stranger's or the Lady's subjective perceptions. The Stranger believes he can hear higher powers meeting to discuss his fate: 'Did you know that just now I heard the gavel fall, the chairs being pushed back from the table and the servants dismissed' (37, cf. 64). The Lady responds by recalling a premonition she has had, which drew her back to him: 'There in the chapel I could not find any peace; a candle went out on the altar and a cold wind blew against my face just as I heard you call me.' The Stranger replies: 'I did not call; I merely longed for you' (37).[1]

However, the Stranger develops a line of reasoning which indicates that he also counts on an abstract reality which does not appear any less 'real' to him, but which is for him a new kind of experience: 'Yes, for some time now I've been noticing everything, but not as before when I only saw things and events, forms and colours; now I see thoughts and meanings' (18). He also testifies to having experienced 'beings that are invisible but tangible and possessing life' (17). Meanwhile, responding to a direct question from the Lady he denies having had 'visions' before (19) and seems determined to dismiss the thought that he ever hallucinates.

Thus, the opening scene in *To Damascus* confronts the audience with someone who is truly disorientated, and who is in contact with a heightened reality. Dramaturgically this heightened reality is represented by light and sound effects, as well as verbal accounts of 'visions' and 'auditory sensations'. This original exposition is designed to allow the protagonist to present his state of mind rather than his background.

One episode in scene 1 is particularly bewildering. According to the stage directions the funeral guests are 'dressed in brown' (31), and when the Stranger asks them why, he is told: 'To our simple minds it is black, but if Your Honour so commands, it shall be brown to him' (32). This scene has provoked Egil Törnqvist to an important observation: 'Here Strindberg, perhaps for the first time in the history of drama, makes his audience doubt their senses.'[2]

In this challenging manner Strindberg questioned the traditional drama of illusions, for which he had sometimes expressed a certain dislike.[3] It may be true that Strindberg did not exploit the consequences of his criticism of illusion to the full in the new form of drama he is developing here, but in those plays he himself thought best of – *A Dream Play* and *The Ghost Sonata* – he does demand that an audience maintain a critical distance to sensory experience. To an ever greater extent his plays will remain suggestive by undermining the reliability of our senses.

In the second scene of *To Damascus*, the audience is again confronted with an extraordinary example of how the senses affect the characters on stage. The Doctor reacts violently to a sound, which the audience understands to be a steamship whistle, but which the Doctor takes for a scream (41). He also hears the Stranger approaching far in advance of his arrival: 'Now they are entering the gate. THE SISTER: I heard nothing! THE DOCTOR: But I, I hear! And now I see, as well!' (42). After such lines the explanation that the Doctor is half-deaf comes as a surprise: 'You may speak loudly, for my husband hears poorly but he can read what people say from their lips!' (50). The Doctor possesses a kind of inner hearing and sight, which is superior to ordinary sensory perceptions. Shortly afterwards the Doctor is within sight of the Stranger and the Lady, who continue their conversation without the Doctor being able to hear, even though he is said to compensate for his deafness by a talent for lip reading. Strindberg has thus complicated the dialogue on stage.

Later on in the play, in the scene called 'In the Ravine' (IV, 1), Strindberg experiments with what might be called a 'disturbed dialogue' i.e. a dialogue that functions poorly, not on account of misunderstandings on the verbal or intellectual level but for acoustic reasons or because one character *is* invisible, either really deaf or mute or *making himself* invisible, deaf or mute. When first the Lady and then the Stranger addresses the Blacksmith and the Miller's Wife, these characters appear to be mute since they only respond with deprecating gestures. On the other hand, the Stranger's question is answered by Echo, since here Strindberg has turned an acoustic phenomenon into a character: 'THE STRANGER: No mercy! ECHO (*in the distance, imitating his voice*): Mercy!' (130).

The Stranger's path to a more humble attitude in the final scene is lined with ominous sounds. Just as he denies, in the first scene, that he has 'visions' (19), he denies 'hearing illusions' (46) in the second scene. In terms of the audience, this establishes that they are to interpret what the Stranger sees and hears not as psychic phenomena but as messages from a higher power.

In *To Damascus* a distinction is made between the various sounds mentioned in the stage directions, which are part of both an internal and an external system of communication, and certain other sounds which, though said to be real, are only apprehended by the Stranger.

Sounds that are audible to everyone are numerous: church bells (15), the funeral march (15, 17, 20, 134), a sound 'like clockwork' (31), organ music (35), choral song (35, 78), women's screams (38), a steamship whistle (41), a whistle (51), a French horn (73, 77), spiritual music (107), banging (112, 120), the wind (120), the roar of a waterfall (120), the sound of a smithy and a mill (129), the tolling of a buoy (136).

Strindberg had never previously assembled so many original sound effects in one drama. These sounds are instrumental in establishing the uniqueness of *To Damascus* as a drama and constitute an innovation within Strindberg's writing for the theatre, and he has recourse to acoustic effects in his other post-Inferno dramas, although their frequency does vary. It is also worth observing that no such wealth of acoustic effects is to be found in the plays of Ibsen or Chekhov. In Ibsen's *The Wild Duck* and *Hedda Gabler*, as in Chekhov's *The Seagull*, pistol shots are heard offstage in the last act. This is a melodramatic and not particularly imaginative way of using an acoustic effect. In *The Cherry Orchard* a 'sound that is like a broken string' is heard on two occasions – in the second act and in the closing scene. This acoustic element has been carefully discussed in Chekhov research[4] while Strindberg's cascade of sound has failed to generate the same attention.

What is interesting in the case of *To Damascus* is the relationship between objective sounds and the sounds that are only perceived by the Stranger. He is beset by a reality that makes a deep impression on him but which does not reveal itself to others. In his attempts to articulate it, he comes to resemble a medium or a seer.

From the perspective of the Stranger, the difference between the objective and the subjective sounds is mainly that the former seem to frighten him while the latter also fascinate. To the latter category belongs, for example, his feeling that a higher power is 'holding a meeting' to determine his fate: 'just now I heard the gavel fall [and] the chairs being pushed back from the table' (37). However, since Strindberg made the Stranger into a poet, such imaginativeness does not seem too far-fetched. In the scene 'By the Sea' (II, 2), the Stranger describes what he believes to be the birth of a poem. The experience gradually turns into a description of a place where he has never been but to which, we subsequently discover, he is on his way:

> Quiet – I hear a poem coming—I call it that when a motif begins to grow in my brain . . . but I hear the rhythm first . . . this time it is like a horse's hooves, and the jingle of spurs and the clatter of weapons . . . but a fluttering too as when a sail is flapping . . . Quiet! – now they are riding over a bridge, but it is a wooden bridge and there is no water in the river, only pebbles—but wait; now I hear someone praying with a rosary, men and women; it is the greeting of angels (69).

The Stranger 'sees' and 'hears' beyond what his senses would normally permit. It begins as an inspiration and turns into 'future sight' (70).

Among the unique features in Strindberg's new drama are the many vague entrances and departures.

> Your mother was here; you talked about me of course; I still seem to hear the sound of her evil words, I can feel how they snap in the air and see how they blacken the sunbeams; I believe I can

even see the impression of her body in the air, here in this room; and she has left a smell behind her like a dead snake (95).

This intense experience of a person *after* her exit is reminiscent of the Doctor's experience with the Stranger *before* his entrance (above, p. 44). In *To Damascus* – as in many of Strindberg's subsequent dramas – a character's entrance or exit is, in a formal sense, often less interesting than the foreboding that precedes his arrival or the presence he leaves behind in the room following his exit.[5] In other cases characters glide in and off stage without there being any strongly marked entrances or exits. These aspects of Strindberg's post-Inferno dramaturgy are used in different ways: often they raise doubts in the mind of the protagonist who is faced with sudden confrontations and risks being seen and overheard without his knowledge. This suspiciousness and a feeling of there being 'witnesses' nearby forms a basic mood and is a dramaturgical trick that often appears in the post-Inferno dramas with their frequently guilt-ridden protagonists.

To a large degree *sounds* both frighten and guide the Stranger on his journey. Through his memories of once-heard sounds he succeeds in returning from the Asylum to his point of departure: 'Do you hear a mill churning? A horn calling? A river that is roaring, a forest whispering, and – a woman who is crying!' (111). On the return journey, the subjective sounds the Stranger hears serve to guide rather than to frighten him.

However, the objective sounds – above all, the nocturnal sounds in the scene in the Kitchen (III, 4) – still frighten the Stranger. This scene of night-time horrors constitutes the drama's peripeteia. The Stranger is frightened into humility, which in turn leads to his conversion.[6] And unlike the first scene of the drama, 'At the Street Corner' the final scene, which has the same location, includes no acoustic elements at all – neither the church bells, funeral music, death-watch beetle, organ music or song which were to be heard when the audience first saw this setting. These disturbing effects are no longer needed and furthermore, the Stranger's subjective experience of sounds is now explained by a religious vocabulary where previously it had been attributed to bad nerves:[7]

THE LADY: Don't you hear the singing?
THE STRANGER: (*Pointing at the church*): Yes, but from in there! (155).

From a dramatic point of view, there is an interesting discrepancy between objective and subjective impressions of sight and hearing in *To Damascus*. On two remarkable occasions – once in front of the brown-clad funeral guests and on another occasion before 'the ghosts' in the Asylum scene – the spectators share the Stranger's predicament and doubt the testimony of their senses.

Advent

In *To Damascus* Strindberg reused his own extraordinary experiences. This is also the case in *Advent*, the third of his plays after the Inferno crisis. However, his distance to the subject matter of the play is greater this time, he chooses not *one* but *two* main characters, and he places the story in a historical context, the early 1800s. The Judge and his Wife undergo the same kind of treatment as the Stranger in *To Damascus*; they are to be frightened into doing penance. As a dramatist Strindberg has become a master of the same kind of horror effects that he himself had been exposed to a few years earlier; his use of supernatural and frightening elements in *Advent* appears to be almost enjoyable to him, now that he himself can play the role of God.

As in *To Damascus*, the main characters in *Advent* appear morally disorientated in the expository scene – but lack any insight into themselves. Unlike the Stranger, their sense of well-being seems boundless. On the other hand, their boasting soon makes the audience recognize their moral decay. It is this discrepancy between appearance and reality, outer and inner, that the drama seeks to demonstrate. The fact that the couple try to find rational explanations for what they experience constitutes part of their pride, even though these experiences become increasingly unreal. For the audience it is clear from an early stage that these experiences have their origin in a moral court, sitting in judgement on the Judge and his wife. The visions and the sounds which become visible and audible in the course of the play have a more objective existence than in *To Damascus* but still serve the same purpose: on the one hand to portray the guilt of the main characters, and on the other to reveal the existence of a reality beyond the visible.

In the exposition, we encounter a feature that is common in the post-Inferno dramas: the protagonists' feeling of being watched or eavesdropped on, or – as in this case – both: 'Don't say that;

somebody can hear it [. . .] Be careful, be careful! Many are jealous of us and we are being watched by evil eyes!' (SV 40:15). And as a whole, the first act includes several strange visions and a rich use of verbal metaphors, all of which are designed to provoke discussion about the reliability of the sense of sight and, by extension, to emphasize the futility of denying a higher, invisible reality.

A reflection of the sun (*solkatt*) also figures in this act, an object which is seemingly directed by a higher will, since it reveals the truth about the person caught in its beam: 'You must have been able to cast spells and distort sight, for now I see how horribly ugly and old you are. [. . .] (*The reflection strikes the Judge.*) Ugh! Now I am being burnt! THE JUDGE'S WIFE: And that's what you look like!' (32). In confronting sensory experiences, the Judge's Wife has recourse to the testimonies of witnesses, or rather, confronted by evidence that she doubts, she relies solely upon the testimony of her own senses: 'Two witnesses behind the bush, that's just as in a court of law. But you see, I know those tricks, and what I've heard and seen, that is evidence enough for me!' (37).

In 'The Procession of Shadows' in the First Act, the Judge's guilt takes shape: those he has humiliated pass across the stage without making a sound. Strindberg has guarded against our interpreting these characters as *no more than* projections of the Judge's bad conscience, since the first time the procession glides by the stage is empty. When the procession passes the same way for a second time, it is in front of the Judge and his Wife. The Judge cannot even shut out the vision by closing his eyes or holding his hands in front of them; the vision penetrates both his hands and his eyelids. His Wife asks herself: 'Are these shadows or ghosts or our own sick dreams?' (41), but the audience is aware that these shadows exist outside the couple's sick dreams. However, the conclusion can hardly be that the dramatist has wanted to show these 'shadows' (that is the word the *reader* sees) as having an objective existence. For a long time Strindberg used the term 'fairy-tale play' as an experimental generic title.[8] Given such a context the ghostlike elements in *Advent* can be more easily explained than in *To Damascus*, where their function was rather to stretch our perception of reality. In *Advent* one is not as surprised; it is true that in the end Strindberg decided to call the play 'A Mystery [Play]' but even so, an audience can accept ghosts on stage without feeling obliged to regard them as the subconscious projections of one or other of the characters. That

Advent is conceived as a kind of 'mystery' or 'fairy-tale play' is also evident in a scene of revenge where the Judge is to be sentenced before a ghostlike court. We now witness what the Stranger only sensed in *To Damascus* – namely, that his fate was decided by a higher order, at which point he heard the gavel striking the table and the chair being pushed back (above, p. 00). In *Advent* the mysterious phenomena simply occur: '*the gavel strikes once; the chairs are pushed all at once against the table*' (99).

In the Second Act of *Advent*, sounds play a large role and, as in the case of visions, they are objective. During the night the Judge runs around his garden chasing the starlings away with a rattle (47), he hears banging from a cupboard and a pendulum that strikes an infinite number of times. He sees and hears a kettle jump (54) and finally he also hears an ominous roar as if of a storm (58).

Other senses are also assaulted. In the Second Act the Judge and his Wife notice that their food tastes bad, whereupon each suspects the other of seeking to assassinate him/her. There is a joint of venison on the table but the Judge takes a piece of bread out of his pocket since he finds the meat tastes of creosote: 'A joint of venison is very good, one can smell it from here, but bread isn't bad!' (53). In the Fourth Act, the Judge's Wife tastes the water in a well: 'Ugh, it tastes just like copper . . . imagine, he's been here and poisoned the water too!' (78). Later she experiences a smell of 'putty' 'linseed oil' or a 'cadaver' and when, in the same scene, she is to be chastised for her vanity, this takes place at a grotesque ball where her escort's hands are 'cold as ice' (93). Other forms of touching include blows and a box on the ears (94) and the scene ends with the Wife going blind. (98)

The Judge continues to search for rational explanations for what is occurring:

> Everything has its reason: *ratio sufficiens*. This cabinet door has a spring that I am unfamiliar with, and because of that I am surprised, but fear not. [. . .] The axe is moving: this has always meant decapitation, but today it only means that it has been displaced from its equilibrium. No, when I get to see my ghost, then I shall begin to reflect, for that is something that this charlatan cannot conjure forth (99).

At that moment a ghost, very similar to the Judge, makes his entrance. He has '*eyes without pupils, completely white like those of plaster statues'* (100). The Judge is confronted by an image of his own moral blindness. Like his wife, he is found guilty, and the next time they meet, they are in hell.

The scene in hell begins with a feature reminiscent of the Stranger's visions in *To Damascus*. In a monologue, '*as in a dream*' (112), the Judge recapitulates what appears to be the moment of his death and burial. Through tactile, acoustic and olfactory impressions, the audience can reconstruct the chain of events before these are understood by the Judge:

> After that everything became black and empty until now . . . I can't tell how long it lasted . . . But now I'm beginning to hear again . . . and to feel. Now it feels as if someone were carrying me; . . . oh, how cold, I think I'm being washed . . . I lie inside a hexagon as in the cell of a bee, and there's a smell of carpentry . . . I'm being carried and a bell is ringing . . . (112).

This monologue[9] is unique in many ways. Dramaturgically, Strindberg uses one of his special devices. He deprives a character of one of his senses, in this case sight. Hence the character is forced to reconstruct a chain of events by using his other senses. Such 'beholding' monologues, possessing a strong sensuous concreteness and built on more or less real experiences, are to be found in several dramas preceding the chamber plays, where they become an integral part of the special nature of Strindberg's new drama.

On the whole, the sounds and visions that confront the characters on stage in *Advent* are also experienced by the audience. Despite numerous special effects, Strindberg has hardly gone any further than in *To Damascus* where letting the spectators doubt the veracity of their senses is concerned. When ghosts are spoken about on stage, they are either visible both to the *dramatis personae* and the audience or are invisible to both parties. Therefore, despite its use of fantastic effects, *Advent* becomes, paradoxically enough, *more* like theatrical naturalism than does *To Damascus* with its creeping sense of unreality. In *Advent* we are told that it is foolish to place too great a faith in our senses or in rational explanations, based on perceptions, but the play does not include the spectator in this discussion, as was the case in *To Damascus*.

Easter, The Dance of Death

Easter (1900), too, is a moral exemplum. In *Easter* different speech patterns are mixed together. Strindberg blends a traditional, well-functioning dialogue that proceeds through question and response, including an interrogation scene, with visionary monologues. And in this play two of the *dramatis personae* possess over-sensitive senses and are capable of 'perceiving' more than material reality. This time Strindberg has returned to the manner of *To Damascus* rather than to that of *Advent*, in that he excludes the audience from some of the extraordinary sound sensations.

The year before Strindberg wrote *Easter* and the year after *Advent* he had written a historical drama, *The Saga of the Folkungs*, which includes a character, 'The Possessed Woman' (*Den Besatta*), whose sensibilities have passed beyond the border of the normal. This type of character is of course not new to drama; she is related to Cassandra as well as to Shakespeare's witches, but Strindberg places her in the Middle Ages. Like her dramatic predecessors, her task is to foretell misfortune. And, as Martin Lamm has pointed out, she is also a forerunner of Eleonora in *Easter*, although the medieval framework of *The Saga of the Folkungs* allows the author to make her less ethereal than the protagonist of the later contemporary lyrical piece.[10]

One original aspect of the Possessed Woman's speech lies in her self-diagnosis; it seems as if the author had partly wanted to depict her as someone who is endowed with extreme sensitivity while at the same time suffering mental illness, since her senses are not separated from one another:

All my senses are joined together as one and function as all five at once. Just now I sensed that Bengt was in mortal danger, but I cannot say whether I saw, heard, smelled or felt it (SV 41:86).

Eleonora in *Easter* is a less turbulent kind of 'visionary' character. For the post-Inferno Strindberg, the quality of seeing what others cannot see and hearing what others cannot hear underwent a change: from being a curse it became a special honour, which was sometimes combined with martyrdom. In *Easter* Eleonora possesses this over-sensitivity, but her brother Elis is also in some respects telepathic:

I *hear* that it is spring! I can hear that the inner windows have been removed – Do you know how I can tell? – Mostly from the cart-wheels – but what's that? It's a chaffinch singing! And they are hammering down at the dockyard, and there's a smell of oil paint from the steamers, from the red lead – (43:245).

In this excursion outside the house, which is undertaken with the help of the senses – and which is made with his *'eyes shut'* – Elis associates with sounds and even smells from up north, where he longs to be: 'It's true that we are *here*, but I was *there*, up there in the north where my home lies' (245). As is often the case in Strindberg's post-Inferno works, a sensory experience has been used to evoke associations – sometimes, as here, with similar sensory experiences linked to other places. The speaker is detached from both time and space. And here again, in a speech that is barely five lines long, one can, for structural reasons, speak in terms of a 'mono-logue'; the speaker is certainly removed from the context on stage and the stage direction emphasizes the difference: *'[remains]silent, shuts his eyes'*.

On another occasion, Elis' ability to comprehend events from afar is certainly remarkable but nonetheless within the bounds of reality. When the ominous figure of Elis's tormentor, Lindquist, walks past in the street outside, he is observed from within the apartment, where he also casts his shadow over the household in a very concrete manner, which is also apparent to the audience: '*On the curtain one sees the shadow of a man approaching indecisively*' (295). Something similar has occurred on two previous occasions before Lindquist finally makes his entrance (259 ff., 292 ff.). On the first occasion, Elis claims he can see him and tells the others: 'I see by his mouth what he is saying . . . ' [. . .] 'listen to his galoshes . . . "wolves, wolves, angry, angrier, angriest, swish, swish"' (260). Once again, and not merely in order to create tension, Strindberg has wanted to delay the entrance of one of the most powerful characters in the drama, but also let him be 'present' both acoustic-ally and visually – not a reflection of the sun this time, but a shadow.

Eleanora, too, is extremely sharp of hearing. When she claims to hear the telephone wires singing, it is within the bounds of reality[11] – yet Eleanora's interpretation is fanciful:

Can you hear the singing in the telephone wires . . . it is the harsh words that the soft, beautifully red copper can't stand . . . when human beings slander each other on the telephone, the copper complains (267).

Eleanora herself describes her sensitive nature; the passage has a clinical tone that was lacking in the speech by the Possessed Woman as she described the way in which her senses were all combined with one another in *The Saga of the Folkungs*:

> Do you know that when I was sick, I had to take Henbane, which has the effect of turning one's eye into a magnifying glass— Belladonna on the other hand reduces everything one sees—Oh well; now I can see further than others, I can see the stars in broad daylight! (269–70).

This speech is based on fact. In his edition of *Easter*, Gunnar Ollén points out that both henbane and belladonna were used in contemporary psychiatry. Apart from their relaxing or stimulating effects on the central nervous system, these substances also affect the appearance of the eye and – to a limited degree – its vision. The atrophy of belladonna enlarges and fixes the pupil, the scopalamine of the henbane focuses the eye on a point in the distance (411).

Strindberg allows Eleonora to associate naturally with other flowers via the daffodil (in Swedish *påsklilja*, literally 'Easter lily') which is her special attribute, and he is being quite objective in letting her talk about her medication. But Eleonora does not mention its effects on the central nervous system herself; she merely mentions the manner in which the eye changes and hence draws the conclusion that her vision has also changed.

Eleonora also reflects philosophically on her vision: 'Now, notice how one person *can* see what others cannot . . . therefore, do not trust *your* eyes!' (270). It is evident that what she means by 'seeing' is not the ability to observe with her eyes but rather a form of beholding in a higher sense.

Eleonora is also sensitive when it comes to aromas. She calls the scent of flowers 'a silent language':

> Every scent expresses a whole range of thoughts, and these thoughts overpowered me; and with my magnifying eye I looked into their workshops, which no one has seen (270).

On two occasions Eleonora perceives the weather in terms of scent: 'It already smells of melted snow in here' (304), 'there are no clouds today, there are only sea mists, for they smell of salt' (308). Here Strindberg is anticipating Eleonora's final line in which she encourages Elis to thank God, something she naively interprets as an acoustic matter: 'Yes, you must say it silently!! For the clouds have gone now, so it will be heard up there!' (337).

Thus, even in the final line of the play, the sensitive sense of hearing is emphasized: this time God's hearing.

In the spatially confined and tightly woven drama that is *Easter*, Strindberg shatters the realistic framework by making two of the play's characters visionaries. But otherwise all is quiet in the small town apartment; the audience does not perceive any of the sounds that are described, and naturally does not smell the scent of flowers, melting snow or lead, to which the characters allude.

The many 'beholding' elements endow the play with a certain dreamlike character. A similar mood is also attained in a different manner at the start of the Second Act, when Benjamin and Eleonora sit mute and appear to sense each other in the manner of Maeterlinck; one is tempted here to speak of a 'mute dialogue'. Verbal communication has been replaced by silence, but the situation is commented on by the other characters: 'Have you noticed how Benjamin is changed! His dark defiance has given away to silent submission . . . ' (282), and again: 'They are probably looking at one another and only pretending to read, for I can't hear them turning any pages' (284).[12] Such lines recall those spoken by the characters left standing outside the house in Maeterlinck's *Intérieur*, but here both those commented on and those commenting are present in the same room.

From now on it is important to recognize that Strindberg's characters do not possess only five senses – they also frequently possess a sixth sense: an inner vision. This means that the characters who appear in different interior settings only seem to live an isolated life; often they are in rapport with their surroundings through sounds, smells and other sensations. Through their senses they perceive more than others do, and they frequently find it difficult to translate their sensations into words. Their speech becomes naive, poetic and dream-like. This tendency reaches a climax in *A Dream Play*.

In *Easter* the senses are largely benignant and the play does not raise the question of sensuality in a more worldly sense. This, however, is the aspect that Strindberg treats briefly in *The Dance of Death* (1900)[13] where there is a long scene without words in which Edgar, the Captain, takes leave of his senses.[14] Earlier in the play he has been portrayed as someone who derives pleasure from his senses, but after his stroke he is seen settling his account with sensuous living. He throws his whisky bottles out of the window and, after having smelt them, his cigars follow. Then he goes over to the piano and after banging on the keyboard, he locks it and throws away the key. Each of these gestures reveals him taking leave of a life of pleasure linked to taste, smell, sight and hearing with an almost allegorical clarity (SV 44:113–14), but given the title of the play with its medieval connotations such an allegorical view seems not too far-fetched.

Written back-to-back during October 1900, *Easter* and *The Dance of Death* are companion pieces. *Easter* demonstrates how sensitive minds may suffer but also be enriched. *The Dance of Death* explores the same theme but from the opposite angle, and exposes the way in which the senses are linked to vice.

Strindberg use both variations of this theme in the future. Most immediately in one and the same piece: *A Dream Play*.

A Dream Play

In *Easter*, hearing had a special function: two of the characters possessed an almost uncanny sense of hearing, so that the world beyond the stage – and even beyond the physical world itself – became uniquely tangible through their reports of it, sometimes in a dream-like manner, sometimes in a threatening way. At the close of the drama the threat was turned into its opposite, whereupon a note of gratitude was directed to a metaphysical addressee.

A similar perception of a divine ear plays an essential role in *A Dream Play* with the significant difference that in this play it is not man's gratitude but rather his complaint and prayers that are directed to the god Indra.

Through its many surprising transformation scenes and its mysterious stage settings and attributes, *A Dream Play* is certainly a very visual drama. As Helmut Müssener has shown, visual metaphors play an important part in creating the special quality of the play.[15] In the analysis that follows, however, I wish to show that the drama is above all a drama about the condition of *hearing*. The type of communication that dominates the play is one in which people transmit messages in the form of incomplete dialogues, in the hope that they will be well received by an invisible listener.

When hearing is to be accorded such importance in the drama, it is necessary that the importance of vision is reduced in terms of the characters. This already occurs in the opening scene when the Mother concludes: 'Imagine, I am also beginning to see poorly . . . yes, it's getting darker—*Polishes the light*' (SV 46:14). Sight as an organ of knowledge is questioned with considerable emphasiz in several scenes, as in the Officer's observation, 'And I have watched this door, two thousand five hundred and fifty five times, without understanding where it leads!' (22) or again when the clover-leaf door is to be opened later on in the drama and the Dean of Theology expresses his doubts in response to the empirical trust of his colleague in the natural sciences:

> You say Bravo, you who see no further than your nose in a magnifying glass, you who only believe in your deceptive senses, in your eyes, for example, which may be long-sighted, short-sighted, blind, purblind, cross-eyed, one-eyed, colour-blind, red-blind, green-blind . . . (104).

At the expense of the defective sense of sight, it is hearing that is now emphasized. Such is the case in the Blind Man's monologue, which, after registering a number of details in a naturalistic manner, turns into an inner vision that ends in compassion for suffering humanity:

> I do not see, but I can hear! I hear when the fluke of the anchor claws the sea bed, like a hook pulled up out of a fish through the gullet, along with its heart!—My son, my only child is to travel to unknown lands across the wide open sea; I can only follow him with my thoughts—now I can hear how the chain is grating— and – something fluttering and flapping, like clothes on a washing line . . . wet handkerchiefs perhaps—and a sighing or sobbing like people crying . . . the waves lapping against the hull perhaps or maybe the girls on the shore—those abandoned . . . and inconsolable (74).

In *A Dream Play*, it is remarkable how frequently 'hearing' is tantamount to receiving complaints and feeling compassion. This is
remarked on by the Daughter during the scene at the Opera near
the beginning of the drama: 'Everyone complains, at least with
their eyes, and with their voices' (19). Moreover, the role of the
Concierge at the Opera is to receive the complaints of the
employees (27) and paradoxically, the singers are said to be jealous
of the fish since they are mute and cannot sing (22).

Thus in *A Dream Play*, life on earth is martyrdom and often a
torture to sensitive minds. The Lawyer says that his clothes 'stink' of
the crimes of others and that he fumigates his office with sulphur in
a vain effort to cleanse it (35). In his home he is forced to eat
'cabbage' (45) while other loving couples are forced to live in 'pig
sties' (63) and in a stench of 'sulphur and carbolic acid' (63, 91).

In *Easter* Strindberg had already used the telephone as a symbol of
confinement rather than a modern means of communication.[16]
The same also happens in *A Dream Play*. Telephoning suggests a
world beyond the stage, and not just in a trivial sense. In an early
scene the Officer is observed telephoning both to the Glazier and
to cancel a supper he has planned (24). Here, the telephone is
shown as an effective instrument that enables the despatch of various errands. But as in *Easter* the telephone also comes to symbolize
the opposite and signifies interrupted communication, in the words
of the Poet, 'a modern tower of Babel' with its wires ascending 'to
inform those Above' to which the Daughter responds:

> Child! Mankind needs no metal wires to transmit its thoughts—
> the prayers of the faithful penetrate through every world . . . That
> is certainly no Tower of Babel, for if you would storm heaven,
> then storm it with your prayers! (98–9).

As in the case of mankind's ability to communicate with the god
Indra, when it comes to communication between human beings *A
Dream Play* is likewise pessimistic. This is stressed by the Poet's
imaginative vision of the 'telephone tower' as a Tower of Babel, an
image that implies a lack of linguistic communication between
people.

The symbolizm of hearing is presented more visually than in this
rapidly etched scene, in the two scenes in Fingal's Cave (40, 87)
and in the shell that the Daughter describes as a Fingal's Cave in

miniature (87).[17] According to the Daughter, this is a divine acoustic organ that receives mankind's complaints: 'It sighs . . . it whines . . . it moans . . . The complaints of the mortals have reached here . . . and no further' (41). When the action returns to Fingal's Cave for a second time, the Daughter distinctly calls the cave: '*Indra's Ear*, for here it is said that the ruler of heaven listens to the complaints of mortal beings!' (87). Like the ear, the cave is shaped like a shell (87).

The complaints of mankind are conveyed to Fingal's Cave by the wind and on this occasion they are interpreted by the Daughter. On a more earthly plane the Lawyer is shown pleading the cause of the condemned. He expresses the hopelessness of his task: 'Oh, that our complaints might reach the gods in heaven' (38) and the promotion scene ends with a Kyrie: 'Have mercy! Hear us! Have mercy upon all mortals! – Eternal One, why are you so distant—From the depths we cry out: Mercy, Eternal One! Do not make the burden too heavy for your children! Hear Us! Hear us!' (40).

On a smaller scale, the same theme of suffering is presented in the scene at Fairhaven in which Lina is tormented by the fact that she does not dare convey her complaints (59), and where the Poet invokes Harun, the Righteous, in what is clearly to be seen as an analogy to the Daughter's visit to Earth: 'Finally the complaints reached his lofty ear. Then one day he stepped down, disguised himself, and went unseen through the crowds to see the state of justice for himself' (60). Meanwhile, in one of the Fingal's Cave scenes we hear 'whimpering cries . . . Oh, woe! Oh, woe! – Oh, woe!' from the depths of the stage (79), representing 'the damned in Foulstrand'. In the second Fingal's Cave scene the Daughter and the Poet also hear a *Kyrie* from the crew of a ship in distress: 'Now they roar; and the sea roars! But nobody hears!' (97).

In a number of scenes, therefore, people get to express their suffering, either directly or through prayer and song. As a drama *A Dream Play* allows the audience to hear 'half-dialogues', i.e. words addressed to a person or authority who is not present, in a unique way. Such 'half-dialogues' can be performed in different ways: as a telephone call where only one party is visible and audible to the audience or as a prayer directed to heaven.

A Dream Play ends with Indra's Daughter returning to her divine abode, carrying with her the complaints of mankind. When asked what has caused her the most suffering during her visit to earth she responds: 'Just – being alive; feeling my sight dimmed by an eye, my hearing blunted by an ear, and my thoughts, my lofty airy thoughts bound in labyrinths of fat ganglia' (117).[18]

To the audience, *A Dream Play* appears as an illustration of the view that all is vanity and deception; life is a wandering among illusions and mirages.

The language of the drama has a lyrical quality – the kind of style that Manfred Pfister describes as directed towards the audience: 'Normally, the poetic functions only apply to the external communications system and not to the communication processes taking place between the various figures.'[19] But *A Dream Play* does not appear to be a 'normal' case. As for the dialogue, the drama is unusually *closed* to the audience, despite its often lyrical nature, something that can be explained by the fact that the dialogue has a metaphysical addressee. If the unique visual elements are there for the audience, it appears that the auditory elements of prayer and complaint are primarily aimed at an imagined, cosmic ear.

3

The Chamber Plays

All things confuse us. These two organs we have for
truth – reason and our senses – mutually deceive
each other, quite apart from the fact that they are not
to be trusted individually.

Pascal, *Pensées*

Introduction

As the previous chapter demonstrated, it is no exaggeration to claim
that the dramas Strindberg wrote after the Inferno crisis were both
enriched and made more complex by the addition of a host of
visual and acoustic elements. Paradoxically, this new direction was
combined with a tendency towards asceticism in the substance of
the actual plays.

Had Strindberg completed the play that was begun in the spring
of 1902 – which he planned as Part IV of *To Damascus* – the picture
might have been different. The play was to utilize, in a more sensual
way, material already partly used in *A Dream Play*.[1] However,
these plans only resulted in the fragment 'Walpurgis Night at
Fairhaven', written in the form of versified monologues which
were later reworked into the poetic cycle entitled 'Trinity Night'
(Trefaldighetsnatten, 1902).

For all its brevity, the dramatic fragment can tell us something about
the different requirements that exist for rendering sensory experiences in a written text (whether prose or poetry) and in the theatre.
One can also gauge Strindberg's not wholly conscious attitude to
the problem.

The dramatic fragment has an optimistic beginning. The scene
represents the spacious interior of an inn; up stage the set includes
'*glass doors and windows opening onto the veranda with a view of the sea,
the beacons and the coast at Foulstrand*'.[2] An event which is almost a
ritual one in Strindberg's world is taking place: '*Young servant girls
in light-coloured clothing are removing the interior windows*'. In the
poem 'Trinity Night' these stage directions have been radically

abbreviated. The description of how the interior windows are removed has been combined with a stage direction from the dramatic fragment which describes how '*The servant girls open the glass doors*' (SV 51:313). In 'Trinity Night' this becomes: 'The inner windows in the back are removed and the glass doors opened on to the veranda'. (9) As a feature in a poetic cycle this is much more expressive than as a scene at the beginning of a play.

The dramatic fragment continues – like the poem – with the Customs Inspector's praise of spring, followed by a long description of a feast. With its sensuous joy this description is an almost shocking contrast to the tone of the dramas from the 1898–1903 period as well as to the chamber plays of 1907. It is as if Strindberg was in the process of creating a counterbalance to the prevailing asceticism of the earlier dramas; however, this attempt became no more than a fragment. In the poetic cycle, on the other hand, the Attorney continues to fantasize over food, exclaiming: 'Oh, the lovely eel, the smoked salmon, good gentlemen' (12) and 'Oh how my mouth waters' (15) as he again conjures up the memory of another enticing meal, only to end: 'Quiet! My hungry mouth!'

The descriptions of sensory experiences in 'Trinity Night' repay further study. They characterize large portions of the poetic cycle whereas in the chamber plays, where the action moves indoors and summer is replaced by winter, this kind of experience is inverted.

Strindberg's world can be clearly divided into 'outdoors' and 'indoors'. The transition from one to the other is often strongly marked, sometimes with ritual overtones. It is not surprising that Strindberg begins his first great prose work, *The Red Room* (1879), with a description of the arrival of spring, and that when he comes to write *The Pelican* as an older, somewhat melancholy author, he describes the longed-for moment of death as an escape from the confines of a city apartment – a journey out to the country and an eternal summer vacation.

As noted, winter and confinement are connected in Strindberg's world with pessimism and misanthropy. Instead of enjoying the scent of flowers, listening to birds and eating succulent food in the open air, in the city apartment one is forced to listen to the noise of one's neighbours and the food that one is served both tastes and smells bad.

'Trinity Night' contains numerous descriptions of scents. Sometimes it is a matter of a pleasant scent in general, as in 'the shyly smelling reseda' (12) or the smell of rye in 'oven-warm bread' (35). Furthermore, there is an example of a 'scent recall' when the scent of lilacs prompts the Attorney to remember another time and another place, a New Year's ball where a certain perfume made an impression on him.

Two other instances where smell is used as a weapon – by man or by nature – are even more remarkable. In the first instance, the lady of the house spreads the smell of 'camphor and wormwood' in the apartment before it is abandoned for the summer vacation in the country (14). In the poem 'The Rye is Smoking', there is a description of a foul-smelling weed which has a similar function.

Poetry enjoys an advantage over drama when it comes to describing sensations of taste and smell. In a drama there exist direct channels for sight and sound, but in general no direct channels at all for taste, feeling or smell. When it comes to visual elements drama has a natural advantage over poetry, and the same goes for sound. The latter relationship is well illustrated when, in the poem, Strindberg seeks to take advantage of a stage direction: '*The steamer is heard whistling, cannon shots and brass music, hurrahs and singing outside*' (314). When staged in a theatre, this provides a considerable acoustic experience. In the poetic version it becomes lame, bordering on the comical: 'Bang! There was a shot! And another! For now comes the boat!' (13). However, Strindberg has enriched his poem in other ways in terms of sound as he includes a number of original onomatopoeic words, as in the description of thunder, which becomes both visible and audible on stage in the Chamber Play *Storm*. In the poem it is said to 'boom and roar,/mangle and wrangle' (18). In 'The Rye is Smoking', the invisible corncrake is described as 'arp-[ing] and knarp[ing]' (36) and in 'The Meadow Barn' the magpie 'screeches, reetches and eetches' (37) while in another poem, 'The Vane is Singing', Strindberg describes the sound of a creaking weather vane and in 'The Song of the Nightingale' he introduces an infantile language in the form of a song that the Customs Inspector of the poem has learned from his nanny.[3]

So as not to appear altogether absurd, the poems 'The Vane is Singing' and 'The Song of the Nightingale' invite or force the reader to read the verse aloud and in the process Strindberg thus succeeds in extracting acoustic experiences from several of his poems resembling those he achieves in his plays.

The return to the city after the summer is described in 'Trinity Night' in sombre words: 'God's peace in nature has run its course,/ Feuding right takes over with squabbles and chores' (20). This is the world of the chamber plays, and it is notable that this sequence of four dramas begins in *Storm* with a depiction of the dog days of summer as they give way to autumn and ends in *The Pelican* with an ecstatic vision of 'the summer vacation'.

STORM

Sight

The principal character in *Storm* is a retired professional Gentleman who has been divorced for five years and who claims to prefer a peaceful life among memories in his city apartment. However, in the course of the play, both his past and his surroundings encroach upon him in different ways, and force him to re-evaluate his situation.

Strindberg uses a very effective dramatic device in reducing the old man's vision while at the same time increasing his hearing. One consequence of the protagonist's reduced vision is that other characters on stage – and at the same time, the audience – *see* more, *know* more and probably *understand* more of what is going on than the main character. As such, the Gentleman in *Storm* is a variation of the disorientated protagonist of *To Damascus*.

The chamber play *Storm* has a realistic framework. From a visual standpoint the viewer encounters nothing that appears to be unreal. But within this framework the drama contains a number of symbols – *the window, the lantern, the eye* – that are related to vision and serve the purpose of questioning not so much the truthfulness of what the sense of sight conveys as its value and worth. Technically *Storm* is among Strindberg's most well-crafted pieces; on the surface the play is a realistic bourgeois *drame* with a suitable number of conventional symbols.

Within the pronounced realistic framework of the play there is an ongoing discussion whether or not a life lived among 'illusions' is possible or even to be recommended, especially where 'illusions' encompass misconceptions, false memories and self-deception as well as sensory illusions.

The First and Third Acts of *Storm* take place in front of an ordinary urban house façade while the Second Act is set in the ordinary drawing-room discerned through the window, in Acts One and Three. In this everyday, well-to-do middle-class world there are a number of mysterious noises which the Gentleman experiences as threatening. He does not know what is going on in the apartment above but, by interpreting the sounds he hears, he is able to make certain assumptions. In this respect he resembles, for all practical purposes, a blind person. But this feature also gives the play an air of unreality in that the invisible – the immaterial – plays a pivotal role. The audience is thus presented with a mildly dreamlike mood in a realistic setting, which is strengthened when the Gentleman keeps both windows and doors open because of the summer heat. This means that entrances and exits from the stage are made soundlessly and sometimes take the Gentleman by surprise. Hence, the play permits a director to accentuate certain dreamlike qualities within a realistic framework.

The Gentleman's vision is reduced. One of the stage directions mentions his '*near-sightedness*' (SV 58:52) which, on a symbolic level represents his resistance to different types of information. On the realistic level, however, it also plays an important role in the dramatic intrigue when, at one point, the Gentleman happens to mistake his relative Louise for his former wife Gerda. Strindberg is explicit on this point, for in the same scene where the mistake occurs, the Gentleman comments on his poor vision in a telephone conversation with his mother:

> My eyes? Yes, I'm getting nearsighted, but I agree with the Confectioner's Wife: there's nothing to look at! I wish I was a little deaf as well! Deaf and blind! The neighbours above make such a horrendous racket at night . . . it's some type of gambling club (53).

This telephone conversation – a kind of 'half-dialogue' – focuses our attention on another character with reduced vision, and of whom the Confectioner also speaks at the start of the play in such a way as to indicate that in *Storm*, blindness also implies a reluctance to know about the surrounding world:

> We old people love the dusk, which hides so many shortcomings in ourselves and others . . . do you know, young lady, that my

wife is going blind, but doesn't want to have surgery: There's nothing to see, she says, and sometimes wishes she were deaf as well (23).

It is clear that at the beginning of *Storm* the senses are regarded as well-functioning instruments for a knowledge of the surrounding world, indeed, they would sometimes appear to function all too well since the protagonist evidently wishes to protect himself from all manner of intrusions from without, but in which the dramatic tension of the play resides:

> It is best not to know anything! (19)
> [. . .]
> I ask to know nothing! (22)
> [. . .]
> I don't want to know anything! (70)

The first line cited above is the Gentleman's response to his Brother, who has just made him aware that a dress has suddenly become *visible* in an upstairs window, and the last line is his reaction when the telephone *rings* while he is waiting to hear his daughter's fate. But it is perhaps the second of these lines that reveals most clearly how he cuts himself off from unpleasant information. The rest of his speech runs: 'Since I had gone through all the horrors of loss, I considered the whole affair buried, and since only beautiful memories remained in the apartment, I stayed on'. The Gentleman expresses his preference for a life among memories, but when these memories turn out to be false, it becomes clear even to him that he has been living on illusions, 'hallucinations'.

It is generally known that while writing the chamber plays Strindberg also read *Hamlet*[4] and there are numerous traces of Shakespeare's play in *The Burnt House*, *The Ghost Sonata* and *The Pelican* as well as in the essay on Shakespeare's play that he dedicated to the members of his Intimate Theatre on its first anniversary, 26 November 1908. However, Strindberg's reading of *Hamlet* is already to be detected in *Storm*. In his edition of the chamber plays in the new Swedish National Edition of Strindberg's collected works, Gunnar Ollén points out that the line which Gerda addresses to her former husband in the Second Act – 'More than your friend' (Mer än din frände, 63) – is a direct quotation from Hagberg's classic Swedish translation of *Hamlet* (Act I, scene 2). The line is in quotation marks in Strindberg's text, suggesting that the borrowing is openly acknowledged. With the help of this quotation Gerda can insinuate that Louise is not only related to the Gentleman but is also his mistress – an insinuation, however, that is not supported elsewhere in the text.

Thus, Strindberg has himself drawn attention to his borrowing from Shakespeare, at least where the *reader* of his text is concerned. However, if one claims that the opening of *Storm* is reminiscent of the opening scene of *Hamlet*, it is no longer simply a question of the borrowing of a single identifiable feature but rather Strindberg's travesty of the effective way in which Shakespeare opens *Hamlet* and creates dramatic tension from the very beginning.

In the Swedish translation of *Hamlet* that Strindberg read, the stage direction reads: '*A terrace in front of the castle*'.[5] In *Storm* the setting is the pavement before '*the façade of a modern house*'. Unlike in *Hamlet*, it is not 'bitterly cold' in *Storm* but rather the stifling dog days of late summer when food rots (13), but in both instances the playwright suggests in words that there is something 'rotten' in the present situation.

However, it is not Hamlet unmasking moral decay that is most clearly foregrounded in *Storm*. Strindberg was tempted to create an opening scene in the manner of *Hamlet* and transposed the Shakespearean model with its rapid dialogue between two minor characters to his own time and milieu, where they provide the exposition in a drama that otherwise opens *in medias res*. But what was, for Strindberg, presumably the most challenging aspect of Shakespeare's play was the exchange concerning the awful events that occurred during the past night: 'HORATIO: What, has this thing appear'd again tonight? [. . .] BERNARDO: What we two nights have seen.'[6]

In Strindberg's *Storm* the opening dialogue between the Confectioner and the Gentleman's Brother echoes some of the eerie features of *Hamlet*, though in a much more subdued tone. The dialogue refers to 'an unknown family, who remained silent all day, but started moving about at night when wagons arrived to pick up something. Not until the end of the second year did I find out that it had been a nursing home, and that what was picked up were corpses' (14). 'However, dramas of life have been performed here [. . .] up there where the red shades are illuminated, that is where the tenant died last summer [. . .] I've seen a great deal, but only late at night!' (15)

In *Storm* what is unseen is frightening, and on occasion connected with sickness and death. The opening scene of *Hamlet* is more problematic: those on stage not only talk about death but also about a ghost who appears and frightens the guards, not least because they are unable to determine its reality. However, they do have difficulty denying what they actually see: 'I might not this believe/Without the sensible and time avouch of mine own eyes'. While it is not until *The Ghost Sonata* that Strindberg incorporates visual spectres on stage, 'spectres' are present in *Storm* in another sense, as ghosts from the past. In that respect, one can speak of Strindberg as engaged in a dialogue with Shakespeare.

Martin Lamm has pointed out a number of similarities between *Storm* and Maeterlinck's one-act drama, *Intérieur* (Interior, 1894). 'It is precisely the same stage setting as in *Intérieur*, where the dialogue on the proscenium stage informs us of the tragic event'.[7] Lamm even goes as far as to complain that Strindberg did not retain this setting in the Second Act as well: 'It would have made a stronger impression if we had been allowed to witness the most distraught meeting at a distance, through a glass window, and not have to hear the lines whose content we can in any case already guess.'[8] Here Lamm actually recommends replacing the dialogue with a dumb show!

There is no doubt that *Intérieur* inspired Strindberg to employ certain dramatic devices in *Storm*, but as for Maeterlinck's influence in general, one must be careful not to over-interpret Strindberg's earlier enthusiasm for the Belgian playwright and make of him the latter's pupil, even if he had translated some of his works in 1901.[9] Rather, it is more likely that in *Storm*, Strindberg is seeking to establish a distance between himself and the author of *Intérieur*.

Lamm is also mistaken when he suggests that in allowing the Gentleman to conduct a conversation with someone through a 'windowpane', Strindberg is merely following the stage setting of *Intérieur*. In Maeterlinck's drama one sees 'three windows on the ground floor [which] are illuminated'.[10] It is apparent that here the windows are closed while the opposite is true of *Storm*: 'above the ground level are large windows which are open' (13).

There will be occasion to return to the important window

symbolism later, but it is a significant difference between *Storm* and *Intérieur* that in the first drama communication takes place in an unproblematic manner between the pavement and the apartment, while in the latter piece one only has a view from outside. While *Storm* begins with the Brother 'knocking with his cane on the windowpane' (13), *Intérieur* establishes a definite barrier between inside and outside: 'Do you want me to knock on one of the windows?'[11]

Maeterlinck's stage setting is intended to demonstrate a distrust of everyday communication. In Strindberg's *Storm* everyday communication functions remarkably well to start with. The Gentleman enjoys not only his everyday gossip with the Confectioner but also conversations with both his brother and Louise. When communication does not work, it is either due to technical mishaps – as when the telephone call with his mother is cut off because somebody is eavesdropping – or to an optical disturbance as when someone is temporarily blinded: 'Don't be afraid, he can't see us here in the dark – the light blinds him, you see' (34). The scene has a parallel in Maeterlinck: 'No, she doesn't know what she's looking at; her eyes don't function. She can't see us; we're in the shade of the big trees'.[12]

With his play Maeterlinck wants to show that the senses are largely useless instruments of knowledge and communication, and this is expressed by letting the characters in the house stare without seeing: 'They have lifted their eyes [. . .] Nevertheless, they can see nothing [. . .] *staring for a long time into the darkness*.'[13] In Maeterlinck's symbolic world people do not comprehend the outside world with their senses and communicate best through silence. The author wants to stress spiritual perceptions at the expense of sensory experiences: 'THE STRANGER: And the second one has eyes full of fear . . . THE OLD MAN: Watch out; one doesn't know how far the soul extends around people.'[14]

Rather than borrowing from Maeterlinck, Strindberg enters into a discussion with him. What is interesting in the relationship between *Intérieur* and *Storm* are certain fundamental differences. It is true that in Strindberg's world view after the Inferno crisis, and definitely in his chamber plays, there exists an ambivalence between 'registering' and 'perceiving' the world around him. His pessimistic point of view tells him that the material world is evil. And yet, at the same time, he registers this debased world with superbly sensitive senses. One could express the same thing by speaking about a conflict between Strindberg the naturalist and Strindberg the symbolist.

In *Storm* Strindberg is still concerned with low or 'complete reality', as he himself calls it in a letter to his German translator, Emil Schering.[15] On decisive points, therefore, *Storm* is a contrast to *Intérieur*: it becomes the response of Strindberg, the truth-sayer, to the symbolist Maeterlinck. The similarities between *Storm* and *Intérieur* can largely be reduced to the house façade of the stage setting in Acts One and Three.

Hearing

Strindberg compensates for the Gentleman's poor eyesight by endowing him with an exceptional sense of hearing. All of the sounds that he registers are also audible to the audience – the ring of the telephone, the chimes of the hall clock, and various noises and the music from the apartment above. Other auditory experiences are subjective and must be communicated orally, as when Strindberg accentuates the Gentleman's good hearing in a line addressed to the Iceman: 'And put the piece on edge, so that I can hear it melting and the water drops falling' (43).

In this scene the Gentleman's good hearing and his poor eyesight are emphasized at the same time. He hears when the Iceman comes but believes that it is his Brother (one of many cases of mistaken identity in this Act), and he continues to speak with the Iceman even after he has departed. Moreover, every time someone enters his apartment he asks them to say who they are, since his own vision is so flawed.

Information as to what is going on behind the closed windows and the drawn shades in the apartment above comes suddenly and in flashes to those left wondering below:

> *Now the blind is drawn up in the window of the upstairs apartment, but only a little, so that one sees a woman's dress, then the blind is quickly lowered again. (18)*
> [. . .]
> *Now a long drawn out 'oooh' can be heard from the apartment. (29)*

The mysteriously glowing red shades provoke an interpretation:

THE GENTLEMAN: Yes, it's so mysterious, but it's worst at night; sometimes there's music, but very poor quality; sometimes I think they play cards, and long after midnight wagons come to pick [people] up ... [. . .] Always waltzes, maybe they run a dancing school, but almost always it's the same waltz; what is it called? (19)

Louise and the Confectioner also speak about these nightly sounds:

LOUISE: [. . .] I've never seen them. But I hear them!
THE CONFECTIONER: I've also heard doors slamming and corks popping, other slams too, perhaps (26).

When the curtain falls on the First Act, it has become apparent to the audience that the characters on stage have interpreted what they hear quite correctly. The red shades mask a gambling club, and the Gentleman's former wife and his daughter are engaged there. However, as yet the Gentleman himself remains in ignorance of this fact. In the Second Act the sounds are still mysterious to him but not to the others on stage or to the audience.

In the Second Act Strindberg has prepared for different sound sensations within the apartment. These sensations complement the sounds heard from the apartment above, and the Act is rich in sound effects. The opening stage direction states: '*To the left, a side-board with a telephone; to the right a piano and a clock*' (38). All three objects will be heard before the Act is over, but to start with, it is the noise from the apartment above that dominates:

THE GENTLEMAN: There's a dreadful noise up there; it's as if someone was stepping on my head; now they're pulling out the drawers of a desk, as if they were intending to leave, maybe escape ... [. . .] It's so noisy up there the chandelier's shaking (38).

There are also sounds from the Gentleman's room, but they do not serve to create an atmosphere; rather, they should be interpreted as 'messages'. Furthermore, on two occasions a '*Rumbling from the hallway*' (42, 43) is to be heard; on both occasions the Gentleman misinterprets the sound, thinking that it is his Brother arriving.

The *telephone* has an important role in both Acts II and III. The withdrawn Gentleman is in contact with the outside world via the telephone, although he seems to favour using it for outgoing phone calls, rather than to receive messages from without. When it signals an incoming call, its sound appears frightening and intrusive, since he remarks that he, 'always get[s] palpitations of the heart when it rings – one never knows what one's going to hear . . . and I want peace . . . peace, above all!' (68).

During the Second Act the Gentleman speaks with his Mother on the telephone. In a formal sense, this is a monologue: a dialogue partner exists but she is not seen or heard by the audience, though of course what the Gentleman says depends on his hidden inter-locutor. Since the invention of the telephone, such 'half dialogues' have been common in the theatre, especially in comedy or in sketches. However, Strindberg's intentions here are serious. He is not merely interested in the telephone as a technological novelty but seems to sense that with its help, he can create a new kind of mysterious monologue. The telephone conversation on stage offers a realistic framework for rambling or fragmentary mono-logues in which information or disinformation can be conveyed to the audience, as the author wishes.

The year before writing *Storm*, in the novella *The Roofing Feast*, Strindberg had been tempted to a similar experiment; he composes a monologue which has the prerequisites of a dialogue but also anticipates, through the words of its freely associating central char-acter who is sedated with morphine, the technique of the inner monologue, or stream of consciousness: 'Now the catch was released, and he lost touch with the nurse, so that the monologue gained speed, became intertwined with *dialogues where invisible absentees gave [him] the cues*' (SV 55:99, my italics).

A telephone in Strindberg's plays is never just a prop. The author has previously utilized the effective stage ploy of letting characters on stage receive messages from outside via technological aids. Both the speaking-tube in *Miss Julie* and the telegraph machine in *The Dance of Death* have the function of letting the outside world sud-denly and dramatically make itself known to those on stage through messages from without. Now, in employing a telephone in *Storm*, Strindberg is both keeping up with current technological devel-opments and acquiring an added bonus in what might be called an advanced variation of the 'half' dialogue.

*

On the other hand, the *piano* is not used a great deal in *Storm*, although the Gentleman does strike '*a few chords*' (42) to express the fact that his peace has been disturbed and indicate his present disharmonious mood. The piano that is heard playing in *Storm* is instead the invisible one in the apartment above. Soon after the Gentleman's disjointed chords, music is heard from this unseen piano; it is Chopin's 'Fantasie Impromptu' Opus 66 – a piece that the Gentleman recognizes as 'his' (43), but which is now played by his former wife in the upstairs apartment. In the First Act, the same piano could be heard out in the street playing Waldteufel's 'Pluie d'Or'. Whether it is a common waltz or 'his melody', the music speaks in different ways about life in the upstairs apartment.

The *clock* is an object that returns with more poignancy in *The Burnt House* and *The Ghost Sonata* and there will be more reason to discuss its symbolic function in relation to those plays. In *Storm* it chimes for Gerda and gives her a sense of discomfort. The chiming of the clock brings back her memories and reminds her of having once been confined in both time and place: 'Oh God! This chiming . . . which I've had sounding in my ears for ten years! This clock, which was never right, but which counted out five years of long hours, day and night' (48). Gerda's lines are related to the other lines in the play in which a character comments on or interprets sound sensations.

The noise and music from the upstairs apartment, the ringing of the telephone, the chiming of the clock, the piano chords – all these sounds are also audible to the audience in the theatre. That is not the case with what the Gentleman thinks he hears; here, sound is discussed but not disseminated by any internal or external communications system. Thus the Gentleman believes, on one occasion, that he can hear his daughter's foot steps: 'I thought I heard "the tiny steps", the tiny tripping steps in the corridor, when she came to visit me' (46).[16] Likewise he tells of the extraordinary auditory sensations that afflict him at night: 'before I go to sleep, when my ear is incredibly sharp, I hear her tiny steps, and once I heard her voice' (47).

Thus, the sense of hearing, which otherwise provides the Gentleman with clear information is temporarily invaded by imagined sounds. These imagined sounds are connected with the memory of his daughter, and it is from these and other memories that the Gentleman builds his own world. This is challenged during the course of the play, and towards the end of the Second Act the Gentleman has gained a new insight: 'I admit that my presumed deafness can go too far and become life threatening' (66).

In the Third Act – which like the First takes place in front of the house – a telephone is heard ringing in the drawing-room no fewer than three times (69, 70, 79). The first call is received by Louise and she is seen – but not heard – speaking on the telephone. The second call is unanswered as the Gentleman relapses into voluntary 'deafness' (70).[17] When the telephone rings for the third time in this Act (79), the Gentleman says that it sounds like 'a rattle-snake' but he nevertheless takes the call, and discovers to his relief that his former wife and daughter are now safe and sound in the country. Meanwhile, the last words to be spoken on stage, 'the silent house', recall an expression that has had its meaning displaced in the course of the play. The house had been called 'the silent house' earlier on in the play, but on that occasion the words referred to the fact that its inhabitants seldom spoke to each other (15). For the audience, therefore, the effect of this repetition of the expression 'the silent house' at the end of the play is almost ironic.

Smell, taste, feeling

No particular emphasis is placed on smells in *Storm*. However, the first of Strindberg's chamber plays contains the embryo of more dramatic elements in the coming works. One example is the reference to the Gentleman taking care of the flowers he has inherited from his former wife. At the end of the First Act he observes that, 'the flowers make my head ache' (36). This motif will return in demonized form in the Third Act of *The Ghost Sonata*. But also in his earlier production – for instance, in the concluding lines to Act One of *To Damascus II* – Strindberg uses flowers as potent olfactory stimulants that affect the mind; the Doctor in *To Damascus II* threatens to poison the Stranger: 'when you sit at your work, I shall come with a poppy, which you can't see, and it will anaesthetise your thought, confuse your mind so that you'll have hallucinations, which you won't be able to distinguish from reality' (SV 39:191).

★

Strindberg stresses the Gentleman's well-developed sense of smell when he lets him perceive the smell from the linen closet in the room next door:

> Is it Louise who is rummaging in the linen closet? It smells clean, and it reminds me . . . yes, of the housewife at the linen closet, the good fairy, who cares for and rejuvenates, the housekeeper with the iron who evens out the uneven and removes the wrinkles . . . yes, the wrinkles (47).

Here a different sense of smell is demonstrated than in the First Act: a scent that acts as a reminiscence.

With these two different types of smell Strindberg has created two olfactory functions that will reappear in the coming chamber plays: smell as a destructive intoxicant and smell as reminiscence. But the sense of smell is also, of course, evoked by its *verbal frame of reference*; this kind of experience reaches the audience encoded within words. In the First Act the Confectioner's business is discussed with a certain sensuous pleasure:

> first there are the strawberries and the wild strawberries, then come the cherries, then we have the raspberries and then gooseberries, melons, and the whole autumn harvest (14).

In the Second Act the Confectioner acts as a purveyor of delicious pastries when he comes with the 'tea bread' (40). With this reference to tea drinking, Strindberg apparently wants to create an atmosphere of tranquility. At the end of the same Act a quiet tea-drinking session is being prepared; here one is reminded that in a drama like *Advent* it was tea and sponge cake that the Judge and his wife longed for in hell (SV 40:121).

Many different types of professions are represented in the chamber plays, but the Pastry Maker comes across as one of the few who is honest in carrying out of his job. In the beginning of the Third Act he shows that he does not want to have anything to do with adulterating the food:

> one must watch the jars with preserves just like mischievous children, there are those who put in salicylic acid, but that's just a trick I won't be party to . . . [. . .] It leaves a taste . . . and is a cheap trick (67 ff.).

The forgery theme that was present earlier in *Advent* is here connected to food.[18] The food motif recurs in yet another variation in
the Third Act when the Gentleman talks about his earlier life, when
his sense of taste was also affected: 'The maids in the house wanted
me to do as they said and eat warmed-up food' (75).

The window

Certain symbols in *Storm* are closely connected to the sense of sight
and the problem of knowledge in general. One such symbol is the
window. Without disputing the commonly held belief that *houses* in
the chamber plays represent 'existence',[19] I want to single out the
window as a more specific symbol.

It is a sign of Strindberg's fascination with the window symbolism that he also uses it in his prose and poetry. In *The Red Room*
there is a reference to the yearly spring ritual of removing the inner
windows, which was still a common custom in Strindberg's time.
This ritual implied a rebirth of the senses:

> At that very moment a gap was made in the wall by a servant girl,
> who had just stripped away the paper pasted over the windows; a
> frightful stench of cooking fat, spilled beer, fir twigs and sawdust
> burst out and was carried far away by the wind which, as the
> cook breathed in the fresh air through her nose, seized hold of the
> paper from the window and whirled away with it (SV 6:8).

It is a similar kind of experience to the one recounted as a memory
fifty-four years later in the novel *Alone* (1903):

> Before one used to remove the inner windows, and straight away
> the noise from the street could be heard inside the rooms, as if the
> connection with the outside world had been re-established (SV
> 52:39).

As we have seen, *Easter* opens with a scene that portrays the same
kind of experience of sensuous release and rebirth:

> The inner windows out, the floor scrubbed, clean curtains . . .
> yes, it's spring again! (SV 43:243)
> [. . .]
> I can hear that the inner windows have been removed – Do
> you know how I can tell? – Mostly from the cart-wheels—but

what's that? It's a chaffinch singing! And they're hammering away down at the dockyard, and there's a smell of oil paint from the steamers, from the red lead – (43:245)

The open window, or the window with its winter insulation removed, is used in all these cases as a life-giving link to the outside world, whose sounds and smells have been shut off for some time. And here the window is seen from *within* the apartment, the perspective from which one should also see the scene in the Lawyer's chambers in *A Dream Play*, where Kristin is gluing paper around the inner windows. For the Daughter this feels as though she is being cut off from the air she so needs and shut in with the others among crying children and the smell of cabbage (46:43).

In his essay 'Ibsen, the Builder', Gunnar Brandell shows how Ibsen strives to escape from 'indoor drama' by the various ways in which he places windows at the back of the stage: 'He attempts in different ways to incorporate a piece of nature, a little fresh air on stage. The easiest way is to open a window or a door at the rear'.[20] It is difficult to disregard the thought that Strindberg was inspired by the term 'chamber play' to allow large portions of these dramas to take place within small, enclosed rooms. In none of the plays that are set wholly or partly indoors – *Storm*, *The Burnt House* and *The Ghost Sonata* – does he prescribe any window or open door at the rear, with or without a view.

Some examples from the historical dramas *Charles XII* and *Gustav III* illustrate the persistence with which Strindberg uses this symbol to represent the border between interior and exterior space. In *Charles XII* the window seen from the *outside* signifies the state inside the house. The condition of the windows signals decay and mystery, and also characterizes two of the characters – the King and Görtz: '*The windows are broken, the roof tiles torn away, the door removed*' (SV 47, Tableau I, p. 15). '*Farthest up to the left towards the rear is Görtz's house with its green shutters closed*' (Tableau III, p. 75).

All four of the tableaux in *Gustav III* take place indoors. The first of them is set in Holmberg's Bookshop: '*To the rear there are open windows and glass doors open towards Skeppsbron; masts and sails are visible*' (SV 48:151). The second tableau takes place at the King's court in Haga Palace: '*The whole rear wall is made up of opened glass doors, through which one can see parts of the park and Brunnsviken*' (181). The third tableau takes place in a room at Huvudsta Palace: '*a large room, with glass doors in the rear opening onto a large wooden veranda facing the garden'* (239). The room in the tableau for the Fourth Act is the Kina Palace at Drottningholm: '*The back doors stand open towards the Park'* (257).

This is the opposite of the closed world of the chamber plays, but as the play proceeds, it becomes clear that the trust which these open windows and doors in *Gustav III* signify is in reality part of the foolish game with danger played by the King with his political opponents. *Gustav III* is a drama about conspiracies. When Captain Nordström makes his entrance in the first tableau, Pechlin has already seen his image mirrored in one of the open glass doors: 'I am no clairvoyant, I can merely see his image in the window pane!' (168).

In the second tableau the conspiratorial elements multiply when Badin first declares his willingness to be the King's 'eye and ear' (191) and then agrees to spy on the police chief. Indeed, the word 'conspiracy' is frequent used, and the King concludes that he himself is being spied on (203), and then arranges in turn to eavesdrop on others when he places Liliensparre to maintain a watch from behind a pillar in the room (214).

In the third tableau Clas Horn offers an explanation of the open glass doors: 'every door at Huvudsta is open – in order to divert suspicion. We must therefore be prepared for a visit, unannounced!' (242). In this way Strindberg is once again able to use the type of furtive entrances that produce unease or create surprise.

The open doors in the last tableau have a clear symbolic function: 'No, they must remain open . . . the people must see that their King trusts them. . '. (278). At the end of the tableau, von Fersen and de Geer exit '*and close the doors behind them'* (297). With this the playwright indicates symbolically that the King's trust has been an illusion, and that he is in fact cornered: '*Then he [the King] stops, crushed, at the upstage doors, drumming on the window panes, with his back turned towards the audience'* (299). And in the final moment of the play, the audience – but significantly not the King, who is masked by his Queen – sees '*Anckarström's face [. . .] in the window pane of the back'* (300). It would appear that in *Gustav III* Strindberg in fact wanted, like Ibsen, to open up the dramatic setting, but his ambition was thwarted by the conspiratorial atmosphere of the play: *Gustav III* ends with closed glass doors and a murderer stalking outside.

After *Gustav III* there is a pause in Strindberg's writing for the theatre, and when he returns to drama, it is to write the chamber plays, in which he continues to develop his window symbolism, but on his own terms.

Storm is relatively optimistic about the ability of people to communicate with each other. The windows in the Gentleman's apartment are 'large' and 'open' (13). The drama starts with the Brother knocking on the window sill, which is followed by a relaxed conversation through the open window.

The mystery of the upstairs apartment appears as an ominous contrast to the open windows in the apartment downstairs: '*four middle windows have red blinds that are lit from within*' (13). The closed blinds invite speculation. As Louise remarks, 'They never open the windows, and in this heat, they must be southerners' (26).

At the end of the drama the light behind the sinful red blinds has been turned off, at the same time as the gaslight – representing order and regularity – has been lit in the street outside. And from the fact that the red blinds are no longer lit up we may conclude that the problematic eroticism which has troubled him throughout the play has now disappeared from the Gentleman's life. What remains after his confrontation with his former wife and the shady dance club upstairs is 'the peace of old age!' (82).

In his dramas Strindberg makes intensive use of the window as a symbol, regardless of whether the viewer is within or outside the house. There is a possible third aspect to this: for someone strolling the streets of a city the window can be interpreted as a stage opening towards a lit-up room from which the fourth wall has been removed.

The autobiographical fiction *Alone* (1903) includes an episode in which the narrator, while out walking, looks in through the window of an older house and sees a drama in embryo: 'At home I planned the drama which I had got from a glance through a shutter!' (SV 52:41). The narrator in this episode sees the window, 'the shutter', as a stage opening. The Brother in *Storm* likewise associates what he sees with the theatre but in his case it is 'the four red curtains [which] look like stage curtains, behind which bloody dramas are in rehearsal' (15). In *Storm* the Gentleman's apartment is open like a peep show while a point is made in not having the intrigues in the upstairs apartment take place on in full view of the audience but instead communicated to the characters via acoustic sensations.

In the last line of the drama Strindberg appears to be distancing himself from his work as a playwright: 'Close the windows, and then pull down the blinds' (82). When the drama in the upstairs apartment is over, the play *Storm* also ends, and Strindberg has ingeniously linked these events with the coming of autumn and the lighting of the first gas lamps in the street, for in his world such events usually signal the opening of the theatre season: 'Oh well, it was August; the lamps were lit again and the theatres were going to open.'[21] In *Storm* autumn is welcomed as the curtain descends upon more than one kind of illusion.

Eyes

In *Storm* the metaphor of sight is richly diversified as the discussion of the way the sense of sight functions symbolically for some of the characters in the drama has already indicated. If Strindberg had retained his original title for the play, 'The First Lamp',[22] this meta-phorical purpose would have been even more obvious to the audience. As it now stands, it only becomes entirely clear in the final scene of the drama when the street lamp is lit, and when, paradoxic-ally enough, people express their joy over the fact that the season of darkness has returned: 'It is getting darker, but then understanding comes and lights its lamp, so no one goes astray' (82).

In *Storm* the sense of sight is not indispensable. Inner sight – which here designates some kind of 'wisdom' – is valued more highly than the ability to observe surface phenomena. Two episodes which the Gentleman tells his Brother about in the Second Act would seem to indicate that the author wishes to suggest that there is always more than immediately meets the eye. On both occasions the Gentleman has looked into other people's eyes, which usually represents the most forthright type of communication and also the most confidential, but the episodes the Gentleman describes both contain shocking disappointments. Firstly he remembers having once seen 'how behind the most beautiful eyes, two unknown glances, as if from an vicious animal, suddenly appeared; I was liter-ally so frightened that I looked to see if there was someone behind her face, which looked like a mask' (46). And later he recalls how, after spending several years abroad, he failed to recognize his own sister: 'I saw with horror two eyes that bored into mine, but with an unfamiliar gaze that expressed the most horrible fright at not being recognized' (47).

These episodes are both pessimistic about the possibility of communicating with the eyes and represent a deepening of the scepticism towards the sense of sight as such that is depicted on various levels throughout the play. In *Storm* the sense of hearing takes over as the dominant organ of knowledge. In consequence, the perceiver is distanced from other people and is forced to interpret his surroundings in a manner that enriches the drama in a purely dramaturgical sense.

Lamp, light and fire

Before the street lamp is lit in the last scene of *Storm* and the paradoxical praise of darkness that accompanies this almost ritual action, the motif of lamp–light–fire has been apparent on several occasions. Early on in the play the Gentleman lights a cigar (16) – a discreet anticipation of the lighting of the street lamp. The reference to the red curtains as a 'cigar lamp' (28) can be said to be a step on the way. Moreover, the sky is illuminated by flashes of lightning and in the basement of the house the Confectioner 'is making a fire' (38, 41). Like the lighting of the lamp, the lighting of the cigar is connected with the peace that the Gentleman is striving for all the time – fire under controlled circumstances. When the upstairs apartment has finally been vacated, it looks as it might 'after a fire' (71). A dangerous fire has been extinguished, at the same time as the longed-for lamp lighter enters and '*lights the [street] lamp*' (81).

In the scene where the Gentleman strikes a few chords on the piano, he also tries to amuse himself in another way: '*is drumming with his fingers; tries to read the newspaper, but tires of it; lights a few matches and then blows them out; looks at the clock*' (42). His lighting the matches here is a somewhat bizarre feature but with reference to a passage in the novella *The Roofing Feast*, in which the protagonist imagines he can see his rival and an erstwhile companion 'sitting at the marble table, striking matches to hide their true feelings' (SV 55:58), it might be considered a means of hiding his irritation. But on stage this behaviour becomes more emphatic, since the flame is visible to the audience. One can see the Gentleman's piano playing and his fiddling around with matches as an attempt to distract

himself by activating one sense after the other. The scene is reminiscent – in miniature – of the Captain's resolute farewell to his senses
in the scene without words in *The Dance of Death* (SV 44: 113 ff.,
above p. 56).

Fire is a recurring motif throughout the chamber plays that is
discreetly established in what Strindberg designates as Opus I,
only to gain increasing importance and develop in a demonic
direction in the coming dramas. In *Storm* one can speak of a
controlled fire and a contemplative attitude towards it. Subsequent
plays deal to a large degree with the sabotaging of this contemplative mood.

The Gentleman's attitude to fire resembles the day-dreaming
that Gaston Bachelard has discussed both in his early work *Le psychanalyse du feu* (1949) and in his last work *La Flamme d'une chandelle*
(1961). In his inventory and analysis of the occurrence of the four
elements as images in literature, Bachelard is interested in literary
works regarded as a form of 'day dreaming'. A particular example of
this kind of daydreaming entails dreaming in front of the fire, which
Bachelard sees as something of a primordial fantasy. In his book on
the psychoanalysis of fire he sees the observing of fire in terms of a
contemplative attitude, the image of wisdom and peace: 'Thus it is a
matter of a quiet, regular, controlled fire [. . .] The fire that is confined to the fireplace no doubt became man's first dream object,
the symbol of rest, the invitation to rest [. . .] It is not for nothing
the attitude of the thinker.'[23] This description could also apply
to the Gentleman's attitude towards the controlled fire in the street
lamp. The drama ends in a contemplative mood. The peace that has
been attained stands in marked contrast to the nervous lighting of
matches earlier in the play.

As attributes on stage, flames and lights are often related to lone-
liness. 'The flame is the world of the lonely man', Bachelard concludes, and goes on to describe the inner world that is attained
through such contemplation: 'The dream and the faint light from
the flame embody the same patience. The dreamer of the flame
unites what he sees and what he has seen. He gets to know the
fusion of fantasy and memory.'[24] Bachelard's description of fire
developing from flame to lamp can be found in *Storm* where the
nervous lighting of matches is replaced by the lighting of the flame
in the gas lamp: 'De la chandelle à la lampe, il y a, pour la flamme,
comme un conquête de la sagesse.'[25]

Colours

The sparse colour symbolism in *Storm* is of a rather conventional kind. The red colour of the blinds obviously represent eroticism, the sinful and secretive life that takes place in the upstairs apartment. To some extent the colour red also represents the theatre – the blinds 'look like theatre curtains' (15). Moreover, when the Gentleman is said to 'hate[s] platforms [*estrader*]' (50), the two spheres are linked as wanton places. The colour red stands for something threatening to the Gentleman's peace of mind: 'I don't like this unknown thing that has entered the house. It's like having a red thunder cloud over me' (30).

This is conventional colour symbolism, but the point behind the numerous references to colours in the chamber plays is of a different kind. The observation of colour may be regarded as an aspect of sight, which can be misled or cheated by painting, or the application of another colour. An illuminating scene in this respect is the one in which the Brother comments on the man in the apartment above: 'With that pale skin he should have had black hair, but it was brown, so it's coloured or else a wig' (19). To colour one's hair implies a form of *dissimulation*, which is precisely what colours represent in the chamber plays. To analyse the colours separately is to miss the point: it is the colouring, the painting *as such*, that is fatal.

When Louise warns the Gentleman that he has lived for too long amongst his memories, she expresses herself in a manner that ought to be seen in the context of this conception of colours: 'You may live another twenty years, sir, and that's far too long to spend among memories that are bound to fade, and which may one day change colour' (39). Strindberg does not invent this use of colour specifically for the chamber plays; the device seems to belong to his post-Inferno period as a whole.[26] In the novel *Black Banners*, for example, Falkenström is described as always writing poetry 'to transform the horrors of reality into something more beautiful, but [he] was then despised by his colleagues and called a gilder. He acknowledged that it was a bit of a joke to present miserable matters in shining colours' (SV 57:56 ff.).

Elsewhere in the novel it is likewise said of a journalist that 'he was to cover the meeting and colour the report in the right colour scheme' (48). Such passages in *Black Banners* anticipate similar discreet allusions in *Storm* and point to an increasingly important thematic emphasis in Strindberg's subsequent plays. *Storm* might be said to contain a brief set of instructions, in which it is made clear that brilliant colours signify not only beauty but also dissimulation.

Gesture

A central theme in *Storm* is that of sight, more particularly the protagonist's development towards an emphasis on inner sight. This theme is expressed verbally in the dialogue, it colours the imagery and determines the symbols. One might add that the theme is also varied visually for the audience in the gesture made by the Gentleman as he listens attentively: '*He covers his eyes with his hand and listens*' (43). This kind of gesture also occurs in the other chamber plays and has a previous history in drama generally. Indeed, this gesture may well be counted among the most common in all kinds of drama, whether it is specified in the author's stage directions or appears as an addition by the director. In Strindberg's case, however, this gesture has a very precise and original implication, which is related to his interest in sensory delusions, and its general importance as well as a particular interpretation of it is to be found in the words with which the Brother sums up the behaviour of the man from the apartment above, as he posts a letter: 'the movement of his hands as he put the letter in the box looked like shuffling a pack of cards, cutting and dealing' (19).

Such gestures are easy enough to interpret; they look like clichés and have, in their very obviousness, a certain melodramatic quality. It is a question of a style of acting from which Strindberg wished to break away from. Such over-emphatic and heavy gestures have no place in an intimate theatre of the kind for which he was now writing. So when he makes relatively frequent use of this gesture in which a character covers his eyes with his hands, it has another significance.

In its original meaning of 'not believing one's eyes', the gesture is found in *Advent* at the moment when the Judge is confronted with his sins personified as ghosts: '*Holds his hand over his eyes*' (SV 40:42). However, the gesture is of no help since he is in the hands of supernatural powers: 'I see through my hand, I see in the dark through my eyelids!' In this way, Strindberg succeeds in extracting a surprising meaning out of a traditional gesture.

1. Delacroix's *Jacob Wrestling with the Angel* (Saint-Sulpice, Paris)

2. *During the Silent Mass.* Oil painting by the Swedish artist Carl Wilhelm-
son, 1895. The painting depicts the holy water stoup and the Angel's face
in the Paris church of Saint Germain l'Auxerrois. It was exhibited at the
Salon in Paris of 1895. In *Legends* (1897) Strindberg describes these details.
(Gothenburg Art Museum)

3. *Hearing*. Detail of the allegorical depiction of the sense of hearing on one of the tapestries *La Dame à la licorne* (Musée de Cluny, Paris). Cf. *The Ghost Sonata*, Act II: 'In the hyacinth room the young Lady is seen with a harp.'

4. *Sight*. Detail of the allegorical depiction of the sense of sight on one
of the tapestries *La Dame à la licorne*.

5. Smell. Detail of the allegorical depiction of the sense of smell on one of the tapestries *La Dame à la licorne*. Cf . Strindberg's drama *Abu Casem's Slippers* which is full of references to the sense of smell and where an ape represent animal sensuality.

6. '*A mon seul Désir*'. Returning the attribute of vanity on the last of the tapestries. Also *The Dance of Death* describes, through pantomime, how the protagonist parts with different attributes representing sensuality.

7. *La grande coupe B*
(Musée National de la Céramique, Sèvres)

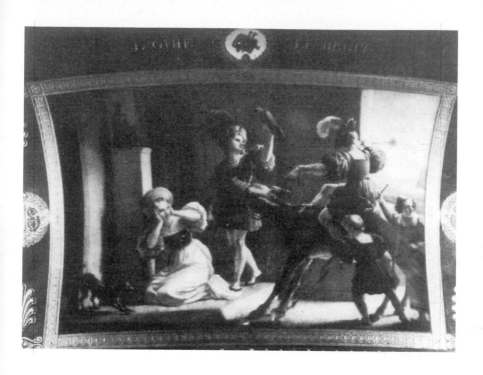

8. Hearing (detail of *La grande coupe*)

9. Sight (detail of *La grande coupe*)

10. Smell – Scents (detail of *La grande coupe*)

11. Smell — Stenches (detail of *La grande coupe*)

12. Sensory illusions. ('Les illusions des sens', *La grand coupe*). In the centre of this painting of *Coupe des sens* an optical experiment is seen. A girl attempts to touch the virtual picture of a flower vase, which in reality is behind the mirror. Another girl to the left illustrates an illusion of touch when she feels a marble with the finger crossed and believes she is is touching two marbles instead of one. See Carl Nordenfalk, *Sèvres et les Cinq Sens*, The National Museum Series N.S. (Stockholm, 1984).

13. Sensory physiologist Professor Hjalmar Öhrvall at the lectern

14. 'The Red House', Karlaplan 40. To the right is Narvavägen. Strindberg lived 4 flats up with an entrance from Karlavägen. It was here that the chamber plays were written. The house was demolished in 1969.
(The Strindberg Museum, Stockholm)

15. The dining room in Strindberg's apartment at Karlaplan. On the mantelpiece of the porcelain stove sits a statue of Buddha.
(The Strindberg Museum, Stockholm)

THE DISTORT VISION (16–18)

16. Julie in the process of seducing Jean in *Fröken Julie*. Julie: Gunilla Johansson, Jean: Jacob Ericksson. Director: Martin Berggren. The Gothenburg City Theatre Studio, 1996 (Photo: Lasse Lindkvist).

17. The Milkmaid bathes the Student's eyes in *The Ghost Sonata*. Ingmar
Bergman's production at the Royal Dramatic Theatre, 1973. The Milk-
maid: Kari Sylwan, The Student: Mathias Henrikson (Photo: Beata
Bergström).
(Drottningholm Theatre Museum)

18. Illustration to Shakespeare's *A Midsummer's Night Dream* by Egron
Lundgren for Queen Victoria's Theatrical Album, 1856. Oberon pours
the juice of a magic herb into Titania's eyes. Shakespeare was part of
Strindberg's reading at the time of the creation of the chamber plays.
Gouache and water-colour.
(Stockholm's National Museum)

19. The First Act of Per-Axel Branner's production of *Storm* at the Royal Dramatic Theatre, 1964. Note the open windows and the Gentleman's eyeglasses! The Gentleman: Uno Henning, The Brother: Tord Ståhl (Photo: Beata Bergström).
Drottningholm Theatre Museum)

20. 'The lamp has exploded but the base is still there.' *The Burnt House* in Alf Sjöberg's production at the Royal Dramatic Theatre, 1970. Civilian: Gösta Prüzelius, The Stone Mason: Erik Hell (Photo: Beata Bergström). (Drottningholm Theatre Museum)

THE GHOST SONATA (21–4)

21. 'Johansson speaks inaudibly.' The 'disturbed dialogue' in the First Act of *The Ghost Sonata* in Olof Molander's production at the Royal Dramatic Theatre, 1962. Johansson: Olle Hilding, Hummel: Anders Henrikson
(Photo: Beata Bergström).
(Drottningholm Theatre Museum)

22. Marble statue in the vicinity of Mondsee portraying Frida Uhl's sister Marie Weyr Brunnen. The statue, which was sculpted by her husband, the famous Austrian sculptor Rudolf Weyr, was destroyed during the Second World War.
(Royal Library, Stockholm)

23. The Marble Statue and the Mummy in Bergman's production at The Royal Dramatic Theatre, 1983. Gertrud Fridh as the Mummy (Photo: Beata Bergström).
(Drottningholm Theatre Museum)

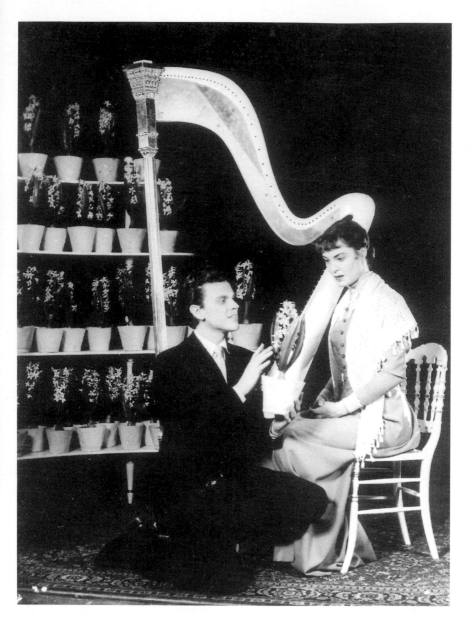

24. In the 'The Hyacinth Room.' Ingmar Bergman's production at the
Malmö City Theatre, 1954. The Student: Folke Sundquist, The Young
Lady: Gaby Stenberg.
(The Strindberg Museum, Stockholm)

25. Strindberg' s own illustration on the title page of the manuscript of
The Ghost Sonata. The illustrations depicts the bulb, which is to be visible
in Act III.
(Royal Library, Stockholm)

26. The first production in Stockholm of *Miss Julie* at The People's Theatre in November 1906. In the role as Kristin the actress Sacha Sjöström fried kidneys so that the odour spread to the audience. Julie: Manda Björling, Jean: August Falck.

27. The Intima Theatre was inaugurated with *The Pelican* on 27 November 1907. This illustration from the *Dagens Nyheter* depicts a scene in the Third Act: 'Gerda in, with the porridge on a tray.'

In *Storm* Strindberg wants to demonstrate that abstaining from participation in external life leads to wisdom and moral insight. In that respect he ends up in an interesting polemic with his own drama *Charles XII* from 1901, where withdrawing from the world is a preliminary to death and where it is said of the King: 'Then Providence pulled his ear and played Blind Man's Buff with him!' (SV 47:139). The expression 'blind man's buff' suggests that the King is disorientated because of his hubris. In *Charles XII* Strindberg makes great play with the fact that no less than four people in central positions around the King are literally one-eyed, information that he could have found in several contemporary histories of Sweden.[27] Besides the Minister of Finance Görtz, General Fröhlich, the Foreign Minister Müllern, and Major General Grothausen are all one-eyed (47:347). Here the sight symbolism is almost trivial; one-sightedness is tantamount to intolerance.

What is more interesting are the King's gestures in his repeated efforts to shut out his entourage. There is a particular reason why he uses gestures in the drama, since he is hoarse to the point of muteness. From a dramaturgical point of view, this is a brilliant strategy, and similar to the Gentleman's poor eyesight in *Storm*. The King makes a mute entrance, gestures at his assembled subjects to rise (43). His indisposition also serves to transfer the main focus from the verbal to the pantomimic. In the second tableau, the King moves his hand twice across his eyes and, in his stage directions, Strindberg has carefully explained how the gesture is to be interpreted:

> *moves his hand over his eyes as if recollecting memories and collecting his thoughts* (50) [. . .] *moves his hand over his eyes as if he wished to free himself from a net* (53).

Later on in the play we encounter the King on numerous occasions with his eyes shut – this too is indicative of his efforts to screen off the outside world. Nothing is said about his inner state of mind; it is not made explicit that he replaces outer reality by lapsing into a state of deep concentration or inner observation, etc. In point of fact, he comes to resemble someone asleep or dead, which is also what those about him come to believe (139, 148). But his method of drawing a sharp line between outer and inner reality does not always work; on one occasion the outer world forces its way into the King's chamber in the figure of a revengeful soldier, and afterwards the King does not know whether the incident has taken place in real life or if he has imagined it. That it might have been a dream is suggested by the stage direction '*rubs his eyes*' (69, 70). But if the King can be characterized as an 'introvert', unlike the Gentleman in *Storm*, he has little to gain from immersion in his inner world. His introverted state of mind is a prelude to death rather than to deeper insights about life.

In terms of visual features, the dénouement in *Charles XII* forms a kind of dialogue with the dénouement in *Storm*. The fiery projectiles that illuminate the stage in *Charles XII* (147, 148) become distant shafts of lightning in *Storm*, while the last stage direction in the history play is reminiscent of the way in which the upstairs apartment is vacated and goes dark in *Storm*: '*the camp fires go out; torches and lamps are carried out! The stage lies in darkness*' (150). The last line in *Charles XII* points to the central symbolism of *Storm*: '*But now a big lamp is visible in the trenches.*'

As in *Storm*, the lamp marks the coming of a new era, which can be interpreted both historically and metaphysically. The King's death in the one play and the death of illusions in the other imply the possibility of a better life. To my mind, it has been too common to glance at the endings of *The Ghost Sonata* and *The Pelican* in reading *Storm* as a drama about the Gentleman's getting ready to die.[28]

The apotheosis of memory

The peace of mind seemingly achieved by the Gentleman at the start of *Storm* which is subsequently threatened by new events is the result of his having withdrawn from the present world: he lives above all among his memories. Therefore, he is disturbed by any information that threatens to destroy these memories, which concern, above all, his former wife who now, five years after their separation, has assumed sympathetic features in his mind. The dramatic reversal occurs when the Gentleman is confronted with her in reality, at which point his memory of her is shattered: '*she* came in and destroyed my memories of her; she wiped out all the beauty I had kept and now there is nothing left' (71).

This recognition and reversal are well prepared; from the beginning, the dramatic purpose has been to discuss the risk inherent in living among memories. The Gentleman's Brother as well as Louise and the Confectioner warn of the danger in this, and even the Gentleman himself seems to be at least partly aware of the risk of living in such a world of illusions:

LOUISE: It's not good to sit for too long among old memories.
THE GENTLEMAN: Why not? When time has passed, all memories are beautiful (39).

In lines spoken by those around the Gentleman, this view of a life among memories is confirmed. Louise remarks that 'he lives with them in memory where there is only beauty'; the Confectioner observes, 'I believe his wife is most beautiful in his memory' (25); while his Brother warns the Gentleman quite directly: 'I believe you are living with a great delusion' (22). In a later exchange where the Gentleman calls his memories 'poems' and thus reveals his own partial insight, his Brother responds by calling them 'mirages' (45).

This exchange opens an interesting part of the drama that illuminates several aspects of the past as remembered by the Gentleman as well as by others. The Gentleman retells two unpleasant memories about his daughter's encounter with evil and his own unfortunate meeting with his sister (see above, p. 80). Both instances refer to disappointing meetings between people; what was perceived as true turned out to be an illusion. Through these recapitulations of past events the Gentleman partly undermines his own thesis that all memories become beautiful with time. The accounts of these painful memories are in turn interrupted by depictions of still other memories – pleasant ones for the Gentleman and produced in at least one case, in a state of confusion. He mentions how he seems to hear his daughter's little steps and also her voice (47) while the smell of his wardrobe reminds him of his wife, probably in an idealized version: 'the good fairy who cares and rejuvenates; the housewife with her iron that straightens out the wrinkles' (47).

This cavalcade of memories continues when the Gentleman leaves and Gerda enters. To her the sight of the apartment awakens memories of an unpleasant kind, as when she hears the sound of the drawing-room clock or finds the thermometer in a box (48). The way Gerda slanders the Gentleman stands in sharp contrast to the way in which he protects and embellishes the memories of his wife; here a particular aspect of remembrance comes into the picture, namely 'honour'. On two occasions the Brother states that Gerda has 'murdered' or 'ruined' the Gentleman's honour (21, 33).

So the Gentleman is slandered by his former wife, who in turn lives on in his memory in an idealized way. After the confrontation scene in the Second Act, this idealized image is shattered by reality, and Gerda's accusations against the Gentleman and against his honour are disclosed as false. In view of this information and the new insight the portagonist has gained, it is certainly not the case that, at the end of the drama, everything returns to how it had been in the past. On the contrary, the final line of the play makes it clear that it is not possible to live on memories, which are then symbolically buried: 'pull down the blinds, so the memories can go to sleep, in peace!' (82). At the start of the play, the Gentleman has been described as 'bound by this apartment through memories' (17). This bondage no longer exists; in the last sentence of the drama, he announces quite logically that he intends to move out of the house.

Thus what *Storm* seeks to demonstrate is the impossibility of living among this type of imaginary notions – what Strindberg calls 'illusions' or 'misperceptions' (*villor*). The word echoes in the Brother's reference to '*vill*farelse', or delusion (22, my italics) and in the Gentleman's penultimate line: '[. . .] then reason comes and illuminates your way with its lamp to keep you from going astray (*villo*vägar)' – (82, my italics).

Ibsen's The Wild Duck

In this context Ibsen's *The Wild Duck* almost invites comment. Its relevance as an intertext is suggested by the fact that in 1903, Strindberg had been reminded of Ibsen's play when his third wife, Harriet Bosse, played the role of Hedvig at the Royal Dramatic Theatre in a production which premièred on 20 March.[29] In *The Wild Duck* Ibsen pleads for the necessity of the 'life-lie'; the person who discloses other people's illusions is said by Dr Relling in the final act to suffer from 'a fever of righteousness'. Strindberg's *Storm* and the subsequent chamber plays, in which various characters suffer precisely from this Ibsenite disease, form a response of sorts to this central theme of Ibsen's play.

In *A Madman's Defence*, Strindberg had once, half playfully, refuted what he understood to be an attack on himself in *The Wild Duck*.[30] In *Storm*, which with its perfect structure, its bourgeois setting and conversational dialogue, is his most Ibsenite drama, Strindberg delivers his final response in his extended dialogue with *The Wild Duck*.

As in Ibsen's play, *Storm* presents two people about to lose their eyesight although in *Storm* no tragic implications are suggested. Old Ekdal's life in the attic among dry fir trees and rabbits that remind him of a more grandiose past among the bears deep in the Højdal woods, becomes in Strindberg's version an old man's memories of his wife. It is Strindberg who tones down the motif and makes the problem less theatrical. Nor are there any pistol shots from the attic in *Storm* – only disturbing piano music from the upstairs apartment.

In *The Wild Duck* Ibsen uses a rich assemblage of metaphors to do with sight through which he comments on the blindness of the characters in a figurative sense. Merchant Werle is said to be going 'blind',[31] but it is also remarked that this might be seen as a form of retribution, since he himself has 'blinded' others.[32] Like Hedvig in *The Wild Duck*, the Gentleman in *Storm* gains insight even as he is going blind. Hjalmar Ekdal's interest in Hedvig primarily focuses on the eyes: 'The eyes! The eyes!'[33] 'Oh, the eyes – !'[34]

Hedvig's gesture is interesting when in the Second Act she '*sits on the sofa, her hands shading her eyes and her thumbs in her ears, reading a book*'.[35] With her gesture she shields two of her senses in order to concentrate on her reading; on the symbolic level her gesture foreshadows her imminent, unwelcome encounter with reality.

Through the characters of Old Ekdal, Hjalmar Ekdal and Hedvig Ibsen shows the impact of the life lie as it impacts upon the representatives of three successive generations. Strindberg also sees the dramatic possibilities of making an innocent daughter the pawn in a cynical adult game, although he doubles the number of young girls (the Gentleman's Daughter and the Confectioner's Daughter) and makes this motif peripheral to the main action. There is only a single protagonist – the Gentleman – who may be observed moving from illusion to clarity as the play proceeds.

Black Banners, *the* Blue Books

It has been common to characterize *Storm* as a realistic play, arising out of the ageing Strindberg's moods during his solitary life in the Stockholm suburb of Östermalm. Scholars have even focused on a specific summer in Strindberg's life, and behind the figure of Gerda they have of course found Harriet Bosse – in fact, she herself made such an identification.[36] But without denying that this biographical background may be of interest, it seems more relevant for an understanding of the play to focus on Strindberg's reflections on the complex problem of 'the world of illusions'.

In *Storm* Strindberg transforms into dramatic form certain ideas he had written down in *A Blue Book I*, which was begun in the summer of 1906 and finished in November that year, only a month before *Storm* was begun. Against such a background, it would have been strange, had *Storm* constituted a return to a naturalistic drama. Nor is that the case.

A Blue Book is far from a systematic presentation of Strindberg's *Weltanschauung*. Nevertheless, the book contains certain constantly recurring thoughts: a religiously based scepticism or aversion to empirical science and a related distrust of the function of the senses in general. Instead, Strindberg asserts – as he did during the Inferno crisis and continued to do throughout *The Occult Diary* – a belief in an invisible world.

Strindberg's first chamber play, *Storm*, has a realistic surface which, together with a certain basic mood of melancholy, may lead the reader or spectator to assess the drama as the adjustment of a tired playwright to the kind of bourgeois conversation pieces that he had always claimed to despise. *Storm* would in that case not contain any new theatrical programme at all but instead be Strindberg's most conventional play.

Flashbacks may be thought to be easier to execute in fiction, but the fact is that Strindberg varies the memory theme with dramatic skill in his chamber plays. In the case of *Storm*, the theme is confined to a man's memories of his wife. That a human being often looks best at a distance is a thought that Strindberg expounds in *A Blue Book I*, where he exemplifies it with an analogy to optics and mental life:

> If an object gets too close to the magnifying glass, it becomes blurred; in the same way one might lose sight of the person dearest to oneself, if she comes too close; she becomes small and blurred, loses her contour and colour; if she is removed towards the focal point, she will be enlarged and clear (SV 65:218).

'Distance' gives a clearer picture, according to Strindberg. In *A Blue Book II*, written after *Storm*, he varies this thought:

When a person near to you dies, he begins to appear as a mirage. All of his less pleasant qualities are wiped out, as if they had been part of this body only, which is now dissolved. His beautiful qualities are enlarged, become distinct (SV 66:881).

The passage from which this quotation is taken, is called 'Apotheosis' – a word that Strindberg often uses about a memory of a person who is only dead in a symbolic sense. In a letter of 8 April 1908 in which he settles his accounts with Harriet, he relates how the process of remembrance started during his recent solitude:

And then began the apotheosis of memory – the whole day, for twelve hours, I simply lived through these [last] seven years. [. . .] Everything at all lacking in beauty was gone, only the beautiful emerged. Before the fact: it is over, I got a distinct impression: dead! I mourned You as dead and could not wish you back, since you did not exist!

Sight is the sense most intensely discussed in the *Blue Books*. Sometimes Strindberg writes in very concrete language about the eye itself, at other times the subject is optics as a science, and in still other instances, he talks about 'an inner sight' that is disengaged from both eyes and optics.

Despite certain exceptions where, apparently without irony, Strindberg points to his own concrete observations, eye witness accounts [*sic!*] and similar matters, he maintains a basic scepticism towards the ability of the eye or any other sense to register reality. From this it follows that he condemns empirical science in its entirety as nearsighted and ungodly.

'My eye sees nothing by itself, for if you take it out and put it here, it sees nothing. Thus it is my inner eye that sees' (SV 65:13). This view is not new in Strindberg's world of perceptions; in *Black Banners* he writes: 'If the surgeon cuts out your eye, then you see nothing, but the eye sees, i.e. gives back images; hence, you need your inner eye for *you* to see' (SV 57:111 ff.). Again, in *A Blue Book I*, he writes under the heading 'The Sixth Sense': 'The material eye can reflect images, the inner eye can interpret them' (198). These are words that could have been spoken by the Gentleman in *Storm* where he affirms that his inner sight is about to take over at the expense of his outer sight. In the drama the Confectioner's Wife is going blind and she sometimes wishes herself dead as well (23). The same wish is expressed by the Gentleman when he exclaims 'I wish I were a bit deaf too! Deaf and blind!' (53). From the realistic surface of the play it is tempting to see this line as a reference to the concretely named senses. But such lines seem to express a somewhat drastic tiredness with reality. Shortly before, in *A Blue Book*, Strindberg used the expression 'deaf and blind' in this figurative sense. In a passage entitled 'Deaf and Blind', he states: 'It is necessary to make oneself deaf and blind, otherwise it is impossible to live life' (SV 65:54). Here the expression signifies less the senses of sight and hearing than a conscious attitude towards the life lie. In *Black Banners* there is a formulation that links such an attitude more closely with the notion of an unconscious life lie: 'There is a Providence that protects the faithful and makes them *blind and deaf* in the right way' (SV 57:24, my italics).

A Blue Book I turned out to be a bank of ideas containing more extensive discussions than those in Strindberg's occasionally lapidarian diary. Many of these ideas are not new but have been expressed by various characters in the novel *Black Banners*[37] where the philosophical concept of 'the world of illusions' comes more and more to colour the contemporary satire: 'Nothing is more uncertain than reports and testimonies, not because people lie intentionally but because everything is so deficient, our senses, our perceptions, our organ of memory' (SV 57:99). Nevertheless, in simpler cases one may be able to convince oneself of the real situation through one's senses.

The penultimate chapter of the novel forms the culmination of this discussion. The occasional sophistry of Strindberg's reasoning seems to have one purpose: to defend experiences of unreality while at the same time discrediting banal reality. The task of the character Kilo in chapter 21 is to defend, with all possible means, the reality of the invisible. Kilo is of the opinion that it is possible to experience 'unpleasant perceptions of hearing and sight in a house of murderers' (210). That not everybody experiences such things is said to depend on the relative degrees of sensitivity in different people. With the help of optics, Kilo makes it clear that ghosts are also a part of reality, i.e. dwell within the domain of visible, if not material reality. In plane mirrors the image becomes virtual – a non-material image which, however, can be perceived by the eye. A ghost is the same as a dead person's illusory image (211). Thus, it is possible to see ghosts!

The purpose of Strindberg's reasoning is to expand reality beyond the purely material world. The subject was close to his heart and it returns in the early sections of *A Blue Book I*, where the eye is momentarily rehabilitated since it can see virtual images: 'Hence, the eye is a good instrument that can make the unreal seem real. Thus it is tempting to believe in ghosts. – What are ghosts? – They are illusory images or unreal images that the eye can perceive under certain conditions' (SV 65:19).

The Gentleman in *Storm* tries to untangle what memory is and this investigation should be viewed against the background of the discussion about visions, mirages and ghosts in *Black Banners* and *A Blue Book I*. With this kind of vocabulary – 'visions', 'ghosts', 'mirages' – we are in that artistically fruitful domain that Strindberg terms 'half reality'.[38]

THE BURNT HOUSE

Introduction

In his second chamber play, *The Burnt House*, which was probably planned at the same time as *Storm* was being written, Strindberg emphasizes yet another aspect of his complex set of ideas about 'the world of illusions'. Instead of the sensory perceptions that he focused on in *Storm*, he now turns his attention to the theme of human deception, represented by a wide scale of actions, from everyday embellishments of the truth to criminal acts. Through this shift in interest, the pessimism of *The Burnt House* becomes virtually misanthropic. In addition, the thematics of memory from *Storm* returns once more. It is, in fact, a theme that unites all four chamber plays but is varied throughout the sequence in different ways.

When reality corrects someone's memories, it often does so by showing that the senses were misled when the reminiscence was established. That is how the senses are discussed in *The Burnt House*. In *Storm*, sensory experiences were treated in the present; in *The Burnt House*, sensory experiences are part of the past.

Sight

Presented in the opening stage direction as someone 'listening to every conversation' (89), the Painter is present as a silent listener throughout the drama. The spectator may in fact gain the impression that he is mute in a literal sense, until – in the second scene – he bursts out in a fit of reproaches directed against the Stranger, the central character who is visiting his burned-down childhood home after having only recently returned to his native country.

In the dialogue between the Painter and the Stranger, the Painter relates a traumatic memory. He accuses the Stranger of having spoiled his future as an artist when he falsely declared the Painter to be colour-blind:

> Mr Arvid, who was then a technician, was to examine my eyes before his father, the squire would support my studies at the Academy . . . So he took two balls of yarn from the dye workshop; one was reddish, the other greenish; and then he asked me. I answered, calling the red one green and then the opposite way round. With that my career was ruined . . . (132).

His bitterness stems from the fact that he really is not colour-blind: 'For this is what happened: I could distinguish the colours but not the *names*. But no one discovered this until I was thirty-seven years old' (137).

This episode may seem to be only very loosely linked to the central intrigue of the play which is concerned with arson, but what is more important than this intrigue is the cavalcade of memories that pass in revue throughout the drama, of which the Painter's bitter memory is one example. For many years he has believed himself colour-blind; hence he has not become an artist but a craftsman. Looking back, he now indicates that he considers his in fact quite normal eyesight has been manipulated.

Judging from a draft outline of the play in the Royal Library in Stockholm which includes the words 'The Deaf Painter speaks',[39] it would seem that Strindberg initially intended the Painter to suffer from a different handicap. Had Strindberg retained his deafness in the finished play, the discussion about his colour-blindness could only have been presented unprompted, which would have been difficult to motivate. On the other hand, for much of the time the Painter does appear to be mute. Strindberg's conception of this character seems therefore to have changed, but what he retained as fundamental to the Painter's role was the fact that he suffered in some way from real or imagined sensory deprivation. This in turn helps evoke the uncertain atmosphere that serves as a framework for a discussion of our sensory illusions.

When it comes to the usefulness of sight, we encounter the same ambivalence in *The Burnt House* as in *Storm.* As early as the opening exchanges between the Mason and the Plain Clothes Policeman, the ability of the eye to register what is to be seen is questioned: 'Has the fire really been extinguished now? THE MASON: At least there's no smoke to be *seen* anymore' (89, my italics).

Juxtaposed to this everyday use of the sense of sight, there is another more original one, which has to do with 'seeing through' something rather than 'observing'. The Stranger recounts a painful memory; how at the age of twelve he tried to take his own life and how, after this 'death', he had gained new skills: 'I saw right through people, read their thoughts, heard their intentions. In company, I saw people naked' (117). Here the sense of sight is connected to a central feature of all of the chamber plays, namely, the complex set of problems surrounding appearance and reality.[40] In his long monologue at the start of the second scene, the Stranger says that in this 'world of illusions and madmen', human beings are unable 'to see what is there but only what seems' (126).

His clear-sightedness and the ability to see through surface reality have led the Stranger to a stance of almost total pessimism and misanthropy:

THE LADY: Do you never enjoy being alive?
THE STRANGER: Oh yes; but that too is an illusion. Let me tell you, my dear sister-in-law, that when you are born without a film over your eyes, then you see life and people as they really are . . . and you would have to be a pig to like this filth – When you have had enough dust thrown in your eyes, you turn them inside out and look into your own soul. There is really something to look at . . .
THE LADY: What do you see there?
THE STRANGER: Yourself! But when you have seen yourself, you die! (150–1).

Clairvoyance is more or less a curse; life on earth is best lived with deadened senses, a thought that has been voiced before in Strindberg's dramas. What is new in *The Burnt House* is that the person serving as the moral unmasker is himself not exempt from scrutiny.

The verb 'to see' is used in yet a third way in this drama – a way that is reminiscent of the praise of wisdom with which *Storm* concludes. Again, it is the Stranger who introduces the idea which adds to the complexity of the drama in so far as one and the same person uses a keyword in different ways. The Stranger now asserts that with increasing age he sees a pattern, where earlier he had only been able to see chance circumstance: 'In old age when your eye begins to see, you discover that all the doodles form a pattern, a code, an ornament, a hieroglyph, which you can only now interpret: This is life!' (109).

Sound, taste, smell

Because Strindberg placed the emphasis in *The Burnt House* on the moral component of his complex idea of 'the world of illusions,' this drama is more silent than *Storm*. There are no additional sound components and the sense of hearing is only related to conversation. In *The Burnt House* one explores and draws conclusions from what one sees; to all intents and purposes listening has been degraded to spying, as when it is stated of the Painter in the opening stage direction that he '*follows every conversation listening in*' (89) or when, shortly afterwards, it becomes apparent that a witness has been concealed offstage from where he hears the whole of the initial dialogue between the Mason and the Policeman (93).

In *The Burnt House*, sensations of taste and smell are associated with discomfort. An inn is visible stage left. It is called 'The Last Nail' since, in earlier days, a man condemned to death received a last glass here on his way to the gallows (107). Nowadays, the Hearse Driver usually fortifies himself here on his way home from funerals. Thus, the inn is not associated with feasting but – in a truly macabre way – with death.

The present *dramatis personae* experience neither taste nor scent, a circumstance which – in combination with the charred remnants of the house on stage – seems to reduce the scope of the drama. In comparison with *Storm* one might even see this as a reduction to an almost ascetic dimension, in which case the image of the flowering garden in the second scene comes to constitute a contrast to this frugality (125).

It is against the background of the garden, with its spring flowers and blooming fruit trees, that the Stranger delivers his darkest monologues. In one of these he remembers how in childhood he was given 'dried cod and beer-soup' for Saturday dinner (126). In the first scene there is a similar recollection of the smells of childhood: 'I remember that I always hated that smell of colour dye, something so sickly sweet' (114). In the Second Act, foul-smelling mankind is contrasted with the beautiful, fragrant spring flowers:

> [Human beings] are a horrible species, ugly, sweaty, stinking; dirty linen, dirty stockings with holes in them, chilblains, corns, ugh! No, a blooming apple tree is much more beautiful; look at the lilies on the ground, it is as if they were not at home here, and feel their scent! (130)

Windows

In *Storm* it was still possible to talk about a certain mutual confidence between people and about a communication that, on the whole, functioned well. This was visualized through different openings in the on-stage scenery.

In *The Burnt House*, the stage is dominated by the charred ruin of a burnt-down house. The initial stage direction, discussed above, is an anticipation, however cryptic, of the subsequently important theme of falsification: '*THE PAINTER is busy painting the window frames of the Inn; he is listening intently to every conversation*' (89). As stated earlier, colour and painting in these plays connote embellishment, faking. If windows may be regarded as symbols of communication and colour as a symbol of falsification, then the juxtaposition of these in the stage direction could imply a warning that communication between people in this play is marred by lies and deception.

The burnt house was never as open as the house in *Storm*; on the contrary, what is emphasized is its *confinement*: 'when they broke open the door to the Student's room, they found heaps of hairpins on the floor, they were certainly discovered, but there had to be a fire first' (98). It is said that the fire might have started in another closed room, in the Cook's 'closet' (100). When the Stranger returns sixty years back in time, he too ends up in a windowless room: 'I sense the smell of a children's nursery, and feel a pressure in my chest' (108).

When, despite everything, a window is mentioned in *The Burnt House*, we find nothing but shame and scandals behind it:

> But one day when Father was away, I found the key. I had seen the books that stood stacked in front before, I had seen through the glass before. There were sermons, the works of great poets, books on gardening, collections of statutes concerning the organization of customs and exercise and the confiscation of goods, law books . . . But then I discovered that behind these books there was room for other things, and I investigated: First, there was the cane – [. . .] But now for it: there were bundles of small booklets with illustrated covers that aroused my interest . . . the memoirs of a certain Chevalier (115).

Thus amidst the ruins of his childhood home, the Stranger conjures forth a number of small, confined rooms, among them the Student's room that had to be broken into and the Cook's closet. The existing windows are either having their frames painted or else they open onto a closed cupboard which, when opened, turns out to contain a great deal more than was visible from the outside.

The fire, the lantern

In *Storm*, the action was to a great degree related to light; the drama takes place while people are waiting for the lamp lighter to turn on the first street lamp of the autumn. In *The Burnt House*, burning light is associated with devastating fire. When the curtain rises, fire has laid waste a house. The unobtrusive lamp lighter from *Storm* has returned in a demonized version, as an arsonist, and the street light has become an explosive lamp.

Thus fire is destructive and less under control here than in *Storm*. In *The Burnt House*, the fire threatens to flare up again; in fact, the first line in the play refers to this: 'Is it really out now?' (89), and it takes some time before it is confirmed that the fire is 'extinguished' (104).

This shift of meaning in the fire and lamp symbolism corresponds to a similar shift with regard to the attitude to enlightenment and information. Fire has a purifying effect in *The Burnt House* in that it brings out the truth: 'a fire must pass first' (98). It sets in motion processes of truth-seeking and truth-saying that do not end until everyone present and several dead people have been unmasked as humbugs or criminals. When the arson was arranged, it was as an act of jealousy, and was intended to facilitate an insurance claim. In reality, however, it initiated a process of unmasking.

As Göran Lindström has demonstrated, the expression 'the burnt house' refers to contextual material from Strindberg's life and he had used the same motif before, for instance in the historical drama *Charles XII*.[41] This practice of reconstructing a past life in a combination of different facets of his experience had also been used by Strindberg in his prose works.[42] His use of it is not only elegiac; he allows his main character to appear as both a Hamlet figure and an examiner of the scene of the crime.

The drama is full of other visual symbolism of mortal decay; apart from the ruins of the house, there are funeral wreaths (98), mourning veils (100), a clock (126); there is also talk of a 'funeral' (94) and the 'morgue' (117)[43] and one of the characters is a hearse driver. These features contribute of course to the pessimistic inflection of the play. The basic tone is vanity – the word is used by the Stranger in his principal monologue about 'the World of Illusions': 'There was nothing there to hold on to! Vanity, vanity!' (126).

Colours

In *Storm* there is a suggestion that to paint – to colour – is tantamount to falsifying (cf. p. 84). The motif as such was not new in Strindberg's writing, indeed, the same idea had been presented with great visual power as early as *Advent*.

In *The Burnt House*, this theme has moved to the foreground, which is apparent even from the list of characters. Two of them are occupied professionally with colours: The Dyer and the Painter. The symbolism of painting is almost too obvious in the drama but not, as in *Advent*, through a visual demonstration; rather, it manifests itself in a series of rather long-winded verbal commentaries on the false surface of everything in this world.

The burnt childhood home is black with soot and though the image of the past that is conjured up amidst the ruins may seem colourful it proves to be false. The dye works that have been the family's livelihood are disclosed as a hiding-place for smuggled

yarn, which was dyed there and then resold (114). The house was
built with double walls between which smuggled goods were
stored. Moreover, colour is not only associated with falsification, it
also arouses memories of unpleasant smell.

In the long pessimistic monologue in the second scene, the
childhood home is depicted as stamped by dishonesty; again,
references to both colour and dye are used:

> It was said to be ebony, was admired as such, and now, after fifty
> years, it stands revealed by me as dyed maple – everything was
> dyed in our house so as to be unrecognizable, and the clothes we
> wore as children were dyed as well, so we always had dye on our
> bodies! Humbug, ebony (126).

Most things in this falsified world are conjured forth out of the past;
however, they occasionally refer to the present, as when, on the
Dyer's first entrance, the audience is made aware of the family's
criminal heritage by his appearance: '*enters, visibly shaken, dishevelled,
his hands a blackish blue*' (104). His condition prompts the Stranger
to ask questions, which his brother feels are insinuating: 'Why are
your hands so black?' – 'Because I handle dyed goods . . . Did you
mean something else?' – 'What would that be?' – 'That my hands
are not clean!' (112). In a later dialogue, this time between the
Stonecutter and the Stranger, it is suggested that the Dyer is hiding
something. This is expressed visually by his dyed hands: 'Yes, he has
a pleasant disposition! I know nothing else, for I can't find out what
he's hiding!' THE STRANGER: 'Excellent! – However! His hands are
always blue, but you know they're white underneath' (143). Shortly
afterwards, a comment by the Stranger's to his brother's wife refers
to imagery that is linked to covering something up with paint and
might be taken to be insinuating: 'Don't I answer to the descriptions, or colorations?' (148) which is, of course the basic theme of
the play – the discrepancy between appearance and reality – in
a nutshell. Following his 'death in life', the Stranger is specially
qualified to make such an observation.

Meanwhile, flowers and trees appear to constitute a contrast to
this false and dyed world. At this stage in the cycle, there therefore
still seems to be a fragrant domain of genuine beauty in the world of
the chamber plays.

Gesture

On two occasions in the drama, a character covers his eyes with his hands. This occurs under similar circumstances and seems to suggest that life is unbearable. On one occasion it is the Stranger who employs the gesture when he observes that the present situation 'is, beyond all description, awful' (140). Likewise, at a subsequent moment in the play, the Dyer's wife reacts with an identical gesture after she hears the Stranger describe the process of looking deep within oneself as a preliminary to dying:

> THE WIFE (*holds her hands over her eyes*)
> *Pause.* (151)

This kind of gesture is strongly underlined in *The Burnt House*, first by the Stranger's line, partially cited above, where in the Swedish original the commas between almost every word invite its slow delivery accompanied by a series of gestures or changes in facial expression in the subsequent pauses. In the second example, Strindberg accentuates the gesture by following it with a pause. On both occasions the gesture implies a desire, albeit a hopeless one, to cut oneself off from painful insights.

The dialogue

In *Storm* there was a confidential relationship, not only between the Gentleman, his Brother, and Louise but also outside this inner circle with a peripheral character like the Confectioner. Conversation and daily small talk constituted part of the cosy atmosphere – hence the drama could be understood as a conversation piece. Such confidential circumstances and relaxed dialogue is lacking in *The Burnt House*. Speech falls apart in a series of rapid exchanges, often between two characters who distrust each other. But in contrast to this aspect of the dialogue, there are several extended monologues, eight in all, which provide a character with the opportunity of expressing his or her innermost feelings, and which also possess a philosophical and meditative content.

The opening dialogue of the play is more of an interrogation with the questions formulated by a policeman dressed in civilian clothes and addressed to the Mason who finally wearies of the conversation: 'You can't pump me any more' (91). He also points out that he feels 'trapped' (92), and in this respect he is not altogether wrong for it turns out that all along the conversation has been overheard by an invisible witness.

The good relationship between the two brothers in *Storm* is replaced in *The Burnt House* by a fraternal relationship that is evidently a bad one. The meeting between the Stranger and the Dyer, who have not seen each other for several decades, rapidly turns into a quarrel in which several injustices that go back to their childhood are revived.

Likewise the dialogue in the second scene between the Stranger and the Student – who is understood to be his son – is marked by suspicion. When the Stranger observes that the Student has 'just lied again. without knowing it!', the Student retorts 'I never lie!' only to be told by the Stranger that he has done so 'a mere three times in this short space of time' (118). Meanwhile the Stranger's dialogue with the Stonecutter, who has been in prison, is more straightforward, but it, too, deals with subjects like 'perjury' and 'testifying' (139).

In this context, the 'mute dialogue' in the second scene between the plain clothes policeman and the Stranger constitutes an interesting feature. According to the stage directions '*The* PLAIN CLOTHES POLICEMAN *enters, speaking slowly to the* STRANGER *who replies in the same manner; this lasts for about half a minute, whereupon the* PLAIN CLOTHES POLICEMAN *leaves*' (147). Here the spectator has to guess the content of the dialogue. The technique seems logical, given the pessimism about human communication that is recorded elsewhere in the drama. Such pessimism is here extended to the relationship between the stage and audience which is left in the dark about what the two characters on stage are discussing.

Elsewhere, the dialogue between the Stranger and his brother's wife, who receives good advice from the Stranger, would seem to demonstrate a greater sense of trust, but the reason for the understanding between them is that they both share the same sceptical attitude to the Dyer. The Stranger's concluding dialogue with his brother has more or less the quality of an accusation.

The monologues and dialogues in *The Burnt House* may seem traditional and indeed, in a letter to Emil Schering (24 April, 1907) Strindberg mentioned Goethe's *Clavigo* and *Stella* as models.[44] But what is interesting is that although, in a formal sense, the dialogues are still dialogues, they are, from the point of view of content, almost completely malfunctioning conversations. In *The Burnt House* it is difficult to exchange information with confidence. Interrogation or eavesdropping are the available methods, which is in considerable contrast to *Storm*.

Childhood memories

In comparison with *Storm*, there is here a distinct shift in the main character's relation to his past. In *Storm* the protagonist lived among his memories, which he embellished in his imagination. In that respect, he contrasts directly with the protagonist of *The Burnt House* whose memory functions in a very matter-of-fact way, and who never attempts to beautify the past.

To a large extent, *The Burnt House* deals with how the truth about people is distorted by posterity for a number of different reasons. This type of falsification is a kind of 'illusion'. As in *Storm*, *The Burnt House* juxtaposes this 'illusion' with the ability of people in old age to survey their lives, something that is now formulated as a capacity to see patterns in what is happening.

As in *Storm*, a world is reconstructed that is partly present and partly past. In *Storm* an attempt was made, through perceptions of sound, to form a picture of possible criminal activity in the upstairs apartment. In *The Burnt House* an attempt is made to use a variety of objects such as hairpins, keys and a lamp stand, to create a picture of the situation that obtained in the house before it burned down. Alongside these efforts, which make use of the senses of hearing and sight, both dramas reconstruct the past. This is done by ensuring that the recollections of the different characters conflict with each other.

The theme of memory is represented in major as well as minor matters. The spectator encounters it most distinctly in a couple of references to the memorializing cult of great men – here there is a suggestions that their greatness might best be likened to humbug. Thus, in the first scene of *The Burnt House* there is talk of a 'memorial' (94) or 'monument' (95) that is to be raised over a bishop's tomb and we are told, in derogatory terms, that the bishop was a collector of insects. The posthumous fame of supposedly great men's is stressed again when the Stranger speaks of his break-down at the age of twelve, which was caused by his being 'sent by the school with torches and banners to celebrate "the destroyer of the country"' (117). The incident implied a kind of fall from grace, which affords an insight into the world as a madhouse – an expression that returns in the long monologue at the beginning of the second scene: 'the world of illusions and madmen' (126).

This falsification of history is seconded in an almost comical way by the everyday forgetfulness of some of the characters. On returning from a funeral the Hearse Driver doesn't even remember the name of the man he has just buried (95). Likewise, the Gardener was supposed to have arranged a bridal bouquet for his son's wedding 'and I've forgotten it' (103) and the Mason is also portrayed as forgetful; to explain his presence in the attic at a certain time he maintains that he was looking for his tools: 'I can't always be there at the usual time to look for tools I've forgotten. When I fixed the Student's porcelain stove, I forgot my hammer!' (104). The Stranger, too, who is the character with the best memory, has difficulty remembering recent events, although he explains it as follows:

> I can't remember that; I often confuse what I've said with what I'd meant to say, and that's mostly because I think so intensely, ever since the day I hanged myself in the closet (116).

On several occasions the Stranger breaks out in longer or shorter monologues. He talks out loud, apparently mostly to himself but according to a pattern that he is aware of: 'I've no purpose with my talk, the memories simply crowd in' (111). His longest and most comprehensive monologue, which ends with the reference to 'the world of illusions and madmen', occurs at the beginning of the second scene. The first scene also contains several similarly constructed outbursts or longer replies in monologue form, in which the Stranger allows his memories to burst out and become audible. The common purpose of these 'memory monologues' is to show that such recollections cannot stand the spotlight of the present.

In six out of eight instances, the Stranger's 'memory monologues' are brought about by different objects that he observes: the ruins of the house (monologue 1, p. 107); the family's photo album (2, p. 109); an apple tree (3, p. 111); the family book cupboard (4, p. 115); the Student's books (6, p. 125); a wreath (7, p. 131). With regard to memory monologue number 5 (p. 117), which deals with his attempted suicide, and memory monologue number 8 (p. 136), which deals with Vesterlund's funeral, visual objects are not the catalysts; rather, these monologues emanate from longer subjective explanations, in response to a question by a dialogue partner.

Memory monologue number 1 concerns the Stranger's home and the occasion is the sight of its ruins. The Stranger remembers moving into the house, but first and foremost his recollection is of a man who killed himself in one of the rooms, and he seems to discern a pattern of accidental circumstances when he states that he later married the suicide's niece. Monologue number 2, prompted by the rediscovered family photograph album, ends with the Stranger observing 'connections and a repetitive pattern' (109) in the relationships between people in general. Monologue number 3 stems from the sight of the garden in which the flowers and trees contrast with ruined human nature and evoke a lost paradise.

Monologue number 4 varies the theme of the Fall, as the Stranger tells of how he gained forbidden access to the book cupboard and discovered the memoirs of Casanova, remarking: 'with that I left the paradise of childhood' (115). Monologue number 5 deals with his suicide attempt, said to have been provoked by celebrations in honour of Charles XII and which led to a lasting ability to distinguish between seeming and being.

Monologue number 6 is the longest and begins with the Stranger searching for the Student's books. He declares Livy's History to be 'nothing but lies' (125). He recognizes another book as his own, although his name has been erased. Then follows an enumeration of fake objects in the house. Some of them break when touched, which results in the mantra: 'Breaks upon touch! Everything broke on touch, everything!' (126).

In monologue number 7, the Stranger remembers old Mrs Vesterlund who used to work in his childhood home: 'When she had been stealing for ten years, she was promoted to housekeeper' (131). The sight of the Gardener's wreaths made from sprigs of bearberry sprigs, 'which he sells as lingonberry' (131) brings the theme of falsification up to date, and in the eighth monologue about Mr Vesterlund, the Stranger learns from Mrs Vesterlund – whom at this point he apparently trusts – that her husband was also a cheat: 'now I see him in his right light'.

Taken together, these precisely formulated remembered vignettes serve to make a clean sweep of the past, to eradicate family and friends from the his childhood. Therefore it is logical that at the end of the drama the Stranger should lay a wreath on the ruins of his childhood home and, after a silent prayer, move on, back out into the world.

As in *Storm*, the protagonist leaves, disillusioned but also purified of his false perceptions. This cannot – any more than in *Storm* – simply be interpreted as a preparation for death. Certainly, the author's pessimism is substantial, and it is possible to find a longing for death expressed in letters written around this time. But author and protagonist are not identical, and in both *Storm* and *The Burnt House* Strindberg keeps a door open for his protagonist. Both the Gentleman in *Storm* and the Stranger in *The Burnt House* possess an element of vitality and a passion for truth that contradict their presumed longing for death. They are clear-eyed moralists and are not lost in the terrible world of illusions. Despite everything, they do not need death as a desperate way out. Both are ready to start anew. The Gentleman in *Storm* will move into a new house with no deceptive memories, and the Stranger leaves like an eternal wanderer: 'And so, out into the world again, thou wanderer!' (157).

Character

Where character in the sense of personality is concerned, *The Burnt House* presents two different aspects. On the one hand, the play stresses man's need to disguise himself, to paint himself as better or different than he is, and the drama as a whole criticizes this art of dissembling on moral grounds. But there is another conclusion to be drawn from the many perceptions of dissimulation in the play, one which has a psychological rather than a moral implication, namely no human being has a solid personality.[45] Nevertheless, this belief can also be formulated morally, as when the Stranger says of his brother that he 'has fabricated a personality for himself out of lies' (149). On other occasions, the author allows the *dramatis personae* to express the idea that it is difficult to assess the personality of a fellow human being:

> THE WIFE: Yes, human beings do each other so much wrong, and they paint each other after their own image . . .
> THE STRANGER: And they walk about like theatre directors handing out roles to each other; some accept the role, others give it back and prefer to improvise (148).

Such views of an elusive personality as a mirage or an illusion[46] are reconfirmed as the play unfolds. In retrospect, the Mason's early line – 'We all know each other' (89) – comes to sound more and more ironic.

The theme of dissimulation is also given a comical twist – or so one is led to think. The Gardener appears to differ from the others in terms of self-knowledge and frankness. He calls himself a 'real oaf', an 'asshole', 'idiot', 'bastard', and 'jerk' (99); he would thus seem to be at odds with the moral humbug displayed by the other characters, at the same time as his comic nature lightens the drama. But it turns out that he, too, has faked his character. His lamentations and self-depreciation were intended to deceive. He is basically 'a wise old man, though he calls himself an idiot' (145). The unmasking is not comical but contributes to a young girl's loosing her illusions and to her difficulty in finding her way morally: 'What am I supposed to believe in now?' (145). This partly accounts for the fact that in the list of *dramatis personae*, Strindberg preferred to identify most of the characters in terms of their profession first, and only then by name. For in an evasive world a professional designation is still something to 'hold on to'. As the Stone-Mason observes: 'Hmm! character! Well, I don't know what that is. Do you mean a profession? Name and character, that's what is listed in the register, but that means profession, not character' (141).

In *The Burnt House*, the view of character/personality is primarily presented in a discursive manner; in his next drama, *The Ghost Sonata*, Strindberg will go one step further.

The material in A Blue Book

The ideas expressed in *The Burnt House*, as well as in *Storm*, are anchored in the philosophical world of the *Blue Books*. It is of interest to study how these notations, originally private, were organized and utilized in the chamber plays where, in a number of fortunate instances, they could be dramatized, and – sometimes less fortunately – they might pop up almost verbatim in scattered lines or monologues. The latter is the case with *The Burnt House*, a play that appears to be more verbally than dramatically conceived, and which is therefore a more rhetorical piece than *Storm*.

The long monologue which opens the second scene, where the Stranger is presented posed like Hamlet with a clock in his hand, corresponds to the essay 'The World of Illusions' in *A Blue Book I*, where the author states that 'everything is lying and deception, all of life is faked, the state, society, marriage, family' (SV 65:39). 'It is surely a madhouse', he adds on another occasion, while invoking Hamlet as someone who could see through such a foolish world. In the same essay, there is a concrete example of folly: 'A nation gathers once a year to celebrate "the destroyer of the country"' which is a reference to the same incident that served as a catalyst in the Stranger's attempted suicide in *The Burnt House*: 'The world was a madhouse! – This I discovered one day when my school was sent out with torches and banners to celebrate "the destroyer of the country"' (177).

As regards respect for great men – the apotheosis – which was exemplified in *The Burnt House* by the raising of a memorial over the bishop, *A Blue Book I* alludes to many such cases. For instance, in the essay 'With the Prince of this World', a statue of 'the destroyer of the fatherland' is mentioned as well as other statues raised on the same false grounds: 'Over there in that park there is one with a laurel on his head; he was the most depraved individual of his time; and way out over there at the harbour there is a third statue of a perjurer' (65).

The Stranger's ability to see through fakery, which he acquired through his visit to 'the other side', has its counterpart in *A Blue Book I* in a more detailed description of a similar situation with the heading 'Somnambulism and Clairvoyance in Every Day Life':

> Sometimes I can awake, however. Then I see the company naked, their dirty linen through their clothes, their deformities and unwashed feet; but worst of all, I hear the thoughts behind their words, I see their expressions, which do not accord with what they are saying (69).

The entry in *A Blue Book* entitled 'Murder Lies' (Mord–lögner) expounds the view that, in a world of falsehood and fakery, life makes people imagine themselves dreaming or losing their substance:

> But your whole philosophy is falsified too; you live in an imagined world, finally you float in the air, you move in a world of false emotions [. . .] It was many years before I could sort out and reorganize my ideas; true and false were all mixed up, lies

became unreal and my whole life like smoke. I was on the verge of a breakdown and was set to lose my mind (173).

In *The Burnt House* the Stranger has such a 'reorganization' behind him: 'However, I got grey hairs that night; and I had to reorganize my whole life' (114). Since then he lives, strangely enough, as part somnambulist, part clairvoyant: 'I walk about like a somnambulist on a cornice – I know I'm asleep but I am awake too – and I am only waiting to be awakened' (149). In an entry whose title is borrowed from a line in *Macbeth* – 'A Tale Told by an Idiot', Strindberg links the somnambulist theme with Shakespeare's dramas:

> To be able to live your life, you must walk like a somnambulist, and you must also be a poet, dupe yourself and others. I have been able to do so quite successfully, and I have walked on gutterings of the thinnest lead (153).

In the entry entitled 'Self-Knowledge' Strindberg describes awakening as something to be worth striving for but also as a brutal experience: 'Then one day you wake up, as it were, from your sleep, see yourself as a ghost, and you are terrified and ask yourself: Is this me?' (68). To see oneself was said to mean death in *The Burnt House* (151). Strindberg's attitude to somnambulism seems problematic. In the Stranger's case, the problem is still there when he points out that he is both asleep and clairvoyant. What might be said about this paradox is that the Stranger is not meant to participate in life on the same premises as others: either he will dream himself away or suffer the torture of seeing clearly.

Experiencing life as a dream world is not altogether negative, but it can be a form of martyrdom for those who suffer from it – a predicament that Strindberg describes under the heading 'Lethe':

> This whole web of lies, mistakes, misunderstandings that consti-tutes the basic content of our life changes life itself into some-thing unreal, dreamlike and should be dissolved when we cross over to the other life (SV 65:166).

Guided by the way in which the colour (dye) motif has been employed elsewhere in *The Burnt House*, the fact that the Dyer has black hands has previously been linked to his criminality. Here it is possible to speak for once of a motif from *A Blue Book I* that has been rendered in visually dramatic terms in the play. In the entry entitled 'The Art of Knowing People', Strindberg says in a reference to Swedenborg: 'the murderer and cheat gets black hands' (90).

The Burnt House ends with the statement that life is a mess more than a patterned web, and that questions of guilt are difficult to determine, which leads to a certain tolerant resignation: 'The case is deleted, the cause cannot be investigated, the parties withdraw' (157). This statement has its counterpart – almost verbatim – in a somewhat fuller discussion by Strindberg in *A Blue Book I* under the heading 'Cannot Be Investigated': 'life is such a web of lies, mistakes, misunderstandings, of debts and claims that a balancing of the books is impossible' (SV 65:186).

The relationship between *The Burnt House* and *A Blue Book I* is thus not one in which Strindberg extracts ideas and motifs noted down in the latter which are then transposed into effective drama in the latter. The somewhat lifeless impression that *The Burnt House* makes on both reader and spectator has to do with its declamatory nature, characterized as it is by a number of monologues, which in turn present ideas from *A Blue Book I* almost verbatim, without any dramaturgical revision.

THE GHOST SONATA

Introduction

The drama that most consistently but also most originally reflects Strindberg's ideas about 'the world of illusions' is *The Ghost Sonata*, written only a few weeks after *The Burnt House*.[47]

In *Storm* Strindberg had stressed the expendability of sensory perceptions in favour of interior beholding and in *The Burnt House* he had illustrated, with almost unremitting blackness, the 'moral' illusion. In *The Ghost Sonata* he combines both of these ideas and in the final Act he also adds a philosophical element by referring to Buddhism both directly and through the mediation of Schopenhauer who, in *Die Welt als Wille und Vorstellung* (The World as Will and Representation), writes of life as 'das Reich des Zufalls, des Irrtums und der Torheit' (the realm of chance, errors and madness).[48] *The Ghost Sonata* thus demonstrates with greater consistency than the other dramas all of the ideas whose pre-history I have previously sought to describe.[49]

When themes and motifs from the earlier chamber plays are presented in *The Ghost Sonata* they occur, as previously, with increasing 'demonization'. This aspect is sometimes taken to such an extreme that it has seemed reasonable to refer to the absurd elements in the play.[50]

With *The Ghost Sonata* Strindberg wishes to show that the sensory world is painful, not least because man's senses can be *sabotaged* in different ways by his surroundings. The title itself already gives an indication of this. Here, two senses are alluded to at once: *vision* ('Ghost') and *hearing* ('Sonata'). This gives rise to a certain unease, in part through the use of the word 'Ghost' but also in the blending of these two senses, which is a strange practice for Strindberg.

Composition

Several attempts have been made to account for the structure *The Ghost Sonata*. The word 'sonata' invites the reader to view the three Acts as the equivalents of the three movements of a musical sonata.[51] A different composition principle will be discussed here. I wish to pursue the thesis that in his demonstration of the philosophy of 'the world of illusions', Strindberg proceeds along a more original path. Thus I claim that the First Act essentially highlights the sense of sight and its limitations. In the same manner, the Second Act describes hearing, and in the compact Third Act, the theme of taste and smell is added. My analysis places the stress on the word 'Ghost' rather than on the remainder of the play's title.

Touch

Where the sense of touch is concerned, bodily contact in Strindberg's dramas is always pregnant with meaning and often originally presented. All touch in *The Ghost Sonata* is clearly accentuated, and it is part of the nature of things that touching is communicated verbally and/or via gestures. The bathing of the Student's eyes by the Milkmaid in the first act is an example of such touching – it is a scene that creates a stark contrast to another scene in the same Act in which the Student grasps Hummel's hand.

When the latter urges him to 'take my hand, and you will feel how cold I am', the Student exclaims, 'That's extraordinary!' and '*recoils*' (177). The Student's problem at the opening of the first act is in turn the result of touch which stems from a time preceding the beginning of the scene: 'My hands have touched the injured and corpses' (165). When, in the Second Act, the Mummy turns Hummel into a parrot by stroking him on the back in a hypnotic fashion (209), it is likewise a question of touch of an original and ominous nature. In the following analysis, however, I am concerned with the less distinct senses.

Act i – Vision

Exposition

There is good reason to examine the opening scene of the First Act in which the Student encounters both the Milkmaid and the Old Man, Hummel, from different perspectives. Gunnar Brandell in particular has observed that the exposition of *The Ghost Sonata* is of an original kind, and that it is likely to create confusion and misinformation, both between the characters on stage and between the stage and the audience.[52] Brandell's analysis focuses primarily on the dialogue but I contend that one can arrive at a similar conclusion by analysing the scene from a more encompassing, physical aspect.[53]

The first question to ask is this: In what way does the opening scene establish the view that the sense of vision is deceitful or problematic?

At first, the audience has no difficulty orientating itself. When the curtain goes up the spectator is introduced to '*the façade of a modern house*' (163) – it is exactly the same setting as in *Storm* (13). So far the setting does not seem to fit the title of the play. According to the stage directions, it is 'a clear Sunday morning'. However, what militates against the idyllic impression and conveys a sense of something serious are the white sheets in some of the windows, the customary way in Sweden of indicating that someone in the house has just died. The stage direction continues: '*a darkly dressed woman stands motionless on the steps*', and the sight of her together with the white sheets tunes the scene to a minor key.

With certain sounds as background – a bell ringing, the whistle of a steamship, the sound of an organ from a nearby church – the play opens without words.[54] The Caretaker's Wife sweeps the hall-way and polishes the brass on the door before watering the laurel bushes in the pots on the pavement. These actions have a symbolic meaning, to which I shall return; however, none of them is in any way problematic from a realistic point of view. Such is also the case with Hummel, who is sitting in his wheelchair, wearing glasses, and reading a newspaper.

The action on stage increases when the Milkmaid enters and crosses to the fountain, though she, too, acts in a mute, yet intense manner. She washes herself, and looks at herself in a mirror (164). The stage direction indicates that there should be as much as '*a couple of minutes of silence*' before the Student makes his entrance.

Several characters are now on stage and there is a predisposition for a dialogue; by now the audience should be impatiently expecting an exposition of some kind. However, what they are given is, as Brandell demonstrates, almost the opposite: an 'erratic' dialogue that risks frustrating and confusing an audience rather than enlightening it.

The characters on stage sometimes react in terror at seeing each other, and this *sighting* is problematic; the Old Man understands that the Student sees someone (the Milkmaid) whom he himself is unable to see. The Milkmaid sees the Student '*with horror*' (164), at which point the Old Man wonders 'who is he talking to? – I can't anyone!'

Sight is also stressed with particular clarity when the Student asks the Milkmaid to bathe his eyes, which he says are inflamed. coming as it does at the start of the drama this eye cleansing has a symbolic meaning: thereafter the play will deal not only with deceitful visions but also with painful clear-sightedness. This is what the Student is being prepared for. Together with certain other elements in this opening scene like the Old Man's glasses, the gossip mirror outside one of the house windows,[55] and the fact that the Old Man does not see what others see (indeed, the verb 'see' is used in many different contexts in the early pages of the play), this confronts the spectator with the problem: to what extent is it possible to trust one's own vision?

Sight, see

The verb 'see' is generally very prevalent in Strindberg's drama. According to Helmut Müssener it is used more than one hundred times in *A Dream Play*.[56] The verb appears at least as many times in *The Ghost Sonata* which is considerably shorter (62 pages in Sam-lade Verk compared with 113 for *A Dream Play*), and in such a way that all of the verb's meanings are utilized. It means not only 'to perceive' in the sense of a vision; it also appears in the context 'to know of' or 'to comprehend, to understand'. Moreover, it is used as an interjection and as a dialectal expression: '*si*' (behold). The song that ends Acts II and III includes the verb and its synonym no less than three times in the first two verses: 'The sun I *saw*, it *appeared* to me/that I *beheld* The hidden' (210, my italics).'[57]

In its use of the verb 'to see', this hymn summarizes much of what the play dramatizes. In the first instance, 'to see' means 'to observe'. The second time it means something like 'I got the impression', and the third time – with the variation 'behold' – the verb has definitely departed from empirical reality. The first two lines of the Song to the Sun illustrate, in a compact way, this development from *observing* to *beholding*, which is a recurring theme not only in the chamber plays but in Strindberg's post-Inferno dramas in general.

But it is in the First Act that the verb is active – almost too active, perhaps, since it prevalence sometimes borders on punning. Thus, the opening short scene directs the viewer's attention to the prob-lematic sense of sight through certain *properties* (mirror, glasses) as well as certain *gestures* (the Milkmaid mirrors herself in the fountain, she bathes the Student's eyes), and furthermore, she states *verbally*: 'I see no one! [. . .] What are you looking at?' (164).

In the dialogue between the Old Man and the Student the verb 'to see' appears in a number of apparently trivial circumstances. Hummel says that he 'saw' the Student as a child (167) and has even 'had his eyes on him' (179); on the other hand he concludes that the Student now 'sees' him as a cripple (169). He enlists the Student's help in crossing to the billboard in order to 'see' what is being performed at the Opera and he uses expressions such as 'Look at that!' (172), 'Well, you see, it is a little complicated' (173). The verb often appears in the imperative, 'Look at her! – Have you ever seen such a masterpiece!' (127) 'But look now, look at the balcony [. . .] Do you see the blue blanket? [. . .] look, at her, look' (179). After Hummel's exit the imperative form is taken over by his servant Johansson who at times uses the dialect pronunciation: '*Si*' (185).

'Look, look at him' (185). It is also Johansson who utters the Act's ominous final line: 'Well, we shall see! We shall see!' (187).

However, on certain occasions the use of the word is of more significant interest. In response to the Old Man's question, 'Do you see that house?' (171) the Student says: 'I have probably observed it . . . I went past here yesterday when the sun was shining on the panes – and I imagined all the beauty and luxury that was inside' (171). His initial statement that he has 'observed' the house makes a matter of fact impression, but this is soon annulled when he explains that 'the sun was shining on the panes', for he thus indicates that he was *blinded* when he fantasized about the interior of the house. And indeed it transpires that he has also created illusions for himself. What Strindberg does here, as was previously the case in *Advent* with the help of a so-called 'sun cat' (blinding mirror), is that he makes the phenomenon of '*blinding*' or illusions concrete.

As in *Storm*, another stage direction suddenly affords the spectator an insight into an apartment after a blind has been drawn, as when we see the Colonel, '*clad in civvies; after having looked at the thermometer, he walks into the room and stands in front of the marble statue*' (172). Here – again as in *Storm* – curiosity is aroused about the lives of those associated with the house. In both cases one can speak of a 'second curtain' that conceals a new staging area.

Just as the Stranger in *The Burnt House* possesses the ability to subject the world to moral scrutiny, the Student is accorded a similar ability in the last Act. Prior to this, another quality has been stressed: a kind of extraordinary foresightedness. He himself concludes that he is 'clairvoyant' since he is a 'Sunday child'. When the play begins he has just saved a child from a collapsing house, and at that moment he maintains that he was guided by some sort of insight:

I came there, and stopped in front of the building which I had never seen before . . . Then I noticed a crack in the wall, heard how it creaked in the foundations; I ran forward and caught up a child that was walking under the wall (174).

In the opening scene the Student has already demonstrated his clairvoyance by being able to see the Milkmaid, whom the Old Man – unlike the audience – cannot see. Likewise, on a later occasion – and again with the audience – the Student can see the dead Consul exiting through the gate. On both these occasions the audience shares the Student's ability to see and can thus experience 'clairvoyance' rather than being struck by an 'altered' vision.

An interesting and almost certainly intentionally cryptic discussion is pursued about the Student as a clairvoyant. Oddly enough, the nearsighted Hummel states that he has *noticed* this trait: 'I saw it in the colour of your eyes' (174). Shortly afterwards it is said of the white-haired old woman sitting at the gossip mirror: 'Yes, she has a beautiful gaze, though I can't see her eyes!' Both comments are based on the notion that the eyes are in some way the mirror of a person's inner self.

Others observe the Student's eyes; they are bathed in water from the fountain at the start of the play. Hummel, on the other hand, hides his eyes behind glasses, and the white-haired old woman looks at the world about her through a two-way mirror: 'this is the only mirror she uses for in it she does not see herself, only the external world and from two directions, but the world can see her, she hasn't realized that' (180). Her use of the mirror to spy on others is a contrast to the young Milkmaid's innocent mirroring herself in the fountain in the opening scene.

A parallel to the scene with the Milkmaid, i.e. a scene in which someone is visible to the Student and the audience but is invisible to Hummel in a ghost-like manner, is the scene in which the dead Consul exits through the gate.

> THE STUDENT: Good lord, what do I see?
> THE OLD MAN: What do you see?
> THE STUDENT: Can't *you* see the dead man in the doorway?
> THE OLD MAN: I see nothing, but that's just what I was expecting! Tell me (180).

This is again a scene in which the Student is clairvoyant but where he also – and one may feel that Strindberg has driven the situation too far – describes what is going on to someone with deficient vision. It is worth pointing out that Strindberg added these 'visions' to the manuscript after the play was completed, most probably in order to complicate the visual aspect of the theatrical experience.

Hummel finds himself in a somewhat similar type of predicament as the Gentleman did in *Storm*, although Hummel is a far more demonic figure than his predecessor. The gesture of shielding one's eyes with one's hand is also found in both *Storm* and *The Burnt House* and emerges in various ways in *The Ghost Sonata* as a

gesture of despair, when the Student is confronted with the Young
Lady and understands that she is beyond his reach: '*with his hands in
front of his eyes*', he exclaims, 'Before hopelessness, there is only
despair' (178). This gesture shields him from the world and is part of
the tendency towards isolation that is a recurring theme throughout
the chamber plays: retirement from the external world and concentration on an inner reality.

The First Act concludes with a third 'vision', but this time there
is a significant difference. Although the Milkmaid is once again
visible to the Student and to the audience, she can now also be seen
by Hummel and reminds him of a crime in which he was impli-
cated in the past. The – to the audience – surprising fact that the
Old Man can now suddenly see the Milkmaid underlines the
capriciousness of the visual sense as it is presented in this Act. And
Johansson's final line, 'Well, we shall see, We shall see!', thus makes
not only an ominous impression but also has an ironic and sceptical
tone.

ACT II – HEARING

The room

As in *Storm*, the First Act takes place in front of a house façade. In
Storm the Second Act took place '*Inside, in the drawing room*'. The
first two Acts of *The Ghost Sonata* follow a similar pattern: the
Second Act takes place '*Inside, in the round drawing room*' (188).

Storm is characterized by a demonstrative lack of confinement,
marked by open windows and doors and an accessible passageway
between the interior and exterior. People communicate with each
other in a largely uncomplicated manner. The opposite is the case
in *The Ghost Sonata*; this tendency is accentuated in the Second Act,
for which Strindberg prescribes a 'round' room. The absence of
corners and right angles suggests both that it is difficult to orientate
oneself with any precision and the idea of captivity. Strindberg had
previously stipulated something similar in the stage directions to the
first part of *The Dance of Death*, which is set in '*The interior of a round
fortress tower of grey stone*' (SV 44:9).

The feeling of confinement and captivity is underlined, when it
is revealed that the lady of the house is kept in a cupboard behind a
jib door and the daughter of the house spends most of her time in a

room filled with hyacinths. The audience is given no direct explanation for these bizarre circumstances; instead, it is said with purpose-
ful mysteriousness to be a question of 'oddities' in both the lady and
the daughter (191, 203). Furthermore, the stage directions for the
Second Act indicate that '*curtains*' can be drawn in front of the
white marble statue and that there is also a '*Japanese screen*' on stage,
which is used as a 'death screen' to be placed around anyone about
to pass away.

In this way, the purely physical arrangement is such that the
characters live isolated from each other even within this apartment
where the *mise en scène* makes the inability or will to communicate,
which is reflected on other levels in the act, visibly apparent to the
audience's eyes.

If the First Act of *The Ghost Sonata* mainly corresponds to *Storm*
through its rich visual metaphors and by its sharpening of the tendency to depict an evasive reality, which was present in *Storm*, the
Second Act of *The Ghost Sonata* takes up the moral theme from *The
Burnt House.*

The Second Act also depicts a number of themes and motifs
from Strindberg's earlier writing. The 'disappointment' motif from
A Dream Play returns. Thus Johansson says that 'it was always [his]
dream to enter this house' (188) and subsequently experiences that
nothing is what it appears to be. Strindberg has already described
one grotesque old couple in *Advent*; in *The Ghost Sonata* we are
offered another such couple, which is even more grotesque: the
man is a cripple, and the woman, who speaks like a parrot, is
described as a mummy – a loving couple that foreshadows aspects of
Beckett's absurd drama. The ghost supper of the Second Act has
been used previously by Strindberg in his prose, in the novel *Black
Banners*, while the scene in which the Mummy transforms Hummel
into a parrot and orders him to go into the cupboard and hang
himself suggests a revival of Strindberg's interest in suggestion and
hypnosis of the 1880s. The Mummy '*pats the Old Man on the back*'
(209), gets him to begin acting like a parrot, and makes him imitate
a cuckoo clock. This is a demonized version of a hypnotic seance
reminiscent of the final scene in *Miss Julie*. The razor blade in *Miss
Julie* is exchanged for a rope, but the command is of the same kind
as Jean's: 'There's a rope hanging in there that looks like the one
you strangled the Consul with upstairs, and that you intended to
strangle your benefactor with . . . Go! *The* OLD MAN *goes into the*

closet' (209). In *Miss Julie* Strindberg ends the corresponding passage: 'It's horrible! But there is no other way out! – Go! MISS JULIE *walks resolutely out through the door*' (SV 27: 190).

The visual metaphors from the First Act are not abandoned in the Second Act. They are revived when the Mummy is said to live in the cupboard because her eyes cannot stand the light (189). She herself concludes that she sits in there in order to 'avoid seeing, and avoid being seen' (195). Likewise, the visual metaphors are revived when the Old Man concludes that the Colonel 'is not who he appears to be!' (200), even as, in the next breath, he emphasizes his own possessive materialism: 'Everything you can see I own, it is mine!' (200).

The Milkmaid's mute and therefore noticeable gestures in the opening scene reappear in different variations – '*The* MILKMAID *[. . .] fixes her hair, mirrors herself in the water*' (164). In the Second Act 'hair' is replaced by 'wig', and 'mirror' becomes firstly a symbol of coquettishness and then an instrument of unmasking; one sees oneself as one is. When Hummel has made his entrance and is alone in the room, he '*fixes his wig in front of the mirror*' (193). The wig is used as a sign of false identity or manipulated age when the Mummy '*grabs at his wig*' (194) and when he himself unmasks the Colonel: 'Take off your hair, and look at yourself in the mirror' (202).

As has already been noted, one can describe the development from *Storm* to *The Ghost Sonata* as a continuing demonization, a tendency to move away from realism towards absurdity. But one can also find the same type of developmental curve within *The Ghost Sonata* starting with the fountain scene in which the Milkmaid is the Good Samaritan and the Student the hero. However, in what follows, emphasis will be placed on how the Second Act describes the theme of hearing in an ingenious and varied way, and thus constitutes another stage in the drama's study of the world of illusions.[58]

Peter Hallberg has identified a connection between the grotesque meal in *The Ghost Sonata* and the feast in Act 1, Scene 2 of Shakespeare's *Timon of Athens*; the latter meal is also characterized by a number of misanthropic outbursts. In his essay on *Hamlet*, Strindberg concludes that in *Timon of Athens* Shakespeare expresses 'a hatred of mankind, or a contempt which is reminiscent of Schopenhauer's or Hartmann's'.[59]

If one turns from the philosophical dimension to what is visually represented on stage, one finds that, as described by Shakespeare, the five senses appear in allegorical costume as an entertainment at the feast:

CUPID:

> Hail to thee, worthy Timon, and to all
> That of his bounties taste! The five best senses
> Acknowledge thee their patron, and come freely
> To gratulate thy plenteous bosom.
> Th'ear, taste, touch, smell, pleas'd from thy table rise;
> These only now come but to feast thine eyes.

However, the performance, the tribute to the sensual world and to frivolity awakens Apemantus's disgust:

> Hoy-day, what a sweep of vanity comes this way!
> They dance they are mad-women
> Like madness is the glory of this life,
> As this pomp shows to a little oil and root.
> We make ourselves fools, to disport ourselves,
> And spend our flatteries, to drink those men
> Upon whose age we void it up again
> With poisonous spite and envy.
> Who lives, that's not depravéd or depraves?[60]

Apemantus rejects sensuous pleasure as immoral and his outburst is directed at a very concrete goal: the personification of the five senses.

Wagner, sound

In the time that transpires between Acts One and Two, the Student is assumed to have listened to a performance of Wagner's *The Valkyr* at the opera. There have been many ingenious and respectable attempts to explain why Strindberg should have chosen precisely this opera; the title is mentioned no less than six times in the course of the play. Leif Leifer contends that *The Valkyr* and *The Ghost Sonata* resemble each other in that in both cases a hero awakens the sleeping daughter of a god.[61] Egil Törnqvist sees a similarity in the fact that in both works, the central theme circles around sacrificial love versus the lust for power.[62] Törnqvist sees similarities even in the details; he associates the shield with which Wotan covers Brunnhilde at the close of the opera to the death screen that is placed in front of the Young Lady at the end of the Third Act.[63] Evert Sprinchorn sees the same parallel between the Student and Siegfried as Törnqvist; furthermore, he argues that Hummel is a Wotan who brings two young people together.[64]

Hans Lindström has – in my opinion correctly – raised doubts about this type of interpretation, when he claims that the *The Ghost Sonata* does not correspond to *The Valkyr* but is closer to the content of the second part of the Ring cycle, *Siegfried*. Furthermore, given Strindberg's hostility to Wagner at this stage of his life, Lindström makes the essential point that it is 'most unlikely' that he 'would paraphrase Wagner, whom he despised', at this point in time.[65]

It is probably misplaced effort to seek out interesting thematic or structural similarities between *The Ghost Sonata* and *The Valkyr* or any other Wagner opera. It is more interesting that the Student is exposed to a maximum degree of *sound* over several hours – music by a composer whom Strindberg despised, and whose music he described as 'cavalry music (trumpets and kettledrums)'.[66]

In 1847 Strindberg's collaborator in the cultural study, *Old Stockholm*, Claës Lundin, published a story entitled *Oxygen and Aromasia* which not only describes experiments made with smells but claims that Wagner is supposed to have had a detrimental effect on people's hearing:

> The celebrated Richard Wagner, the inventor of the music of the future, had belaboured people's eardrums so violently, that they were finally unable to receive any impressions, and his pupils had sent trumpet blasts through phonographs over the entire earth. Humanity was for a long time deaf, stone deaf, and the ear was finally regarded as a superfluous limb.[67]

It is *hearing* that is the central theme in the Second Act – an Act that is paradoxically characterized by muteness. Regarding the ghost dinner which is its centrepiece, the servant Bengtsson explains how: 'They drink tea, don't speak a word, or the Colonel speaks to himself; and they nibble away on biscuits, all at the same time, it sounds like rats in the attic' (188). As this quotation indicates, other sounds emerge in such silences, in the absence of conversation. The result is an Act acoustically rich even when the conversation ceases. It is not like Maeterlinck's dramas in which silence favours communication between souls.

Certain acoustic attributes are employed in especially tense scenes. The introductory stage direction to the Second Act mentions first an '*ornamental clock*' (188) and later (202) a '*bell*' of the type used for summoning servants. The ticking of the ornamental clock is obviously intended to be heard when there is silence on stage, for example when the characters drink tea after the Colonel has tried in vain to start a conversation. In this context, the Old Man utters a long monologue in which he pays tribute to silence as more honourable than speech, which is false:

> I prefer silence, when one can hear thoughts, and see the past; silence can hide nothing . . . which words can do; I read the other day that the different language really arose among primitive peoples in order that each tribe might conceal its secrets from the others (205).

In 1901 Strindberg had himself translated the following lines from Maeterlinck: 'In a chamber five or six people sit talking about the weather; but above this dismal conversation, these six souls are engaged in a conversation that no human wisdom would dare to approach without danger.'[68] The difference in attitude towards silence of the two writers is apparent here: in Maeterlinck the souls converse in silence whereas in Strindberg silence is revealing. There are two reasons for speaking out loud in the world of illusions: to lie and disguise oneself or to speak brutal truths. The pleasant small talk between the Gentleman and the Confectioner in *Storm* is completely absent here while in *The Burnt House* the conversation was already largely replaced by questions and answers of an interrogative nature.

Hummel's long monologue about telling the truth is interrupted five times by the stage direction '*Long silence*', and after the last of these interruptions Hummel draws attention to the ticking clock: 'Listen, how the clock is ticking, like the Death-watch Beetle in the wall!' (206). Then a sound is heard that heralds the striking of the clock: 'I can also strike . . . (*He strikes at the table with his stick*). Do you hear?' (207).

Here, the conversation has been penetrated by dramatic sounds. The words are blended with sounds in a way that undermines the dependence on language. The dramatic tension increases when the Mummy stops the clock and utters a monologue against a backdrop of total silence, at which point the Old Man is himself accused of the same type of deceit that he has identified in others. The Mummy rings the bell on the table twice in order to summon Bengtsson who can testify about crimes in Hummel's past, and after firstly imitating a parrot and then a cuckoo clock, Hummel goes into the cupboard to take his life: 'Cuckoo, Cuckoo, Cuckoo!' (206). He has been deprived of his language and is totally robbed of his humanity. Unmasked, the Old Man is transformed under some kind of hypnosis: '*The* MUMMY *pats the* OLD MAN *on the back.* Parrot! Is Jacob there?' (209). He acts like a parrot, a creature devoid of independent self-expression that only echoes the words and sounds of others. Despite an invitation to supper with accompanying conversation, people fill this Act with multiple sounds of a less communicative nature. There is an indication of the same type of distrust towards speech at the beginning of the Act, when it is said of the Mummy that she '*crows*', '*babbles*' and '*whistles*', and when the dialogue between her and Bengtsson becomes a caricature of an exchange of ideas:

> BENGTSSON (*babbles*): Ta, ta, ta, ta! Little Dolly must be nice now, for then she will get something nice! – Pretty parrot.
> THE MUMMY (*as a parrot*): Pretty parrot! Is Jacob there? Crrrrr! (190)

The parrot imitates the human voice, and people in the parrot's surroundings imitate the parrot in their turn. One can hardly descend deeper into meaninglessness than this.

When the verb 'listen' is used in the Second Act, it is in combination with Hummel's *eavesdropping* on the conversation, consisting entirely of gossip, between Bengtsson and Johansson. He steps forward and '*pulls Johansson by the ear*' (192) so that the attention of the audience is directed towards the ear and hearing, and not, as at the start of the First Act, towards the eye and vision.

ACT III – SCENT, TASTE

Smell

There is a danger that the spectator will become disorientated in the Third Act, firstly because of the way in which the dialogue frequently oscillates between a passionate lyricism and brutal truth-saying, and then because of the bizarrely decorated stage where a room in 'oriental style' teems with hyacinths. Even so perceptive a theorist of modern drama as Peter Szondi reacts against this Act and regards it as a failure,[69] while Martin Esslin, in a more positive spirit, speaks of its elements of 'absurdity'.[70]

However, if one chooses to see the different acts of *The Ghost Sonata* as demonstrations of how our confused senses render life on earth as insecure and full of disappointments, the Third Act appears as a consistent, albeit intensified, consequence of the two preceding Acts. To demonstrate this Strindberg makes great play in the Third Act with the addition of the senses of smell and taste. The Student comes to experience how powerful smells confuse all his senses and the Young Lady describes how the food she is served has been diluted. However, it is probable that Strindberg did not take the difficulties of communicating sensations of smell and taste to the audience into account. In consequence, the Act is extremely difficult to perform.[71]

In the Third Act of *The Ghost Sonata* the opening stage directions emphasize the non-realistic décor of the set. In the preceding Acts, non-realistic elements were presented within a realistic frame. In the Third Act, however, even this realistic frame has been elimi-nated. The author prescribes '*A room decorated in a somewhat bizarre style, with oriental motifs. Hyacinths in all colours everywhere.*' This is the atmosphere in which the lovers – the Student and the Young Lady – finally encounter one another. The former seems at last to have reached his goal, but in doing so he loses control of his senses as he succumbs to the power of the hyacinths:

> Their fragrance, strong and pure from the first winds of spring that have passed over melting snow, confuses my senses, deafens me, blinds me, drives me from the room, assails me with poisoned arrows that make my heart faint and my head hot. (212)

At the end of this Act the Student returns to this notion of poison-ing: 'To think that the most beautiful of flowers are so poisonous, are the most poisonous, their curse rests upon all creation and life itself' (224). He is referring to the hyacinths that thus also illustrate the notion that nothing is as it appears to be. Beauty is illusory; in reality it hides a poison.

The scene in which the Student is poisoned by the hyacinths is a turning point in the drama, but the unique olfactory experience to which the Student is exposed has rarely been given due attention. Just as previous accounts of the play have focused on Wagner's *The Valkyr* and not on *sound as such*, so the choice has been to concentrate analysis on the hyacinths[72] and not on *scent as such*. There is good reason to expand the analysis of this 'scent scene' and to consider it intertextually in terms of a number of earlier works by Strindberg himself, on the one hand, and several texts by Romantic authors such as Goethe and Hoffmann, on the other. In every case, it emerges that texts which describe *scents* are of more interest than those which merely describe flowers.

In the story 'Pioneering' from the collection *Utopias in Reality* of 1885 Strindberg allows the girl Blanche to lose herself in dreams with the assistance of an assortment of perfumes. The situation is reminiscent of Hans Christian Andersen's 'The Little Match Girl', but, in Strindberg's case, it is not burning flames that kindle reminiscences but scents:

> First there came a shower of scent from the . . . narcissus that filled and anaesthetized the room. Blanche opened her nostrils and with wide-open mouth breathed in the intoxicating air while blood rushed to her cheeks made pale by vinegar. Then followed a shower of *muguet* fresh as the clean spring scent of lilies of the valley. Now she closed her eyes as if she saw visions, early summer landscapes with unharvested fields and blooming fruit trees, children playing and sailing clouds; she heard alpenhorns and babbling brooks, steamship whistles and boys' choirs. Her whole drab, grey youth was forgotten (SV 19: 21).

The form of this passage is still naturalistic; Blanche resembles someone performing a vivisection on herself. But even here there is a tendency towards the visionary.

In the post-Inferno drama *Easter* the form is not naturalistic but symbolist. The heroine, Eleonora, perceives the scents as languages, but it is also typical of Strindberg's use of scents in the years following 1900 that these are described as 'attacking' a person:

> Each scent expresses a whole range of thoughts, and these thoughts overwhelmed me; and with my enlarging eye I looked

into their workshops, which no one has seen. And they spoke to me about the sorrows that the foolish gardener had caused them (43:270).

In the Hoffmann-inspired 'The Pilot's Trials' in *Fairy Tales* (1903), the main character is exposed to strong, mind-numbing impressions in a perfume boutique: 'The boutique was rather similar to the shell boutique, but the smell was so strong that he got a headache and had to sit down in a chair' (SV 52:119). The 'oriental' element, represented in the décor of *The Ghost Sonata*, is also represented here in the shape of a Persian tablecloth, and the scents are administered by a woman who turns out to be a magician endowed with the fatal ability of 'altering the senses'.

In a passage in *The Gothic Rooms* (1904), in which Count Max describes the experience of being separated from Ester Borg in terms of smells, and then doubts the experience as such, scents possess a more particular meaning:

> At a distance I sense your mood towards me as three different scents, two of which are especially pleasant to me. The first is like incense, and is sometimes so strong that it seems like bewitchment and lunacy, while the last is like fresh fruit. The second one is nauseating like perfumed soap and is unpleasant to the senses. But in your closeness I never sense these scents or any others; *therefore they are not olfactory perceptions in the real sense but seem to be a translation* (SS 40:243, my italics).

What is most pertinent to *The Ghost Sonata* are sensations of smell rather than olfactory hallucinations, but the above passage may be of interest as an example of the importance that Strindberg generally attaches to smells and their ability to bewitch. It may also be worth remarking that the above example relates to private experiences of an intimate nature.[73]

Goethe's *Faust*

Egil Törnqvist has noted certain correspondences between Part Two of Goethe's *Faust* and *The Ghost Sonata*. He points to a striking similarity in the function of the clock in the death scene of the Second Act in Strindberg's play and Faust's death scene.[74]

Strindberg's own essay entitled 'Goethe's *Faust*', which is included in *Open Letters to the Intimate Theatre* (*Öppna brev till Intima Teatern*), bears witness to his interest in Goethe's drama. He relates there how two years earlier he had been commissioned by the impresario Albert Ranft to edit and cut down Goethe's text to produce a stage version that could be performed over the course of two evenings (SV 64:228). *Faust* is beyond doubt an important intertext in *The Ghost Sonata*. Törnqvist is mistaken, however, when he advances the witch in 'Hexenküche' as a model for the Cook in *The Ghost Sonata* and the threat she poses to the Student:

> Certainly there is something grotesque, perverse and witch-like about the Cook, whose poisonous soya bottle recalls the poisonous aphrodisiac drink the Witch prepares for Faust and which makes him see a Helen in every woman; in *The Ghost Sonata* the smell of the poisonous hyacinths seem to have a corresponding aphrodisiac effect.[75]

In the first place, Strindberg's text never states that the soya is 'poisonous' – its destructiveness has to do with its colouring and the way its falsifies whatever it is added to. In the second place, where the aphrodisiac effect of the hyacinths is concerned, there is a more probable inter-scene in the second half of *Faust*. In this case, too, one can find verbal similarities. In the scene titled 'Grablelung' in Act Five, a chorus of angels takes care of Faust's dead body by poisoning Mephistopheles with the scent of roses: 'Roses spreading their blinding scent' (*Rosen, ihr blendenden,/Balsam versendenden*).[76] Mephistopheles tries to defend himself against the flowers: '*Striking out in the rain of roses.* Be gone you will-o'-the-wisp! You may shine splendidly, but look, when captured you become a speck of jelly.' (*Sich mit den schwebenden Rosen herumschlagend.*) Irrlicher, fort! Du leuchte noch so stark,/Du bleibst, gehascht, ein ekler Gallert-Quark').[77]

The situation here certainly differs from *The Ghost Sonata*, but there is a similarity in that both dramas achieve a kind of peripeteia when their key figures fall under the influence of an intoxicating scent. In *Faust*, too, scent is associated with earthly love: 'Is this the element of love' (*Ist dies das Liebeselement*)?[78] The reaction of Mephistopheles, whose question this is, closely resembles that of the Student: 'My head is burning, my heart and liver burn' (*Mir brennt der Kopf, das Herz, die Leber brennt*),[79] Mephistopheles exclaims, while the Student in Strindberg's play experiences how the hyacinths shoot at him with arrows that 'make my heart ache and my head hot!' (212).

Hoffmann's 'Der goldene Topf' (The Golden Jar)

Another of Strindberg's familiars since the Inferno crisis was E. T. A. Hoffmann in whose clearly depicted fantastic tales he could find a model for his ambition to expand the range of his own writing. However, in this respect Strindberg is bolder in his dramas than in his fiction, except, that is, in the tales from 1903, which he called *Sagor* (Fairy Tales).

One text by Hoffmann that he returns to on several occasions is *Das Teufels-Elixir* (*The Devil's Elixir*). He refers to it in letters dated 17 September 1892 and 28 June 1894. On 17 September 1896, in the midst of the Inferno crisis, he writes to Torsten Hedlund: 'I am now reading Hoffmann's Teufels-Elixir and feel that every word is true.' In a letter to the author Henning Berger on 10 December 1906, he pinpoints the particular quality in Hoffmann that captures his interest: 'Hoffmann saw the supernatural as something completely natural and thereby rescued poetry (atmosphere).' A quotation from Hoffmann's *Serapions-Brüder* (*Serapion Brothers*), which he transcribed in the original language in *The Occult Diary* on 6 May 1899, also appears in the first part of *A Blue Book*:

> In the last century E. T. A Hoffman [*sic*] writes as follows: 'In olden times we had a pious, generous faith; we recognized a dimension above us but also knew about the inadequacy of our senses; then came "enlightenment", which made everything so clear that one saw nothing for very clarity's sake; and now the transcendental is to be grasped offhand in flesh and bone' (SV 65:160).

It is obvious that Hoffmann's fantastic tales exerted an influence on Strindberg's *Sagor*, for instance in 'The Pilot's Tribulations', and that 'Klein Zaches genannt Zinnober' (A Small Thing Called Zinnober) inspired the portrait of Zachris in *Black Banners*.[80] When it comes to *The Ghost Sonata*, the Hoffmann-like traits of the opening scene have often been noted, for instance by Sven Söderman in *Stockholms Dagblad*.[81] In a letter to the theatre director Victor Castegren, Strindberg himself uses a vocabulary that points to Hoffmann as a source of inspiration: 'What I aimed at was a fairy or

fantasy piece in the present with modern houses.'[82] As Göran
Lindström suggests in his valuable commentary on the play in a
student edition from 1964, the designation 'fantasy piece' is reminiscent of Hoffmann's first collection of short stories, *Fantasiestücke in
Callots Manier* (*Fantasy Pieces in Callot's Manner*).[83]

Göran Lindström also highlighted the similarities between *The
Ghost Sonata* and Hoffmann's piece 'Das öde Haus' (*The Vacant
House*), which describes how the hero is tempted by a secretive
power

> to become interested in a given house in a prominent big city
> street. He ventures inside and, after a terrible argument, discovers
> what is hidden behind the façade. An old lady of the nobility
> lived there, who had gone insane after an unhappy love affair and
> now hid from the world, cared for by an old housekeeper with a
> mummy-like face. The love affair had resulted in a child who had
> grown up as someone else's daughter.[84]

Strindberg's long-standing affinity with Hoffmann's writings is
relatively constant as regards its content. Initially it seems to have
been the German author's natural attitude to the supernatural in
which Strindberg found consolation, much as he did in his reading
of Swedenborg. At a later stage, however, when he was again
engaged in writing literature, he viewed the same narrative
approach as something to be emulated. In a tale like 'The Pilot's
Tribulations' the moral gist is 'not to let oneself ever be astonished';
i.e. the reader is not to ponder where realism ends and the fantastic
begins. In that respect the tale turns into a paean of praise for the
imagination.

At the end of *The Ghost Sonata* when both the Student and the
Young Lady break down, Strindberg does, however, restore the dis-
tinction between the real and the fantastic. What contributes to the
tragedy of the play is above all its equation of fantasy and 'illusion':
'Where is honour and faith? In fairy tales and in children's fantasies!
Where is loyalty and promise-keeping? . . . In my fantasy!' (224).

Göran Lindström is of the opinion that Strindberg borrowed
'several of the motifs in *The Ghost Sonata* from "Das öde Haus" and
other short stories by Hoffmann.' There is reason to dwell somewhat on one of these stories, 'Der goldene Topf' (The Golden Jar).
The tale is included in the third volume of *Fantasiestücke* from 1814.

In his last library Strindberg had Hoffmann's *Sämtliche Werke in fünfzehn Bänden* (Leipzig, 1900).[85] We do not know to what extent Strindberg made use of these texts; only one of the volumes (the first) contains his marginalia; it is, however, precisely the volume that contains 'Der goldene Topf'.

In Hoffmann's tale about the student Anselmus, whose name of course recalls that of Strindberg's student Arkenholz,[86] we are presented with what appears to be an everyday bourgeois milieu, in a series of references that locate the events to Dresden. But early in the tale this realistic surface is broken by the most fantastic features. Often the unreal visions are caused by different kinds of elixirs – a standard Romantic ingredient that appears in the title of the one Hoffmann text alluded to most frequently by Strindberg, *Das Teufels-Elixir*.

On the realistic level the plot of 'Der goldene Topf' describes how Anselmus is taken in hand by Superintendent Paulmann, who arranges for him to meet the Archivist Lindhorst and receive an invitation to the latter's home. This arrangement is reminiscent of the Student's visit to the opera in *The Ghost Sonata*. The fantastic aspects of Hoffmann's plot consists not only of visions and moments of ecstasy under the stimulus of a variety of drinks. Smells, too, constitute an important aspect in this part of the story. Early on in the narrative Anselmus falls asleep under an elder bush. He then has visions and imagines the elder bush talking to him: 'You lie in my shade, my scent embraces you but you don't understand me. Scent is my language when love inflames it.'[87] Moreover, Lindhorsts's home contains not only the beautiful Serpentia but also a room full of plants:

> From the hallway they entered a large room or, rather, a gorgeous nursery where all kinds of wonderful rare flowers, big trees even, stood on both sides all the way up to the ceiling [. . .] Anselmus stood spellbound by this sight, intoxicated by the sweet scents of this fairy-tale garden.[88]

In this room, which is conceivably a source of inspiration for the Hyacinth room in the *Ghost Sonata*, there is also a creature who is at the same time a human being and a parrot, and who speaks a kind of parrot language: 'Rette – Raug – raub.'[89] Hoffmann, like Strindberg in *The Ghost Sonata*, facilitates a collision between innocence and the demonic, but above all, the two texts are related to each other through their use of olfactory sensations, which deprive each of the young students of their equanimity.

Taste

In the first chamber play, *Storm*, a Confectioner refuses to add salicylic acid to his preserved fruits: 'it leaves a taste . . . it's a trick' (68). In accordance with the tendency towards demonization to which attention has been drawn above, the theme of taste also appears in Opus 2, *The Burnt House* in a more unpleasant variation. Eerily enough the inn is named 'The Last Nail' and the Stranger recalls with some discomfort the Saturday afternoons of his childhood 'when we got dried cod and small beer for dinner' (126). In *The Ghost Sonata* the Cook is said to deprive the food of its nourishment, thereby manipulating both the vision and the taste of the eaters by colouring the water with soya sauce: 'we get one course after another, but deprived of all nourishment . . . She boils the meat until there's nothing left but sinews and water while she drinks the stock herself; and when there's a roast, she boils all the juice out of it, eats the gravy, and drinks the broth' (215). 'She's Soya the witch who turns water into broth that replaces the gravy in which the cabbage is cooked, and which we make mock-turtle soup of' (220). Thus the descriptions of food in *The Ghost Sonata* are not only used to create distaste through the senses but also include a moral component: they describe acts of fraud and forgery.

Thus the comments on tasteless food are very much more interesting than the passing private irritation of a pernickety person.[90] The use of colour symbolism, or rather of symbolism associated with the idea of painting, culminates in this example and in the example of the strongly scented flowers which happen to be hyacinths. These are also features of both *Storm* and *The Burnt House*. In *The Ghost Sonata* the theme of decorating, of 'painting an inch thick', is combined with a recurrent motif that is established as early as the opening scene: water.

Water

At the start of the play the audience is immediately confronted by a '*street fountain*' (163) in the right foreground. It is alongside this fountain that the action subsequently begins. In addition, the

Caretaker's Wife is also to be seen, watering the laurel bushes after having swept the landing and polished the brass.

This is described by Strindberg in an unusually long stage direction. When the action really begins, i.e. when the step is taken in the text from this opening stage direction to the moment in which a character is named, it is the Milkmaid who makes an entrance and crosses over to the street fountain, where she drinks out of a scoop, washes her hands, and examines her reflection mirrored in the water (164).

The water in the fountain functions here as a life-giving element whereas one might see the watering of the laurel bushes by the Caretaker's Wife from a different perspective: laurel is a traditional symbol of honour, and is nurtured here by someone who has just been seen polishing brass, i.e. engaged in a kind of gilding.

But the water in the fountain is stressed in a positive fashion. The Milkmaid *tastes* it, *washes* herself in it, *looks* at herself in it, in short, she engages with the water with three of her senses. The water symbolism is important in the play and there is good reason to trace its development from the life-giving element of the introduction to an image of immobility and decay at the end of the play.

In the opening scene, the fresh as well as life-giving quality of water is stressed when the Student asks the Milkmaid for a scoop of water to drink and goes on to ask her to bathe his eyes in 'the fresh water' (165).

The next time water is mentioned is at the end of the First Act, when Hummel and the Student observe the Young Lady who is watering the hyacinths in the window. Hummel notes: 'She's giving them a drink, only pure water, which they turn into colours and fragrance' (179). Like the chamber plays in general this play includes a repetitive scene in which the implications of the first occasion are changed in the second. Just as the Milkmaid gives the Student water to drink in the opening scene, the Young Lady now gives the flowers a drink, but the implication of the scene seems to have changed from a life-giving gesture to aesthetic contemplation. In the language of the chamber plays, this scene means that in conjuring up colours and fragrances the Young Lady is engaged in a kind of forgery, something that is stressed in a draft for the play in which Strindberg notes that the Young Lady is 'a teacher of makeup at the conservatory' (4:4, 2).

During the Student's first meeting with the Young Lady he is subjected to the influence of sound – it just happens to be Wagner's *The Valkyr*. During their second meeting, he is subjected to the influence of various fragrances. His senses seem to be constantly under attack, and in this way he is helplessly drawn into the world of illusions, an existence that is in stark contrast to the refreshing scene with the Milkmaid at the outset.

The hyacinths represent a kind of aesthetic shallowness and temptation. Through the vocabulary that is used, the audience is encouraged to suspect that these flowers are not what they appear to be. Through the way in which they transform pure water into colour and scent, they too appear to be related to parasites, vampires and counterfeiters.

In Bengtsson's monologue about Hummel's antecedents, there is a further reference to water. Hummel is described here quite directly as a 'vampire' who was once a parasite in Bengtsson's house where he was in the habit of drinking the best broth. The scene Bengtsson describes is in stark contrast to the opening scene with the Milkmaid. That scene was about giving; for Hummel it is about taking. And when it is said, of the Cook, that she turns water into broth 'with [the aid of] colouring', there is a parallel to what the Young Lady does with water and hyacinths. This sequence of scenes reaches its climax in the Third Act where it is stated that 'Mrs Soya [. . .] turns water into broth' (220). Reading retrospectively, therefore, it is clear that we are to understand the hyacinths as also falsified.

The water symbolism is employed a final time in the Student's closing monologue: 'Remaining silent for too long creates a pool of stagnant water, which rots, and so it is with this house too' (223). This time the imagery may seem forced, but reading the words in the context of the previous references to water, it is possible to see why the author has chosen this image: 'rotting water' becomes an expression of total destruction.

The dialogue in Act III

In the Second Act it seemed as if Strindberg had tried and had radically rejected most possibilities of communication. The Act – at the centre of which is the ghost supper – ends with the Student reciting a version of the Icelandic 'Song of the Sun' while the Young Lady accompanies him on the harp. Music and poetry have replaced conversation. 'What's the point of talking, we still can't fool each other'? – with this quotation of her father's words, the Young Lady expresses, at the beginning of the Third Act, what she has learned in the previous one.

The dialogue that opens the last Act can hardly be expected to be an ordinary functional dialogue. Strindberg had to choose between continuing a depiction of the impossibility of human conversation, risking tedious repetition, or attempting an expansion of the scope of conventional dramatic dialogue. He chose the latter with a dialogue that tends towards different types of monologues, sometimes with lyrical, sometimes expressive features. It also contains elements of prayer and incantation in situations that appear desperate.

Flowers make up the subject of the initial dialogue (211–13). The stage directions indicate that they are visible to the audience, both the variously coloured hyacinths and a shallot bulb with a stem and a crown of flowers that is placed in the lap of the statue of Buddha which stands on the mantelpiece.

The flowers form the basis of a lyrical dialogue that seems to begin right away with the Young Lady's opening line when she asks the Student to 'Please, sing for my flowers!' (211). What might confuse a spectator who is not completely intoxicated by this lyrical outburst, is a longer passage by the Student, in which he states that he will be poisoned by the smell of the hyacinths; this is followed, however, by his interpretation of the shallot bulb and its flower rather than of the hyacinths. There is no clear transition from one flower to the other. The reference to the hyacinths ends with the Young Lady wishing to hear their 'fairy tale'. What is implied is probably the classical tale of the youth Hyacinth from whose blood grew the Hyacinth flower, i.e. a variant of the vampire motif that is so central in *The Ghost Sonata*. But it is a tale that the audience will have to supply for themselves, for instead of relating it the Student expounds on the meaning of the shallot bulb and its flower as metaphors of the earth and the stars of heaven. To add to the confusion, the Young Lady asks the Student if he has seen the shallot bloom, when, in fact, its flower has been visible on stage the whole time, resting in the lap of the Buddha on the mantelpiece.

The only plausible explanation for this confused conversation is that Strindberg deliberately strove for an even more capricious dialogue than in Act I. Attempting to analyse the botanical context in this scene is futile; besides, the dialogue seems to defy most attempts at a logical explanation. It is more fruitful to view it as having an associative rather than a rational structure, which suggests that it is closer to modern poetry than to the conventional naturalistic dialogue of turn of the century drama.

The Young Lady, inspired by the exalted Student and his 'vision', exclaims after listening to his analogy between the shallot and the earth and its link to the universe: 'Oh, that is grandiose, where did you get that, how did you see it?', to which The Student replies, 'Let me think! – in your eyes!' (212). In this way they continue to inspire each other. The Student exclaims: 'We have given birth to something together, we are married' (213). In a way the dialogue has been *fruitful*, though difficult to follow, resembling most closely a love duet in some romantic opera where emotions and harmonies are more important than logic and information. An additional factor to take into consideration is that the Student – as he himself states – has become 'confused' by the smell of the hyacinths.[91]

What complicates the matter – but also makes the Student's lines more original – is the fact that while describing an aspect of the setting in the Hyacinth Room, the Student also interprets it and is inspired by his own interpretation to the point of being spellbound by it.

'Interpretative meaning'

The Student's 'interpretation' is complex, for he uses two interpretative methods at the same time. His detailed account of the bulb (including both the hyacinth and the shallot) is in accordance with Swedenborg's concept of 'correspondences'. But he also talks about the flower's 'interpretative meaning' (*tyda*) – an expression that Gunnar Ollén understands as a synonym for 'interpretation, meaning'.[92] The word *tyda*, however, has a special meaning in folklore, which Strindberg probably knew since he was an avid reader of *Wärend och wirdarne* by the celebrated Swedish ethnologist Ragnar Hyltén-Cavallius.[93]

As a concept in folklore *tyda* belongs to the same family as 'omen' and 'premonition'. To this might be added 'clairvoyance' of the kind that the Student possesses in *The Ghost Sonata*. Strindberg's attitude to the ideas of folklore remains to be explored and would surely prove extremely rewarding.[94] In keeping with its title, *The Occult Diary* can be read as a compilation of occult phenomena, but a reader is also likely to associate it with folklore where a similar world full of ominous encounters, inexplicable lights, smells and sounds emerges, and which is characterized by strange experiences involving birds, magic objects or meteorological matters. A hypothesis well worth testing would be to see if the diarist Strindberg ought not to be called 'a recorder of *tydor*' as much as a 'mystic' or an 'occultist'. The word *tyda* suggests such a level of meaning in the Student's interpretation of the phenomena in the Hyacinth Room. For even if his exposition of the shallot bulb is pedantic and detailed, it does not exclude the possibility of his having access to its hidden message.

The final monologue

One can judge Strindberg's experiments with the dialogue in Act III in different ways. In *Theorie des modernen Dramas* (1956) Peter Szondi argues sternly that 'the Third Act cannot but fail since without epic support, he would have had to reconstruct the dialogue anew'.[95] 'Epic support' refers to Hummel, who in Szondi describes as 'the epic presenter' of Act II and whose role, he sees as anticipating epic drama. Szondi continues: 'The shattered, desperately meandering speech full of pauses, monologues, prayers, constitutes a painfully failed ending of a strange work.'[96]

However, one can see the matter positively from the opposite perspective. It is true that the Third Act of *The Ghost Sonata* has little to do with epic theatre, but since Strindberg never had any ambitions in that direction, there is no need to judge it a failure. Another objection is that in his analysis, Szondi only concerns himself with the *dialogue* of the play and thereby misses characteristic traits in the drama, aimed at other senses.

The introductory lyrical dialogue is interrupted after three pages of printed text by a dialogue of a more conventional variety, in which the Young Lady relates her difficulties with the servants. This dialogue is not erratic but consists largely of questions and answers (214–21).

Beginning with Act II, one can trace a monologic tendency in the dialogue.[97] However, the conversation between the Student and the Young Lady about the customs of the house does not display this tendency; but, at the end of the drama, the matter-of-fact dialogue is interrupted by the Student's powerful monologue in which he sums up his experiences in the house in a clear-sighted, but logically and linguistically confused manner. With what one might call a necessary paradox, the Student becomes a 'visionary truth-teller'.[98] His outpouring here shatters all boundaries and leads to the Young Lady's invisible but audible death: '*a whimpering can be heard from behind the screen*'. In the meantime, the stage changes radically when '*The room disappears*' and the background opens up to reveal a picture of Böcklin's *Toten-Insel* while music replaces speech: '*faint music, quiet, agreeably sad is heard from the island*' (225).

The Student's final monologue becomes an eruption of truth-telling, more associatively than logically structured. In this cascade of accusations, there are certain breaks which have the quality of a religious prayer: 'Woe! Woe! Thou Saviour of all of us, save us, we perish!' (224) It is hardly a surprise when this Christian prayer is shortly followed by a prayer to Buddha, for it is in keeping with the way that Strindberg has sought to sow confusion in the audience's mind ever since Act I: 'Wise One, mild Buddha, who sits there waiting for a heaven to grow out of the earth, grant us patience in our tribulations, purity in our will, so that our hope will not come to nought!' (225). The final line once again has a Christian quality: 'Lord, Our Father in Heaven be merciful to thee on thine journey' (225). Although naturally difficult to digest for a logical or religiously rigid mind, this is a perfect example of syncretism. Instead of saying that Strindberg mixes religions, one ought to say that he associatively jumps between them.

When the Student exclaims 'Now I'm sinking! *Cor in aethere!* Song!' (217), two of the elements of Christian prayer are combined with a prayer for music, which is said to be a link to the divine that will save the speaker from everyday material misery. And in the final monologue he prays in a similar manner, using a Catholic phrase on music: '*Sursum corda!* Try once more to make fire and brimstone from the golden harp [. . .] (*Takes the harp, but the strings make no sound.*) It is mute and deaf!' (224). The final prayer: 'Heavenly Father, be merciful to thee on thy journey', which brings the drama to a close, is followed by gentle music as described above. With this, a large portion of the visual elements on stage have been transformed, and speech has been replaced by music. The conventional elements in a drama – dialogue and the scenery – are replaced by an invitation to contemplate a suggestive painting to the accompaniment of music. The dialogue is replaced by a combination of pictorial art and music.

Visual and auditory elements

An analysis of *The Ghost Sonata* that restricts itself to a study of the dialogue risks being seen as too limited. As I have argued above, Strindberg imagines the scene in Act III to be filled with the scent of hyacinths. In this Act, the Young Lady loses her will to live when the Cook manipulates her sense of taste. These sensory impressions that impact immediately upon the young couple must nevertheless still be experienced by the audience to the best of their ability.

But the Third Act also contains more obvious visual and auditory features. In the opening stage direction, Strindberg mentions not only the harp as an emblem of music but also '*a large statue of Buddha with a bulb in his lap*' (211). Strindberg was apparently inspired by an illustration in an advertisement from Paul Peters's import business on Vestmannagatan in Stockholm. The so-called Green Sack which is now the basis of the Strindberg archive in the Royal Library in Stockholm, contains a copy of the advertisement,[99] for a 16 centimetre high statue of Buddha, 'artistically produced in ivory after an original piece located in the Grassi Museum in Leipzig', which exactly accords with Strindberg's stage direction. Its advertised function is also as it is in the play, namely to accommodate a bulb 'at the feet of the idol'.

As elsewhere in Strindberg's theatre, displaying this statue of Buddha on stage is intended to signal a religious mood. In *Advent*, he allowed pagan ideas to materialize on stage in a statue of Pan (SV 40:87, 90 f.,98, 112, 125) and in *Gustav III* a bust of Rousseau is placed on the porcelain stove in Holmberg's Bookstore in the First Act, where it serves as an emblematic critique of the autocratic monarch. In the Second Act, which takes place in the King's Office, there is also statue on the mantelpiece, this time of Voltaire, the admirer of Charles XII (SV 48:151, 181).

This method of stylizing a set of ideas in a visual image, or doing so in part, is certainly typical of Strindberg in his efforts to achieve concrete representation.[100] The approach is familiar from as long ago as his youthful drama, *The Outlaw* (1871), where the action takes place in thirteenth-century Iceland and '*the seats of honour are carved with images of Wodin and Thor*' (SV 3:47).

In *The Ghost Sonata* the harp, as stated, becomes an emblem of music, which in turn represents the immaterial and unearthly. That the harp refuses to function in the Student's final monologue illustrates how visual impressions and sound impressions no longer harmonize, which in turn is the result of the broken relationship with the higher spheres that the play as a whole dramatizes. Thus the Student '*goes up to the harp but the strings make no sound*' (224). When the harp sounds again at the end of the act, it is without any one visibly touching it. Strindberg's stage directions are formulated in an impersonal way: '*There is a whispering*', '*the room is filled*', '*The room disappears*', 'Toten-Insel becomes the background' (225). One gets the impression that higher powers have taken over the management of sound and light on stage.

The presence of a harp in a middle-class home at turn of the last century seems a somewhat unlikely feature. However, here too *The Outlaw* might be used as an intertext, since there a harp also '*stands by the seat of honour*' (SV 3:47). To the accompaniment of '*harp playing*' the poet Orm sings a poem about the life of the Vikings. The link between *The Outlaw* and *The Ghost Sonata* is present in this Icelandic poem. In the latter play, the Student recites the medieval Icelandic *Song to the Sun*,[101] accompanied by the harp. In *The Outlaw*, the poet Orm is without his own harp and is encouraged to use another one. When he does so, however, he exclaims that 'There is no sound! All this Christian church silver is no good for the strings – I'd rather have my old steel strings' (71). Late in life Strindberg responds to this passage from his earliest playwriting by letting an old Icelandic poem in *The Ghost Sonata* be infused, not with pagan Viking deeds but with Christian Catholic thoughts about the value of good deeds.

The breaking up

All the chamber plays end with a departure or leave-taking. In *Storm* and *The Burnt House* it is still a question of departing from a geographic location. The Gentleman in *Storm* is going to move out of 'the silent house' – these are the last words of the play (82). In *The Burnt House* the Stranger says to himself at the very end: 'And so: out into the world again, thou wanderer!' In the final lines of *The Ghost Sonata*, it is also a question of a journey, but this time a departure from life itself. When the Young Lady dies, the Student utters the last words of the drama: 'Lord in Heaven, show mercy on the way' (225). The theme of moving–travelling–dying is thus treated with increasing seriousness.

Windows

The opening scene in *The Ghost Sonata* is visually reminiscent of the opening scene in *Storm*: '*a modern house façade*' where some of the windows are open. But the interiors visible through the windows are more original in *The Ghost Sonata*. In one window a great many blue, white and pink hyacinths are to be seen. In another window a blind is drawn and remains thus until well into the first scene. However, in the first stage direction Strindberg has prepared us for what subsequently becomes visible, a form of preparation that is unusual for him: '*When the blind is drawn up, a white marble statue of a young woman appears by the open windows in the round drawing-room; she is surrounded by potted palms, strongly illuminated by the rays of the sun*' (163).

In *Storm* the windows of the upstairs apartment had red shades; in *The Ghost Sonata* the corresponding windows are covered with white sheets, signalling death rather than sinful living. On the ground floor there is yet another window to which the audience is denied visual access but which is combined with a gossip mirror, thus suggesting a complicated form of communication: '*To the left of the entrance on the ground floor there is a window with a gossip mirror*' (163). There is thus considerable variation in the detail which the windows of a house façade present to the spectator at the start of the each play.

During the opening dialogue, mute action continues in the background, especially behind the windows. In the exchange between Hummel and the Student one reference seems rather meaningless in the context unless one sees it as an invitation to the spectator to look at the windows in the background: 'I had a friend in my youth who couldn't say "window" but always said "wundow" – I've only met one person with that kind of pronunciation and that was him; you're the other one' (167). What puzzles the spectator here is that the Student has not previously pronounced the word.[102] What happens in the background – at the windows and elsewhere – illustrates visually, through mimed action, a lack of communication between people and becomes a complement to the meandering dialogue in the foreground. What the audience sees and hears is a depiction of the isolation of people even when they are together.

When the blind is drawn in the Round Room, the Colonel becomes visible: '*after having looked at the thermometer, he goes into the room and stops in front of the marble statue*' (172). Shortly after this brief scene in which attention is focused on the thermometer, something becomes visible behind another window; indeed, each of the windows can be seen as a miniature stage, sometimes even equipped with a curtain.[103] '*Now a White-haired Woman is seen sitting down by the window with the gossip mirror*' (175). Like the Colonel she has an instrument outside the window. Both of them seem interested in what is occurring outside their respective rooms in a matter-of-fact way, but they have no real contact with the external world – rather, it is a question of controlling and registering it.

A longer speech of Hummel's ends with a stage direction: '*The YOUNG LADY, who has now changed her clothes, is seen watering the hyacinths in the window*' (179). Hummel encourages the Student to look in through the window while he informs him and the spectators about what goes on inside the house. But he also *interprets* the silent gestures of the Young Lady even though they are clearly visible to everyone. The approach is reminiscent of Maeterlinck's method in *Intérieur*. During the same extended speech the interest of the spectator moves from one window to another: '*It grows overcast and dark; the OLD WOMAN at the gossip mirror closes the window*' (179). Even this everyday and silent incident is expounded by Hummel: 'seventy-nine years old . . . the gossip mirror is the only mirror she uses, for she doesn't see herself in it, only the external world and from two directions; but the world can see her, she hasn't thought about that' (180). In *The Ghost Sonata* windows seem to exist mostly to disclose the inner life of the house.

In another scene when the Young Lady '*has lost her bracelet through the open window*' (183), the Student makes contact with her for the first time, but without words; he reaches up to the window and gives her back her bracelet. With this gesture – though stiff and lacking the more jovial mood of *Storm* – the barrier between outside and inside has been passed. The Young Lady '*thanks him haughtily*', and the scene hardly suggests that the ice has been broken.

The First Act ends in accelerated tempo as Hummel enters,

riding in his carriage, standing up and exhorting the others to greet the heroic Student. The reaction of those in the house is still marked by silence and haughtiness: '*The* COLONEL *stares out the window. The* OLD WOMAN *gets up by her window*' (186). The Young Lady, who is described as being '*By the window, waving a handkerchief*' (186), is somewhat more active. This silent and somewhat lame reaction is probably experienced by the audience as an anti-climax – as yet another example of stalled communication.

The Second Act, which takes place inside the Round Room, includes no windows; one must assume that the window to the room that is mentioned in the initial stage direction is now replaced by the forestage opening. Hence, the room affords an exposed impression. In the Third Act, the action moves from the Round Room to the Hyacinth Room; no window is mentioned here either, which suggests that in this case, too, the window faces the audience.

It is clear that a reduction of sorts has taken place in *The Ghost Sonata* when compared with *Storm*. This is reflected in the use of windows to illustrate the communicative and informative conditions of the characters, their degree of participation in life, their trust in each other, etc. *The Ghost Sonata* provides open windows, but what these let us see turn out to be mere illusions. When Hummel is described as '*crawling in through the window*' (183), this constitutes a demonization of the window motif. The world inside the window is a world of semblance, a world of illusions, and it is clear that for the Student it would have been better, if the windows had never glistened so seductively in the sun when he passed by, thus leading him to imagine 'all the beauty and luxury that existed inside' (171).

Strindberg's prose in the form of the fairy tale 'At Midsummer time' (1903) offers an example of how the window motif can be developed in a way that is difficult to realize in a drama. At the beginning of the tale we meet a ninety-year-old woman who has been bed-ridden for two decades. She is separated from her surroundings by a window, which nevertheless provides her with vignettes of life outside and functions as a magnifying glass:

. . . through the window she could see everything that happened outside on the farm, which her two sons cultivated. But she saw the world and its people in her own special way, for the windows had oxidized in all the colours of the rainbow; all she had to do was turn her head a little and everything appeared in turn red, yellow, green, blue, purple. [. . .] But the magic panes had yet another gift; for they were curved so that they showed what was outside, sometimes magnified, sometimes diminished (SV 52:87).

In this tale the window has a function similar to that of the Student's first encounter with the house in *The Ghost Sonata*: to activate the imagination in an embellishing way. The window serves as a kind of optical lens, which gives colour to visual impressions and magnifies them. Strindberg utilizes the window motif to its maximum: at times it becomes a stage opening, at others a channel or a curtain between outside and in, and it can also be employed as a magnifying instrument of sight.

Plato's Phaidon

Whether or not death entails an overcoming of the sensuous in the sense that the body is now abandoned leaves Strindberg torn between different ideas. His reading during the period when he was writing the chamber plays includes two texts that are especially important for him: Plato's *Phaidon* and Swedenborg's *Heaven and Hell*.

That aspects of Plato's thinking feature in *The Ghost Sonata* is evident. The world is appearance and illusion, the soul reaches upwards from this lowly, worldly existence. In the *Blue Books* one finds numerous examples which indicate that, even during this period, Strindberg emphasizes the doctrine of reminiscences that sometimes colours his speculations on memory in general. In the collection of short stories on historical themes, *The Memories of Chieftains* (1906), he discusses this doctrine in a quotation that provides an interesting background to the chamber plays:

> The human being who has retained faint memories of the primary images will always feel disappointed at the sight of their representations, such as life offers them to him. [. . .] The primary images are reversed representations in the mirror called the world; therefore the world will appear in reverse to the awakened

mind, which has lively memories from the other side, or from above (SS 43:363).

In the first of the *Blue Books* Strindberg writes: 'My thoughts have lately been occupied with death and life hereafter. Yesterday, I read Plato's *Timaeus* and *Phaidon*. Am currently writing "Toten-Insel"' (SV 65:431).[104]

This entry stems from the period closest to the writing of *The Ghost Sonata* and it appears as if Strindberg is seeking to give dramatic life to Plato's *Phaidon* in *Toten-Insel*, a fragment about death and life hereafter, i.e. a play that begins where *The Ghost Sonata* ends. As stated in *A Blue Book II*, what is of interest to Strindberg appears to be the fact that the dialogue 'so beautifully describes the immortality of the soul' (SV 66:861) and also contains – here with similarities to Swedenborg – a detailed geographical and topographical description of the earth. His reading of *Phaidon* in April 1907 was not his first contact with this text; according to *The Occult Diary* he had reread this dialogue on 25 November 1904.[105]

Plato's *Phaidon* expresses a scepticism of the sensory with great clarity:

> I mean it this way: does for example the sense of sight or hearing give any truth to man? Or is it that our poets incessantly repeat to us that neither through hearing nor through sight do we receive any knowledge? And yet, if these, our bodily senses, sight and hearing, are not safe or reliable, then the other senses cannot really be so, for they are lower and worse than both of these. [. . .] philosophy [shows][. . .] that all observation with the eyes is full of deception, and so is all perception by the ears and the other senses.[106]

This is the same sceptical attitude towards the senses that Strindberg propounds, repeatedly, in the *Blue Books*, and it is this vision that comes more and more to colour the chamber plays where it is combined, oddly enough, with the view that human beings sabotage each other's senses.

Unfortunately, Strindberg's copy of *Phaidon* is missing from the library at the Strindberg Museum in Stockholm; hence, it is impossible to draw upon any marginalia he may have made in this

Platonic dialogue. However, his copy of the *Timaeus* in Dalsjö's translation is preserved,[107] and here Strindberg's pencil markings are of some interest.

Through Socrates Plato describes how the gods created mankind: 'Of the sensory tools, they first created the light-catching eyes'.[108] After this, there is a detailed description of sight, which Strindberg has partially underlined; Plato prefers a medical-physiological description of sight, and the argument – with its mixture of concrete detail and imaginative superstructure – is reminiscent of Strindberg's short essays on the same topic in the *Blue Books*:

> Now when daylight surrounds the light-waves of the eyes, these light-waves fuse with the same and form a body of related parts in the direction of the eyes, whereby the waves from within strike and are united with those coming from the outside.[109]

Dalsjö has commented on this difficult passage and is of the opinion that 'Plato's attitude in this question [is] altogether too unclear for us to be able to decide precisely to what extent he knew about the eye's construction and the real process of seeing.'[110] Dalsjö points out that Plato's ὄψισ in Swedish can be translated with numerous related words: 'sight', 'vision', 'sight ability', 'eye', etc. However, the conclusion of Dalsjö's commentary was apparently too matter-of-fact for Strindberg, since he drew a line through the text, under which he wrote:

> What is really meant by 'the sight organ is expanded and con-tracted', must be difficult to decide. Probably he meant the eye's 'ray of light', possibly the pupil. That Plato did not know of any image of the seen object projected onto the cornea of the eye was quite clear from the last passage.[111]

However, a passage in Plato's own text that clearly expresses Platonic idealism has also been marked by Strindberg:

> Or are these exterior objects that we see with our eyes or observe with the body's other senses the only things that have a real and true existence, and is there nothing else except these things, so that it is simply nonsense when we say that as a foundation for each thing there exists, for the mind, a cognizable idea?[112]

Swedenborg's Heaven and Hell

When it comes to the immortality of the soul, Strindberg thus refers to the *Phaidon* where there are no less than three proofs of this immortality; but when it comes to the life of the body after death, it is not Plato's but Swedenborg's vision that inspires him, most probably because it takes a concrete form, which makes it more rewarding for portrayal on stage.

Plato's dialogue includes the death of the body and all of the senses. The opposite is the case in Swedenborg's world of ideas, which is evident from the heading of a chapter in *Heaven and Hell:* 'After death man possesses all the senses, every memory, thought and fancy, just as in this world, and leaves nothing behind but his earthly body.'[113]

However, after death, man does comprehend that the body is now spiritual, since it otherwise looks just as it did before. Strindberg had successfully used this situation in which it seems almost as if mankind is exposed to some kind of blind man's buff in the second scene of the last Act of *Advent*. The senses perform as before, but now with 'spiritual' instead of 'natural' material:

> When man has become spirit, he does not know but that he is in his worldly body, and thus that he does not know that he has died. The human spirit can also take pleasure in having every outer and inner sense that he has enjoyed in this world. He sees as before, hears and speaks as before, he also has smell and taste, and when he is touched, he perceives it with his feeling as before.[114]

It is responding to these kinds of ideas that enable Strindberg to depict people after death in a dramatic form: they appear as they had done in life, and it is of special interest that they do not realize their changed situation. In *Advent* the venture was successful whereas in *Toten-Insel* his attempt to set an entire drama in a *post mortem* situation remained a fragment. The Judge and his wife in *Advent* have been evil people in their earthly life and therefore did not pass through the three stages that, in most cases, precede a descent into hell or ascent to heaven.[115] But the wretched teacher in *Toten-Insel* ends up in a preparatory state, somewhat like Dante's Ante-Purgatory. How Strindberg intended the play to continue, we do not know, however. Retaining the Swedenborgian idea of this *post mortem* state throughout an entire play, instead of as in *Advent* merely making it the culmination of a drama, might possibly have lead to problems that would have been difficult to overcome artistically.[116]

Strindberg was not a systematic thinker; philosophical precision and systematic logic were foreign to his temperament. His genius was essentially associative. In addition, he was highly receptive and had an exceptional eye for what might be dramatically useful in different thinkers. This explains why, in *The Ghost Sonata*, we can trace influences not only from Plato but also from Schopenhauer and Buddhism, Christianity and Swedenborg, sometimes quoted almost verbatim. The least common denominator in these systems is that they direct our attention to this world's illusions. Therefore Strindberg no doubt felt that he had the right to choose, with great freedom, *illustrative material* from one source or another.

The Upanishads

Great scepticism towards sensory experience is also an enduring theme in the *Upanishads*. In his final book collection Strindberg had the *Rig-Veda* in a German translation by Hermann Grassmann and, to judge from his pen-markings, he had paid close attention to its mythological discourse on the rainbow, a subject that he had himself speculated on in his diary as well as in the *Blue Books*.[117] The library also contained the *Kâthaka Upanishad* in a Swedish translation by Andrea Butenschön. Here, the only marking in Strindberg's hand highlights 'the learned', who are criticized in a manner that is reminiscent of Swedenborg; according to the *Upanishad*, the learned are conceited in their belief that they know something, when they have only scratched the surface of reality:

> Those who dwell deeply in ignorance, self-righteous, consider themselves learned; confused, stumbling hither and dither, they walk about like the blind leading the blind.[118] (Marked in the margin by Strindberg.)

In this *Upanishad*, as in most of the others, the criticism directed at sensual experience is repeated with variations or formula-like expressions. The following formulation in the *Kâthaka-Upanishad* is typical:

Not through words, not through the mind, nor through the eyes can he (The Brahma) be understood. 'He is!'[119]

Strindberg also owned the three volumes of *Främmande religions-urkunder* (1907–8), published by Nathan Söderblom, which had been procured after the writing of the chamber plays. Nevertheless, certain annotations here are also of interest. It seems as if in these texts Strindberg is mainly seeking confirmation of ideas that he had himself been acquainted with for a long time, and which he might use to illustrate his own arguments.

In the first volume there is a marking in Söderblom's text explaining a difference between Buddhism and Hinduism:

> But – unlike Buddhism – there exists something real, the atma-brahma. The reason for the optical illusion that *distinguishes between me* and you, sees the world's bounty, is maya, the illusion, or avidya, ignorance.[120] (Strindberg's underlining)

In the margin Strindberg has also marked the following passage where his Christian standpoint leads Söderblom to distance himself from the teachings of the *Upanishads*:

> Knowledge is not an inclination to pursue research, rather it is a liberation from illusion, a freedom that stops in the great void. This speculation has swept clean and has seated itself with crossed arms – a gospel of liberation, but also of paralysis.[121]

Judging from the markings in Strindberg's hand, there is a method to his reading: he pays attention to formulations regarding 'illusions'. One of the texts that Strindberg read – *Ayaranga-Sutta* I, 2.3, includes the following line: 'Avoid wisely both the top and roots of sin'.[122] Strindberg has underlined Söderblom's commentary on this line, which confirms his own interest: 'The root of sin is illusion, mirage, its top the remaining sins' (Strindberg's underlining).

In this manner the *Upanishads* thus provide the eclectic, associative Strindberg with material for his own view of the 'World of Illusions'.

THE PELICAN

Introduction

Strindberg wrote his first three chamber plays in a sequence and over a short period of time, from January to the beginning of March 1907. During the better part of March he was occupied with a planned Opus 4, a drama entitled 'The Bleeding Hand', which, according to a letter to Emil Schering, he burnt on 2 April. Later that month he started *Toten-Insel* but did not complete the drama.[123] Exactly when the final Opus 4 – *The Pelican* – was begun is not clear, but it was completed on 19 June 1907.[124] Five months had now passed since he finished his first chamber play, *Storm*. There is a gap between *The Ghost Sonata* and *The Pelican* of a little more than two months.

From a formal point of view, *The Pelican* marks a retreat from the advanced dramaturgy of *The Ghost Sonata* with its use of 'half-reality' and absurdism *avant la lettre*. For reasons unknown, Strindberg found it better to return to a dramatic structure that was well tested: the bourgeois *drame*. *Storm*, too, had some of the features of a *drame*, and in this respect, *The Pelican* can be seen as an intertext: In his fourth chamber play Strindberg opens a dialogue with his Opus 1. In so doing, he drastically refutes the relative optimism of the drama he had written not fully a half-year earlier.

The room/space

Space – the drawing-room – in *The Pelican* has the same confined character that Strindberg had previously used in order to provide an anxiety-ridden framework for, for instance, sexual and family conflict in *Miss Julie, The Dance of Death* or in the chamber scene in *A Dream Play*. In *The Pelican*, the Mother begins by saying: 'Close the door' (231). It also becomes apparent that she lacks the opportunity open to the Gentleman in *Storm* of moving elsewhere since, when asked why she doesn't move, she says 'We can't. The landlord won't let us . . . ' (232).[125] From the opening stage directions it appears that the apartment has a balcony, so that it is clear that this time Strindberg has located the action to a set of rooms that are above ground level. In both *Storm* and *The Ghost Sonata*, the upper floor seemed mysterious to an outside observer; it was screened off by either red and white curtains. In *The Pelican*, the audience is given access to such a secretive upper floor.

Like Ibsen, Strindberg wrote his plays before the era of large apartment buildings, where a claustrophobic feeling is created almost spontaneously. For a long time it was natural to Strindberg to let the action take place on the ground level and give a possible upper floor a more symbolic function, as in *Miss Julie*. Ibsen works in a similar way in *The Wild Duck* where a curtained-off attic serves as a symbolic space. However, the chamber plays were written by a playwright who himself lived in a large apartment house. Strindberg no longer lived on the ground floor but could note sounds from both the floor below and above his apartment. He had used this situation artistically in the novella *The Roofing Feast* a year earlier. A large apartment house with several floors – where the house itself becomes an important precondition for the intrigue – does not appear until the play *The Black Glove*, two years later, when Strindberg was inspired by his new domicile in the so-called Blue Tower on Drottninggatan in Stockholm: 'A tower of Babel with all kinds of people/And languages; six flights up plus the ground floor/ Three apartments on each level' (313).

When it comes to the relationship between outer and inner space, Strindberg does not proceed as Ibsen did; Gunnar Brandell has pointed out how, in Ibsen's later plays the outdoor surroundings become increasingly visible and impinge upon the consciousness of his characters.[126] Strindberg does precisely the opposite; he opens the stage vertically by letting those who live in an indoor space become aware of the apartments above or below them. In that respect, *Storm* appears a remarkable exception, in that the characters in the room enjoy good relations with the world outside the window, but are also disturbed by the lifestyle of their neighbours: 'There's such a ruckus up there that the chandelier's rattling . . . and the confectioner's lighting fires down below' (38).

Confinement is given a realistic inflection in *The Pelican*. The Mother wants the door to the kitchen closed in order to keep out the smell of 'carbolic acid and fir twigs' (231). For the same reason she wants a window kept open, which contributes to the coldness of the apartment. Thus, the open window has no function as a channel of communication. The impression of confinement and stagnation is increased by the fact that the Mother is not allowed to move the furniture prior to the inventory of her late husband's estate. There is a hidden drawer in the escritoire (248) and incriminating papers have also been secreted away behind the closed shutters of the tiled stove. Thus, the closed room itself also includes a number of enclosed spaces.

In *Storm* the Gentleman lived in tranquil comfort among his drawing-room memorabilia until his life was disclosed as a life lived among illusions. In *The Pelican* every chance of comfort has been removed. Compared to the drawing-room in *Storm*, a metamorphosis has taken place of the kind that Strindberg depicts under the heading 'The Spellbound Room' in *A Blue Book*. There 'The Teacher' tells of a beautiful room, furnished as 'a temple of memories' (SV 65:26). This temple undergoes a change, the result of a matter-of-fact remark by an unsentimental visitor: 'When he said that, the chamber grew dark, the walls were pushed together, the floor shrank [. . .] the gilding blackened; the brass shutters of the tiled stove dimmed.' Strindberg not only describes how ugly the room becomes but also how the room appears to shrink. The chamber plays were written for a small theatre, although exactly how small, Strindberg did not as yet know. In any case, the fact that the stage at the Intimate Theatre only measured six times four metres cannot have spoiled the sought-after claustrophobic impression.[127]

The Mother who has opened the drama by demanding the door be closed three times, repeats the line 'Close the door!' once more, when her son enters (237). Later on in the First Act when she closes the door upon herself and her son-in-law, her daughter is roused to jealousy:

THE SON-IN-LAW: Why did you have to close . . . we're lost!
[. . .]
GERDA: Why have you closed yourselves in? (250).

In their first dialogue, the Mother and the Son-in-Law urge each other to open the *sealed* escritoire. In the Second Act, the Son reminds his sister of how their father had been *locked out* of their home: 'You locked yourself in the drawing-room, played music and read' (265). The animosity and suspicion of the family is made starkly visible by the way in which doors are closed and objects of various kinds are shut away. In *The Pelican* brings to a climax the way in which the chamber plays as a whole depict a series of closed rooms that began with the double walls and the cupboard in *The*

Burnt House and continued with the screen and the cupboard in *The Ghost Sonata*.

The theme of confinement culminates in the final Act when the Mother closes the window, which she has kept open until now on account of the smell. The room is now hermetically closed and the tension inside becomes so great that some kind of release is necessary. Strindberg brings about this release by employing the same motif as in *Storm* – fire.

Fire

The leitmotif in *Storm*, *The Burnt House* and *The Pelican* is fire. In the third of the chamber plays – *The Ghost Sonata* – fire was replaced by another element: water. The function of these two elements is related; they symbolize purity, but fire has a more actively purifying function than water.[128]

In *Storm*, fire/light was directly connected to the dramatic tension. In an early draft the drama was given the title 'The First Lamp'. Waiting for such a lamp to be lit creates tension and expectation in the play; in the opening scene, the Gentleman states: 'If only they could light the first lamp, then I'd feel calm again' (18). At the end of the play, this expectation is fulfilled: 'Look, there comes the lamp lighter, at last!' (81)

In *Storm* fire was a matter of an element kept under control: the Gentleman lights his cigar and toys with the matches, etc. Beyond that, however, there are references to fires he does not control, such as the fire stoked by the friendly confectioner below or the air filled with fiery thunder and lightning. With regard to the apartment above, there is no real fire, but the Gentleman uses the word itself metaphorically when, the activities in it having been disclosed and after the tenant has moved away, he describes the apartment as looking 'like after a fire' (71).

The Pelican, too, may be called a drama whose characters are waiting for the fire, but here it is only in part a question of a warming fire, under the control of one or other of the characters. The fire at the end of the play is a fire let loose. Strindberg has at last stopped using 'fire' metaphorically. *The Pelican* ends with a highly realistic fire, reminiscent of the one whose devastation is visible when the curtain rises upon *The Burnt House*. In *The Pelican* a fire is raging at the end; like the one in *The Burnt House*, it is the result of arson. The final stage direction – '*The doors in the back are opened, a red light is clearly visible*' (297) – is reminiscent of the first stage direction in *Storm*, where the upstairs apartment was described as having '*four middle windows with red blinds that are illuminated from within*' (13). This stage direction connoted something secretive but as yet hidden and under control.

The Gentleman in *Storm* could be characterized as someone who wishes to control his world. Eventually he realizes that this was done at the expense of truth. But the end of the drama still breathes a certain harmony, brought on by the sense of security that is signified by the rhythm of day, the seasonal change and the almost ritual lighting of the lamp.

In *The Pelican*, too, the end is longed for, at least by the morally pure characters in the play, the Son and Gerda. But here a strong dramatic escalation has taken place when compared with *Storm*. The fire that occurs on stage in *The Pelican* at first brings warmth, then a crackling sound and exotic smells, and finally a red light. But it is caused by arson committed by the Son, who intends to burn both the house and its inhabitants.

This final scene in *The Pelican* is also prepared for in another way. Just as *Storm* depicts people waiting for the first lamp to be lit, so the action of *The Pelican* is endowed with a particular tension when the Mother refuses to light the tiled stove, while the others characters – Margret, the Cook, the Son-in-Law and the children – try to persuade her to do so:

ACT I

Shouldn't I make a fire up for you, Madam? It's so cold in here. (234) [MARGRET] [. . .]
Shan't I make a fire? (235) [again, MARGRET]

ACT II

I'm freezing, make a fire (264) [GERDA] [. . .]
Perhaps there's a fire in the stove; Mother sometimes used to put some wood in just to fool us (265) [GERDA] [. . .]
A letter! Torn, we can make a fire with it . . . (265) [THE SON] [. . .]
Well, then I'll light it, no matter what! (267) [THE SON]

In the Third Act the turning point occurs when the Son-in-Law forces the Mother to do what she has refused to do all along and has also prevented others from doing, i.e. to make a fire in the tiled stove:

> THE SON–IN–LAW: [. . .] however, you will make a fire in the stove!
> [. . .] No, but wood has to burn first in order to make it warm!
> Quickly! [. . .] Light it! [. . .] Now, you watch the fire while we
> go into the drawing-room to eat . . . [. . .] Now, light it! – Blow
> on it! (279–80)

Here the Mother's imperative command 'Close!' has been replaced by the 'Light!' demanded by the other characters. On a realistic level, we witness a struggle between the Mother's miserliness and the cold felt by all the others. It is also possible, as Egil Törnqvist has shown, to interpret the cold as an absence of human warmth,[129] but to this one ought to add a further aspect, for as in *Storm*, the fire in *The Pelican* seems connected with the notion of *truth*. The Mother robs her children of warmth, but she also fuels their deceitful perceptions of their father. One could say that the Mother is miserly with the truth, and it is significant that the truth about the dead father only comes out when the Son finds a letter he has written in the stove, which the mother has tried to burn.

With its closed shutters, the tiled stove is a secretive space, related to the clover leaf door in *A Dream Play* and the cupboard in *The Ghost Sonata*. But the equivalent space in *The Pelican* is more specific than in either of these dramas: it is a fireplace. From the Mother's point of view it is a space that is never to be used; she makes a pretence of wishing to warm the room by placing a few sticks there, but she also snatches them away, and uses the space as a hiding-place for the letter.

In *The Pelican* there is a tension that is fuelled by a fire that is held back as long as possible but which is finally allowed to burn. In that sense, fire becomes a symbol of truth. Traditionally, fire stands not only for the annihilation of earthly life but also for enlightenment. Strindberg seldom works with mythological *patterns*. But he sometimes lets his characters identify with mythological *figures* like Prometheus and Heracles, both of whom are associated with fire, though in different ways: fire as knowledge and death through fire.

'There was nothing else to do' (295), the Son declares with the same laconic attitude towards death that Jean had displayed his final lines in *Miss Julie*: 'It's horrible! But there's nothing else to do!'

(SV 27:190). In Miss Julie's final ecstatic lines one also recognizes the combination of death, warmth and fire, despite the fact that in the earlier play, there is no fire in any manifest sense in the setting:

> the whole room appears like smoke to me and you look like an iron stove that resembles a man dressed in black with a top hat – and your eyes are gleaming like coals when the fire goes out [. . .] it's so warm and nice (27:189).

Senses

In the analysis of *Storm* it seemed logical to focus on the importance of *sight* and *hearing*. Strindberg had thoroughly exploited the same senses in, for example, *Advent*, and he does so again in the first two Acts of *The Ghost Sonata*. We have also seen what a disturbing and frightening role visual and auditory impressions could play for Strindberg himself during a critical time in his life – the Inferno crisis – and how passionately he discusses them in non-literary contexts both in his diary and in the *Blue Books*.

In 1907, too, during the composition of the chamber plays, Strindberg experiences a crisis. This time he is especially disturbed or confounded by sensations of taste and smell. These experiences in his private life manifest themselves in the dramas he is writing, although hardly in the way that Martin Lamm claimed when he described the many references to food in the chamber plays as merely embarrassing reflections of Strindberg's ongoing problems with a succession of housekeepers and the food they served him.[130] Another explanation is closer at hand, namely that Strindberg had found that these banal but real experiences also testify, in their own way, to the fact that he lived in a world of illusions. Sensations of odour and scent penetrate the dramas, and do so with increasing force. This force is so great that Strindberg ignores the problems that sensations of smell, taste and feeling present in the theatre. In fact, *The Ghost Sonata* and *The Pelican* have continued to strike posterity as 'strange' even though Strindberg may have believed that the way he had incorporated the elements of smell and taste in the Third Act of *The Ghost Sonata* was innovatory from a dramaturgical point of view. In any case, he used such features again in *The Pelican* where he adds yet another sense that has only previously figured in passing, the sense of touch, or feeling. This is the realm that includes such ordinary sensory experiences as the ability to feel warmth and cold.

Taste

In Strindberg's one-act comedy from 1892, *Playing with Fire*, the friend in the house – having declared his love to his host's wife, and after she has asked him to stay with her and her husband, exclaims: 'What a devil of a thought! – And you think that after this, I would want to live in this house on crumbs from the rich man's table, swallow air, drink the scent of flowers' (SV 33:264). To swallow air and drink the scent of flowers is tantamount to living on surrogates or, stated more directly: to not having one's love satisfied.

The children's hunger in *The Pelican* has, as Egil Törnqvist has pointed out, a similar symbolic function; the children are expressing 'a hunger for love'.[131] But in *The Pelican* Strindberg is more detailed in his description of food; its role in the drama is not only to express lovelessness, together with the cold in the apartment. Food has also the function of contributing to the depiction of how a person with power – an evil mother – can control those around her by manipulating their senses.

In *Storm*, the kind Confectioner refused to put salicylic acid in his preserve. 'That's only new tricks,' he states (67). In *The Pelican* the Daughter and the Son accuse their Mother of precisely such tricks. She 'made discoveries; that was the soya sauce and the cayenne pepper!' (269) 'The inventions' consisted of various tricks which enabled her to serve food that lacked any substance but in which this lack was concealed by the plentiful use of spices as substitutes. In a very concrete way, the children have grown up in a world of illusions.

The descriptions of food in *The Pelican* are aimed at arousing disgust. According to the Cook, the Mother has sent her children to school on 'a cup of chicory and a piece of bread' (233), while the Daughter draws the following picture of earlier times:

> No, you gave me a glass bottle and stuck a rubber dummy in my mouth, and then I had go to the cupboard and steal, but there was nothing there except stale rye bread, which I ate with mustard, and when it burnt my throat, I cooled it with vinegar (292).

The food mentioned in *The Pelican* consists either of substitutes, so that it tastes like 'air' or else it tastes only of spices (244, 277), which have the same function here as colour had in the earlier chamber plays; it covers up, distorts, falsifies, creates an illusion. When it comes to spice, it is taste rather than sight that is deceived.

In other instances, food is simply unappetizing because of the Mother's stinginess. The Son-in-Law does not want to stay until evening: 'I don't drink tea water and never eat rancid anchovies . . . or porridge' (257). This line comes at the end of the First Act. At the end of the Second Act, he also turns down, and again with brutal frankness, a meal consisting this time of porridge: 'No, thank you! If it's oats, then give it to the watchdogs, if you have any; if it's rye, then put it on your boils . . .' (274). The Act ends with Gerda's rebellion against her Mother which takes the form of offering a tasty alternative to porridge: 'Courage, gentlemen, you'll get a sandwich and a steak from me . . .' (274).

Food – and here it is not a question of food as something substantial but its taste – forms the leitmotif of the drama. But it is not until the final act that the much talked-about porridge is seen on stage: '*GERDA enters, with porridge on a tray, which she puts down [on the table]*' (289).

Smell

In the exchange with Margret that opens the First Act of *The Pelican*, the Mother already confirms the 'smell of carbolic acid and fir twigs' which pervades the apartment. She tries to shut out the smell from the drawing-room by keeping the window open and closing the door to the other rooms with 'that terrible smell' (232). It is obvious that the smell also represents her bad conscience towards her dead husband: 'The memories . . . all those unpleasant things, and the terrible smell . . .' (232). As in *Hamlet* and in several of Strindberg's previous plays,[132] a bad smell stands for rottenness.

In the Second Act of *The Pelican*, there are no features referring to smell, but at the beginning of the Third Act, we are told how the Mother had cooked a ptarmigan in the kitchen: 'the first hour, the whole apartment was suffused with a wonderful odour of game', but after that she herself ate the gravy and served the ptarmigan cold: 'when the food was served, it had no smell and tasted only like air!' (277).

Before an odour is described in more attractive turns in Gerda's final monologue (to which we shall return) a pleasant odour is actualized in an original, although perhaps far-fetched way, in one of the Mother's lines, the source of which is a verse that was dedicated to her on her daughter's wedding day and which began: 'In Ginnistan . . . ' The Mother herself tells us that the word 'Ginnistan' comes from the Persian and means 'the Garden of Eden'. It is characterised by 'beautiful Peri who live on pleasant fragrances' (291). A 'peri' is a lovely fairy descended from a fallen angel.[133] The Mother's account of Ginnistan is a hubristic recollection of her own beauty and youth, but this does not explain the expression 'living on pleasant fragrances', which was seemingly of importance to Strindberg even though it runs the risk of making the line incomprehensible.

The stingy Mother describes paradise to her daughter as a place where one lives on pleasant fragrances. To the Mother herself, these fragrances constitute a contrast to the present smell of carbolic acid and fir twigs that pervades her home. But the circumstance of *living* on pleasant fragrances can also be understood as a defence of her own poor housekeeping. On an earthly level, she has attempted something similar without receiving any gratitude, so that her account of Ginnistan may be seen as a strained defence of it.

Feeling, warmth – cold

In the chamber plays, the sense of feeling is used, above all, to register sensations of cold and warmth, in the air or through direct contact. In *Storm*, there is oppressive heat, in *The Ghost Sonata* Hummel turns out to have an ice-cold handshake. In *The Pelican* everyone is freezing except the Mother. Often such freezing is linked to the lack of food: 'I've frozen, I've starved' (236), the Cook bursts out, and Gerda expresses herself in a similar way: 'I've always been cold and hungry!' (264). But it is the Son who seems to have suffered the most in this respect. Among other things, he plays the piano in order to keep warm (234), thus articulating a pessimistic view of the purpose of art.

In the chamber plays, vampire-like people – Hummel and the Cook in *The Ghost Sonata*, the Mother in *The Pelican* – are associated with cold. Hummel admits that he is freezing: 'push my chair a little, so it ends up in the sun,' he asks the Student, 'I'm so dreadfully cold. When you can't move about, your blood congeals [. . .] take my hand and you'll feel how cold I am'. To which the Student responds 'But that's incredible! *Pulls back*' (176–7). Like the Cook in *The Ghost Sonata* the Mother in *The Pelican* keeps warm by eating the nourishment in food that will later be served up to others overcooked. This is stressed in the following exchange: 'The Mother; I can't drink blue milk, it makes me freeze! Gerda: After you've skimmed the cream for your morning coffee!' (290).

In both cases it is a miserly character who feels the cold whereas in *Storm* the Gentleman and his friends are described as generous people who live in an almost oppressive heat. According to Gerda in *The Pelican*, the atmosphere resembles the 'coldness of the tomb' (267), an expression which refers both to the chill that exists for real and signifies the lovelessness that emanates from the Mother.

Sight

Where the senses of sight and hearing are concerned, it is clear that they do not have the same dominant role in *The Pelican* as in the earlier chamber plays.

Several of the *dramatis personae* — the Mother, the Son and the Daughter — are described as 'somnambulists', implying an attitude towards life that the Daughter describes as follows: 'If that is so, I don't want to live, but if I have to, then I want to walk through this misery deaf and blind, but hoping for a better hereafter' (293). This somnambulistic attitude which may, according to Leif Leifer, signify a different moral dimension,[134] is characterized by the way in which one or even several senses have been more or less shut off. The Son-in-Law says to the Mother about her Daughter: 'she's beginning to wake up from her somnambulistic sleep. Beware, when she opens her eyes!' (254). But the Mother is also described by Gerda as a somnambulist: 'You still walk in your sleep as we've all done, but will you never wake up? Don't you see how they laugh at you?' (291). And again the Son says of her: 'She's sly as an animal, but her self-love often blinds her' (271).

Here deafness and blindness are to be regarded both literally and metaphorically. The Mother is morally blind but is increasingly plagued by a bad conscience over her newly deceased husband. In *The Pelican* sight and hearing, like smell, have the function of arousing unpleasant memories.

'Do you think I'm afraid of ghosts?' the Mother asks the Cook in the First Act (234). Later on she turns out to be exactly that and with good reason. She is reminded of her dead husband through two pieces of *furniture* – a new device for Strindberg. Previously he has used other objects – especially clothes – as a surrogate for absent people, but furniture can also serve the same purpose very effect-ively, namely to dramatize the presence of an absent person. The furniture in question is '*a chaise longue with a crimson cover in velvet pile, and a rocking-chair*' (231). The husband died on the chaise longue and before that, the rocking-chair was his favourite piece of furniture. Its crimson colour is associated with blood, as was the case in *Storm*. In that play there was talk of 'bloody tragedies' behind the red curtains. In *The Pelican*, the Mother makes a similar allusion which may be designed to point up her resemblance with Lady Macbeth: 'Ugh! It is a bloody butcher's block!' (255).[135]

In a fatal way, the Mother is caught in the vicinity of the chaise longue. It must not be moved before the inventory of the estate has been completed (232), and the rest of the family wants to force her – as a final act of revenge – to use it as a bed (255). She is even more plagued by the rocking-chair which reminds her of her dead hus-band. The rocking-chair really does move on a number of occasions in the play, but unlike in *Advent*, real objects are not endowed with supernatural causes in *The Pelican*; to the extent that supernatural phenomena do occur in the chamber plays, they are confined to *The Ghost Sonata*. In the opening scene of that play, certain people are able to see a deceased person (The Milkmaid, the Consul), but by no means everyone can. In *Advent*, Strindberg wished to demon-strate the hubris of the Judge and his Wife as they sought natural explanations for supernatural phenomena, but in *The Pelican* he himself provides careful natural explanations. In a stage direction at the end of the First Act, it is stated: '*The rocking-chair moves*' (252), but immediately beforehand, it is possible to conclude from the same stage direction that it is the wind from the open window that sets the chair in motion. This is reaffirmed shortly afterwards: 'THE MOTHER: [. . .] Look at the rocking-chair!' THE SON-IN-LAW: 'It's the draft!' (253).

Towards the end of Act Two, the Mother enters the stage just as the Son gets up from the rocking-chair '*which remains rocking until the MOTHER enters*' (273), at which point the Mother 'gasps in hor-ror'. Here too there is a natural explanation, but the Mother reveals her bad conscience by her reaction.

The dead man never appears as a ghost in any real sense; he is never visible as a spectre to the audience or to other characters and yet he is in a sense a spectre to the Mother at times when her conscience misinterprets events in her immediate surroundings, which have a rational explanation. A certain set of visual metaphors is woven into this circumstance. The Mother wants to rid herself of her husband's portrait on the wall: 'I don't like it; his eyes look evil.' (241) When the children realize the truth about their mother through the father's posthumous letter, they describe the experience as follows: 'Gerda and I have become clairvoyants, we have been visited by a dead ghost' (273). But these are only words; no 'real' ghost appears ever on stage in *The Pelican*.

Hearing

It is by no means a new trait in his repertoire of dramatic effects when Strindberg allows the wind to whistle and objects to fall to the floor in order to frighten the protagonist,[136] and play upon his nerves. Such uncanny effects played, as we have seen, an important part in *Advent*, where they were designed to frighten the main characters into humility. In *The Pelican* Strindberg does not seem to count on any corresponding possibility on the part of his protagonist. In the world of the chamber plays there is no longer any room for divine intervention. When Strindberg wrote *Advent*, he was much closer to his own nightly terrors and his own conversion. Death was still something to be feared and to terrify.[137] But to Strindberg as the author of the chamber plays death is more of a gain, and so the need for supernatural effects disappears. In the world of the chamber plays, there is little room for moral improvement; rather, what dominates is now a primitive desire for revenge.

In such a world one cannot trust anyone. The Mother's suspicious frame of mind makes her hypersensitive to certain *visions* and, especially, to certain *sounds*. She reacts with terror and suspicion to both real or imagined sounds: 'Is there someone out there?' she asks in terror. 'No, not that I can hear!' her Son responds (240) Even the latter's piano playing seems to terrify her: 'Who's that playing?' (231 'Is it my son playing?' (232). As in *Macbeth*, a play to which Strindberg devotes an essay in *Open Letters to the Intimate Theatre*, there is famously a knocking on a door (250, 288) that terrifies those on stage. In Shakespeare's play, the royal couple share a bad conscience; at first it is Macbeth who is frightened by the knocking: 'Whence is that knocking?/How is't with me, when every noise appals me?' (Act II, scene 2).[138] According to the stage directions in *Macbeth*, there are three knocks that scare the King. In the Fifth Act Lady Macbeth is also frightened by her recollection of these knocks and the Doctor concludes: 'Infected minds/To their deaf pillows will discharge their secrets.' (Act V, scene 1).[139] In *The Pelican* the Mother is described as '*walking round and round in the room until she falls head-long on the chaise longue, burying her face in the cushions*' (288).

In *The Pelican*, the first knocks turn out to come from the Daughter who wants to get into the drawing-room. The second instance of knocking is not quite as clear but points mostly to a trivial explanation; here again there is talk of 'the wind'. The Mother is alone on stage, ready to throw herself out the window, when '*there are three knocks on the upstage door*' (288). The Mother talks to herself: 'Who is it? What was that? [. . .] Come in!' After this, the double doors to the rear are opened but there is no one to be seen. There is no spectre visible in this scene either, but in her general state of fright, the Mother seems to sense a one: 'It's him, in the tobacco field! Isn't he dead?' (288).[140]

Before the action continues, Strindberg has added three asterisks in his manuscript, in addition to a brief musical interlude: '*Il me disait is played within*' (288). The action moves on when Gerda enters bearing the tray with the porridge, and it is likely that Strindberg – despite the indicated pause – intended the knocking to be the Daughter's, who now makes a delayed entry. In the world of *The Pelican* one does not make spontaneous entries.

As in, for instance, *The Dance of Death*, the wind is used to create a frightening atmosphere. It happens in the First Act when no one is present on stage:

> *The stage is empty; outside the wind is blowing, howling about the windows and in the tiled stove; the door to the rear starts to bang, papers on the desk fly about the room, a potted palm on the console is shaking furiously, a photograph on the wall falls down. Now the SON's voice is heard: 'Mother'. Soon thereafter: 'Close the window!' – Pause. – The rocking-chair begins to move* (252).

This stage direction, devoid of people, has a sequel in the Third Act when the Mother is placed in a similar setting. The reason for the wind is that she must have the window open on account of the smell. Both scenes end with her request that the window be closed, which means that, like the Young Lady in *The Ghost Sonata*, she locks herself in among smells.[141] She seems to be caught between unpleasant smells and unpleasant sounds, and appears to prefer now the one, now the other.

The sounds in *The Pelican* are seldom harmonic. The piano music comes from the freezing Son who tries to keep warm by his playing. The most brutal sound is when the Son-in-Law hits the table with his cane as he forces the Mother to make a fire (279). Another sound becomes brutal in the Mother's ears, namely the sound of the rocking-chair: 'It always sounded like hacking knives when he sat there . . . and hacked my heart to pieces' (285). Some of Strindberg's refined uses of sound consist of sharp contrasts, as when he interrupts the whistling of the wind and the Mother's shrieks with piano music (288), or when the music suddenly stops to allow for the Son's 'howling' to be heard (294).

The dialogue

In the chamber plays, there is a mood of growing pessimism, not only in terms of the ability of the sensory organs to register the surroundings in a reliable way or the quality of sensory experiences in general; there is also a growing pessimism about the communicative ability of language. The distrust of dialogue takes numerous forms. In the chamber plays there are regular references to people as liars, and there are a number of violent, monologue-like outbursts in which one character accuses another of not speaking the truth. Parallel to this type of monologue, there is another kind which differs from everyday conversation or logically structured speech. This form of dialogue – what might be referred to as a lyrical monologue[142] – is found in the Third Act of *The Ghost Sonata* and at the end of *The Pelican*.

In this kind of monologue, Strindberg tends to reject everyday dialogue, except for arguments, insinuations or misunderstandings. This is more evident in *The Pelican* than in any of his earlier plays, and it transmits a sombre picture of a human predicament, at the same time as it anticipates the theatre of the absurd.[143]

The imperative 'Quiet!' is heard in different contexts in the play; it means either that someone should remain silent in order not to reveal his presence (250, 271) or because speaking might lead to the revelation of unpleasant truths about oneself or others. Thus Gerda remarks, 'Quiet! I walk in my sleep, I know that, but I don't want to be awakened! Then I would not be able to live!' (263). On other occasions, remaining silent may be a way of preventing a painful memory from surfacing (266). The very frequency of the imperative 'Quiet!' reveals a pessimistic attitude towards spoken language.

With one remarkable exception in the dialogue between the Son and Gerda in the Second Act, the dialogue in *The Pelican* is subverted in an almost comical way by the unwillingness of the *dramatis personae* to speak the truth.

The family servant Margret has never dared complain before about the food (233) but in the First Act she suddenly blurts out the truth, whereupon the Mother responds: 'I don't understand a word of what you're saying' (235). Here, to 'understand' means not to accept an accusation, a type of strong-willed inability to understand, that leads to further arguments. This feature is not unique in itself in a dramatic dialogue, which lives on tensions and contrasts, but what is original in *The Pelican* is that alongside these arguments, there is a meta-level commentary about the way in which people talk past each other. It appears impossible to enter into an intimate relationship with another human being through language; this is an increasingly clear insight in the chamber plays, an insight that runs parallel to the growing pessimism with regard to sensory experiences. Neither language nor the senses function well.

The Son has been provided with certain *speech impediments*; he enters '*coughing. He stutters slightly*' (237). He 'howls' on at least three occasions (268, 288, 294). These inarticulate howls seem to be his answer to an impossible life situation.

In *The Pelican*, painful insight into the vileness of existence leads to speech impediments or inarticulate howls rather than grandiose monologues of the kind found in *The Burnt House*. The Son's predicament seems to have been shared by his father. The Mother recalls his behaviour outside the Son-in-Law's house when she was invited there for dinner:

> we were sitting at a splendid dinner table when we heard those terrible cries from the garden, which we thought must come from the prison yard or the madhouse . . . do you remember? It was him walking about down there in the tobacco land in the dark and the rain, howling from his wife and children (256).

Earlier, in the poem 'Chrysaëtos', Strindberg had used 'howling' as an expression of total despair.[144] With the Son, it implies an insight into the miserable conditions of life rather than a concrete loss, which was the case with the father. Another flashback testifies to a symbolic speech impediment in the father. The Son recalls how 'when I went out walking with the old man, he seemed to want to speak, several times, but the words never passed his lips' (266). On the other hand, the father can communicate after death through the letter in which he discloses that his wife tortured him to death. 'Just imagine, he clambers out of his grave and speaks – he isn't dead! I can never live here', says the Mother (253). A letter that reveals a secret is certainly an old trick in the theatre,[145] but the episode in *The Pelican* may also reveal Strindberg's confidence in the written word as a better form of communication than speech.

The speech impediment which link the Son with his father is one thing, lacking the will to engage in real conversation is something else. There are numerous examples of the latter in *The Pelican*. The first dialogue between Mother and Son in the First Act contains lines like 'Is that the way to answer me?', 'Why do you ask that?' (237), 'How you talk!', 'What do you mean?' (242), 'No, but what's that I can hear?' (244) – a series of exclamations by the Mother in which she seeks to manifest her authority as a mother. The Son's last line in this dialogue shows that he has found the conversation meaningless: 'Yes! . . . I'll go! I'd like to say something, but that's enough for today!' (244).

This dialogue – a communicative failure but interesting from an expressive point of view – is interrupted by an exchange between the Mother and the Son-in-Law. This is an effective dialogue where the Son-in-Law pressures the Mother into opening a panel at the rear of the escritoire. Before that, however, the Son-in-Law has admitted to having derived little pleasure from his wife's conversation during their honeymoon: 'Well, it was a bit long, you know, when you've exhausted the subject, the solitude becomes oppressive' (245).

The Second Act opens with a more successful dialogue between the Son and Gerda, who also comment on their conversation. It turns out that this is the first time that the two siblings have carried on such a meaningful conversation:

GERDA: [. . .] Sit down and talk, Fredrik, keep me company!
THE SON (*sits down*): Yes, I believe we've never talked before, we avoided each other, there was no sympathy between us (259).

During their conversation the Son happens to disclose to his sister that her husband has gone out to a tavern instead of to a meeting (261) and that the Mother has kept herself informed about the honeymoon: 'Well, you know, Mother is curious, and she can use the telephone like no one else!' GERDA: 'What! Has she been spying on us?' THE SON: 'She always does . . . she's probably listening behind one of the doors to this conversation' (262). Thus the Mother uses other methods, such as gossip and eavesdropping, rather than regular conversations in order to get information.

Without intending to, the Son has hurt his sister with the truth. He struggles with the same problem of telling the truth that pervades all the chamber plays and that is given an extra dimension by pointing, intertextually, to Ibsen's polemics against the rage for disclosing the truth in *The Wild Duck* (see above, p. 88–89). 'It's best to gloss over the faults and flaws of your neighbour, that's true . . . but the next step is called "flight" and "flattery" . . . It's difficult to know what to do . . . sometimes it's your duty to speak out' (263).

Just like the Gentleman in *Storm*, Gerda prefers a life among illusions. The interesting thing is that she consciously chooses such a life, though at one time she seems to comment on its predicament: 'Do you know what the greatest pain is? – *Pause* – It's to see the futility of the greatest of happiness!', to which The Son replies 'Now you're talking!' (264). To 'talk' is here synonymous with telling the truth and nothing but the truth.

Language has the opposite function in the flattering verses directed to the Mother on her daughter's wedding day: 'Yes, probably no mother-in-law has ever received such verses at her daughter's wedding' (246). She was given the same homage on her silver wedding: 'What speeches and verses they got!' (265).

Almost throughout his career as a writer, Strindberg had an eye for official celebrations that often seemed to him like public lies. In *The New Kingdom* this view constitutes a leitmotif, and the letter in which he addresses the Norwegian writer Bjørnstierne Bjørnson as 'as false as a speaker at a feast', are well known.[146] In *The Pelican* it is suggested that, on two separate occasions, the Mother has been paid undeserved tributes in festive circumstances.

In a dialogue between the Mother and the Son in the Third Act, the Son is '*somewhat drunk*' (281, which prompts his outspokenness (282). In a series of hot-headed words the Son accuses the Mother of lying, and he refers to his father's claim that unlike other children, the Mother did not learn to speak first but instead learnt to lie from the beginning (284). It is on this occasion that the Son's pessimism become fathomless: 'My contempt for life, humanity, society, and myself is so boundless that I can't be bothered to go on living' (285).

It is quite clear that the dialogue in *The Pelican* is exposed to sabotage. When the Son – coughing and stuttering – fails to have an intimate talk with his Mother in the First Act, he returns drunk in the Third Act and succeeds in directing his *accusations* at the Mother and her inability to tell the truth.

The dialogue functions better in the Second Act – not in the sense of 'dramatic' dialogue but in the sense of establishing 'communication between people'; it is here that Gerda 'speaks', i.e. says something which is true.

The final scene

In the final scene of *The Pelican* the text is broken up by three asterisks and opens with the Son's line: 'There . . . is smoke . . . in – the kitchen!' (294). This is a demonized version of the Young Lady's reply in *The Ghost Sonata* when the Student asks her why she doesn't make a fire: 'Because it fills the room with smoke' (217). What happens in *The Pelican* is that the Son sets the apartment on fire. The window motif in the chamber plays also reaches a climactic finale here, as the Mother throws herself out of the balcony door.[117]

The Pelican ends with two short and two longer lines between Gerda and her brother, which might rather diffidently be called 'summatory monologues'. Applying the so-called 'situation criterion',[148] these lines should perhaps not be regarded as monologues since two people are present on the stage at the same time. But by employing a 'structural criterion' which is based on the length of the lines and their independence from the surrounding dialogue, it is possible to call them monologues.

But it is also possible to call the last two lines in a dialogue a monologue. Gerda is *talking to* her brother the whole time: 'Hold me tight, little brother. [. . .] we're suffocating [. . .] don't you feel [. . .] Little brother! Don't be afraid. [. . .] Hold me tighter [. . .] Oh, that smell' (296). And the brother *talks to* his sister: 'Do you remember when we went down to the white steamers [. . .] we went around like little aristocrats . . . Gerda, hurry up [. . .]'.

These are lines in a dialogue that tends towards a monologue both on account of its length and because the two speakers, though talking to each other, do so almost rhetorically, without expecting an answer. At the same time, they report to each other – Gerda about the burning apartment and her brother about his memories of childhood summers. Finally, he conveys a vision of a new 'summer holiday'. The language is at one and the same time informative, expressive and lyrical. It is more complex than the language elsewhere in the play, where it has been mostly a case of telling the truth or not.

In the exalted 'final monologues' of Gerda and the Son the problems connected with the five senses reach their climax in a somewhat surprising denouement. It is not simply that the dying are relieved of their unbearable sensory impressions. On the contrary, Strindberg demonstrates quite clearly how the dying are compensated for their suffering in this life.

Feeling. Coldness–Warmth. Life in the home has been characterized by coldness – metaphorically and literally – and is now replaced by warmth: 'do you feel how warm it is, how pleasant, now I am no longer cold', 'Hold me tight, little brother'.

Smell. The smell of carbolic acid and fir twigs is replaced by a wealth of scents: 'don't you feel how nice it smells, the potted palms are burning and so is father's laurel wreath, now the linen cupboard is burning, there's a smell of lavender, and now, the roses! [. . .] feel the scent, it's the sideboard burning, with the tea and the coffee, and all the spices, cinnamon and cloves . . .'

Sound. The frightening sounds and the hysterical piano playing is replaced by pleasant sounds: 'listen how it's crackling out there, now everything old is burning, everything old and nasty and ugly . . . [. . .] Gerda, hurry up, there's the steamer's bell.'

Taste. The falsified food and the feeling of always being hungry is replaced by its opposite: 'It's like Christmas Eve, when we used to eat in the kitchen, and dip in the pot, the only day we got enough to eat.'

Sight. The ugliness in the apartment is replaced by a vision of summer and vacation, and finally also by a redeeming image of the Mother, whose presence seems necessary to complete the picture of summer holidays: 'I don't see her, it's no fun without Mama, oh, there she comes!'

The last line of the play: 'Now the summer holidays are beginning!' constitutes a reply to the arrival of autumn that ended Opus 1, *Storm.* That play was a farewell to the sensuousness of life while the subsequent chamber plays have depicted the pain caused by the senses. But for Strindberg death reveals a summer landscape, where the senses are restored with such emphasis that one seems to experience a younger and more life-affirming Strindberg, enjoying his life on a summer's day.

Notes

Introduction

1   From Alain Erlande-Brandenburg's *La Dame à la Licorne* (Paris, 1993) it is clear that the inaugural exhibition of the tapestries occurred with great pomp on 21 April 1883 (p. 12). The tapestries were well known and had been frequently written about. George Sand, for example, drew attention to them while they still hung at the Château de Boussac. They are mentioned in her novel *Jeanne* (1844), are discussed by her in an article in *L'Illustration* (1847), and are mentioned again in *Autour de la Table* (1862) and in *Journal d'un voyageur* (1871). They were subsequently the focus of a loving description by Rilke in *Die Aufzeichnungen des Malte Laurids Brigge* (1910).

2   See Carl Nordenfalk, *Sèvres et les Cinq Sens*. Nationalmusei Skriftserie N.S. 2 (Stockholm, 1984). Strindberg had long been interested in china. In the essay 'Porslinsbilder' (Porcelain Pictures) in *Kulturhistoriska studier* (Studies in Cultural History, 1881), originally published in *Dagens Nyheter*, 28 April and 9 May 1877 – the year after his first visit to Paris – he reveals considerable knowledge on the subject and also treats Sèvres china in some detail.

3   The title of the essay in full is 'Woman's Inferiority to Man, and Her Justifiably Subservient Position. (According to the Latest Scientific Results)'. The manuscript was offered for publication in Verdandi's edition of shorter studies but was refused after Hjalmar Öhrvall, an assistant professor of physiology who was a member of the editorial committee, had criticized its supposedly scientific content. In 1889 Öhrvall, an old friend of Strindberg's, defended his doctoral dissertation in Lund; his topic was *Studier och undersökningar öfver smaksinnet* (*Studies and Research Regarding the Sense of Taste*, Uppsala, 1889). He subsequently published several studies on the subject of sensory physiology. Only two letters from Öhrvall to Strindberg survive. In one of these Öhrvall criticizes Strindberg's theories about colour photography, observing: 'I suspect that your conclusions are the result of a mirage' (letter from 13 December 1890, KB).

4   'The five senses' are well known as a topos in older Swedish literature through such poems as Samuel Columbus's 'Lustwin Danssar en Gavott mäd de 5. Sinnerne' (Lusty Dances a Gavotte with the Five Senses, 1687), Johan Gabriel Oxenstierna's 'De fem Sinnen' (The

Five Senses, 1772) and Johan Henric Kellgren's 'Sinnenas förening' (The Fusion of the Senses, 1778). See Louise Vinge, *The Five Senses. Studies in a Literary Tradition*, Skrifter utgivna av Kungl. Humanistiska Vetenskapssamfundet i Lund LXXII (Lund, 1975).

5　There are many indications that Strindberg employed the expression in colloquial language while using it at the same time as a philosophical formula. See, for example, a letter to Birger Mörner, 7 April 1896: 'You must live in a complete world of illusions with regard to the value of my scientific work.'

6　Cf. Johan Cullberg, *Skaparkriser. Strindbergs inferno – och Dagermans* (Stockholm, 1992) pp. 118 ff. and Gunnar Brandell, *Strindberg in Inferno*, translated by Barry Jacobs (Cambridge, Mass., 1974), chap. 4 *passim*.

7　See Gunnar Brandell, 'Forskning om drama' in *Nordiskt drama – studier och belysningar*, Skrifter utgivna av Svenska Litteratursällskapet 43 (Uppsala, 1993). In this context Brandell defends an interest in the playwright's intentions: 'Here we have an elementary case where the author's intentions must be taken into account, in order not to lose touch with common sense. If the author has written his drama with a staging in mind, every interpretation of the drama, every reading of it, must be predicated upon this circumstance' (p. 13).

8　See Manfred Pfister, *The Theory and Analysis of Drama*, translated by John Halliday (Cambridge, 1988), chap. 3: 'Sending and Receiving Information' *passim*.

9　Pfister, 1988, p. 7.

10　Pfister, 1988, p. 8.

11　In some extreme naturalistic productions food has occasionally been cooked on stage. This was the case at the successful Stockholm première of *Miss Julie* at the Folketeatern on 13 December 1906. In *Dagens Nyheter* on 19 December, 'Floridor' (Beyron Carlson) reported that there was a smell of 'beefsteak in the whole playhouse', while Carl Laurin in *Ord och Bild* observed more specifically that 'the scent of grilled kidney was agreeable' (*Ord och Bild* 1907, p. 6). It is the presence of such experiments that leads Pfister to a parenthetical statement about smell. Cf. Gilles Girard, Réal Ouellet and Claude Rigault, *L'Univers du théâtre*, 3e édition revue et corrigée (Paris, 1995): 'au théâtre, les messages, en plus d'étre sonares et visuels, peuvent également être tactiles, olfactifs ou gustatifs' (p. 26, but cf. 21 ff).

1 The World of the Senses

1　In his letters, Strindberg often reported on the sense of freedom that the open window gives him. For example, in a letter from Grez on 22

September 1883 he writes: 'Bathed in the river yesterday! Full blown summer with open windows', while from Stockholm he writes to Harriet Bosse on 4 April 1906: 'I've my spring coat on, the window open the whole day – one can breathe again!' Cf. Bertha's line in *The Father*: 'when you come, father, it is like having the inner windows removed on a spring morning!' (SV 27, p. 41).

2 *Le plaidoyer d'un fou*, ed. Lars Dahlbäck and Göran Rossholm, Svenska författare utgivna av Svenska Vitterhetssamfundet XXIII (Stockholm, 1978) p. 14. The novel contains a number of references and depictions of the senses: 'Gullible, unsuspecting, he would have lost his honour during a ten year sleep in the arms of an enchantress, lost his manhood, his will to live, his intelligence, his five senses and more' (p. 9). Compare also the account of Axel's nightly walk in the woods: 'But under the influence of a primitive fear my senses were sharpened, so that I could discern the different types of trees solely by listening to the rustling of the leaves. [. . .] I would have considered myself capable of discerning a pine cone from a fir cone by the sound of it falling to the ground. Through smell alone I felt mushrooms nearby, and the nerves of my toes seemed to me able to discriminate between the pressure of club moss and hair moss' (p. 68 f.).

3 In his memoirs Dr Ludwig Schleich writes of their acquaintance in 1890: 'At that time Strindberg was a convinced monist, a mechanic of life of the purest kind. Everything I myself could contribute to the mechanics of biology interested him in a most vivid way'. *Hågkomster om Strindberg*, translated by Gustaf Lindelöf (Stockholm, 1917) p. 12.

4 See Karl-Åke Kärnell, *Strindbergs bildspråk. En studie i prosastil* (Stockholm, 1962) p. 113.

5 Kärnell, 1962, p. 115.

6 Ekman, 'Strindberg's senses, symbols and synesthesia'. *Strindberg: The Moscow Papers*. Proceedings of the XIIth International Strindberg Conference, ed. Michael Robinson (Stockholm, 1998), pp. 27–35.

7 Kärnell, 1962, p. 229.

8 Cf. Kärnell, 1962, p. 229.

9 KB, SgNM, unnumbered.

10 Strindberg also took two cameras along with him on the journey, but like the earlier expedition through France in 1886, he failed with his photography. See Per Hemmingsson, *August Strindberg som fotograf*, 2nd ed. (Stockholm, 1989), pp. 16–25 and 57–65. Hemmingsson also observes how Strindberg's interest in the art of photography undergoes a change during the Inferno crisis: 'The most startling fact is that in the 1890s he wanted, by means of photography, to expose man's view of the world as a subjective optical illusion. In the same bold spirit he had, with a poet's intuition, hypothesized about the

camera's ability to capture other dimensions of reality than the visible' (p. 12).

11 See Eklund's comment on the letter of 13 December 1900, note 1.

12 See, for example, 20 May: 'It was generally said that sweet-smelling fields between Kristianstad and Åhus appeared in the summertime on the sand-filled pastures that lay only ½ mile from Åhus. People said that this divine smell was most notable at midsummer and especially in the evenings and mornings. They also believed that both rosemary and lavender would grow there as in the fields in Spain; we were curious as to what caused the scent. When we came to the place, we found that all this scent came from the blossoms of a carnation, such as we had never seen further north in the country.' *Carl Linnæi Skånska Resa förrättad år 1749*, ed. Carl Otto von Sydow (Stockholm, 1982) p. 104. Or 26 May: 'A delightful smell rose from the fields just before we arrived in the afternoon at Vittskövle. This smell came from the many sand carnations [. . .] which bloomed in the sand' (p. 135).

13 Georg Brandes, *Wolfgang Goethe* II. 3rd ed. (Copenhagen, 1920) p. 77.

14 See Brandell, 1974, p. 280.

15 Adolf Paul, *Min Strindbergsbok* (Stockholm, 1930) p. 129.

16 Paul, 1930, pp. 130 ff.

17 Paul, 1930, pp. 133 ff.

18 Cf. Brandell 2, 1985, pp. 303 ff.

19 A typewritten copy was made by Strindberg's friend, Professor Vilhelm Carlheim–Gyllensköld, KB, I:SgNM:17.

20 'Fifth Letter' p. 4.

21 Brandell, 1974, pp. 189 ff. Cf. Stellan Ahlström, *Strindbergs erövring av Paris. Strindberg och Frankrike 1884–1895* (Stockholm, 1956), p. 276. Cullberg interprets the text like Brandell. See Cullberg 1992, p. 24.

22 Brandell, 1974, pp. 189 ff. Cf. a letter to the painter Richard Bergh, dated 26 November 1894, in which Strindberg claims that 'in a scrutinising disposition [he] sought to anticipate the abilities of a future more highly developed spiritual life'.

23 Kärnell, 1962, p. 264.

24 Manuscript in the Royal Library in Copenhagen, sign Ny kgl saml. 2943.4.

25 Regarding Strindberg's agoraphobia, see Brandell, [1950] 1974, pp. 190 ff. Brandell admits that 'agoraphobia's character of factual experience cannot be disputed'.

26 'The Fifth Letter'; p. 4.

27 'Des Arts Nouveaux! Où Le Hasard dans la production artistique'. Manuscript, SgNM 6:17, 12, p. 6.

28 See, Brandell, [1950] 1974, p. 191.

29 Cf. Harry G. Carlson, *Genom Inferno. Bildens magi och Strindbergs förnyelse*, translated by Gun R. Bengtsson (Stockholm, 1995), p. 321.

30 Brandell points out that in 'Études funèbres' Strindberg is on his way to finding his new style (3, 1982, pp. 139 and 143). Brandell sees the text as a sign that Strindberg wanted to be free of his obsession with chemistry and return to literature.

31 Dated Paris, 20 February 1896, published in *Göteborgs Handels- och Sjöfartstidning*, 11 March that year (Brandell, 1974, p. 321).

32 See Brandell 3, 1983 p. 88.

33 See Abbé l'Epée, *Institution des sourdes et muets par la voie des signes méthodiques* (Paris, 1776).

34 As fate would have it, Strindberg would later on in Lund be in the vicinity of a deaf-mute institute. See Olléns's comments on *Easter* in SV 43, p. 372. Ollén believes that a notation in the fragment 4:23,I indicates Lund: 'Deaf-mute institute where the nightingale sang!' cf. Eleonora's line: 'Because those who have hearing can't hear what the nightingale says, but the deaf-mute hear it!' (p. 269). A passage in the first chapter of *Black Banners* points to a direct connection between Strindberg's impression of deaf-mutes and a mute scene described in prose: 'Now the company around the table became as in The Silent School. They nodded and drank, and drank and nodded' (p. 9). Cf. the explanation, p. 356, where The Silent School is identified as a private teaching institution for deaf-mute children, which at the turn of the century was situated at 51 Nortullsgatan in Stockholm.

35 However, his interest in mimed action preceded this period and was expressed in, for instance, *Miss Julie*. Cf. Carl-Olof Gierow, *Documentation – évocation. Le Climat littéraire et théâtral en France des années 1880 et 'Mademoiselle Julie' de Strindberg*, Acta Universitatis Stockholmiensis. Romanica Stockholmiensia 3 (Stockholm, 1967). – The brief prose sketches 'Pantomimes from the Street' (Pantomimer på gatan, 1883) constitute another example; here the narrator describes people's actions without being able to hear what they are saying. Hence, it is up to the observer/author to attempt to supplement what appears to him as pantomime but which in reality is a real, albeit inaudible dialogue. This is reminiscent of the situation where a spectator might be confronted with active, yet inaudible characters performing on stage: 'She looks around the cemetery as if she were looking for someone. Yes, indeed! There he sits. She immediately rushes forward to her melancholy – almost surly – father. He looks disappointed and impatient. The girl begins to speak, briefly, rapidly, and receives short and clear answers. She speaks at greater length, pointing behind her (homeward!), clasps her hands (her mother's despair!), wipes her eyes with her apron (the siblings' miseries!). But

her father is adamant. Then she gets angry, shakes her fists at him, grabs him by the jacket so that the buttons come undone. The father turns his back and gives her his deaf ear is while buttoning up his jacket again (SS 22, p. 70).

36 Cf. the discussion of the child's drawing in the diary from the journey in Västergötland (above, p. 16) and 'The Fifth Letter', p. 6.

37 During 1898 there are still many entries regarding sensations of sound and smell. In 1899, as in 1900, they are notably fewer. Harriet Bosse's arrival in his life that year eventually results in what appear to be powerful hallucinations related to the sense of smell of a kind that also reappear after their final divorce. Hence they appear during the period when the chamber plays were written. Private experiences have presumably affected the olfactory elements in the chamber plays as well as in later dramas like *Abu Casem's Slippers* (*Abu Casems tofflor*) and *The Great Highway* (*Stora landsvägen*). The important difference lies in the fact that more or less dramatic sensory impressions are no longer interpreted in a paranoiac way; instead they are occult or symbolic.

38 Cullberg has a medical explanation for the cricket's singing in the pillow; the symptoms that Strindberg also complains about on occasion in the future may be indicative of so-called ear hissing. Cullberg, 1992, p. 45.

39 Thus it is not a question of hallucinations but rather illusions. Cf. Cullberg, 1992, p. 76.

40 *Ögonvitten. August Strindberg. Mannaår och ålderdom*, ed. Stellan Ahlström and Torsten Eklund (Stockholm, 1961), p. 105.

41 Brandell, [1950] 1974, p. 17.

42 Emanuel Swedenborg, *The Five Senses*, translated from the Latin by Enoch S. Price (Philadelphia, 1914). Cf. Lars Bergquist, *Swedenborgs drömbok. Glädjen och det stora kvalet* (Stockholm, 1989), p. 21.

43 Regarding Strindberg's identification with Swedenborg, see Brandell, [1950] 1974, pp. 126 ff. and Göran Stockenström, *Ismael i öknen. Strindberg som mystiker*. Acta Universitatis Upsaliensis. Historia litterarum 5. (Uppsala, 1972), pp. 76 ff.

44 SgNM 9:2, 3.

45 See, Stockenström, 1972, p. 57.

46 Swedenborg, *Vera Christiana Religio*, § 569.

47 Swedenborg, *Vena Christina Religio*, § 569.

48 Such descriptions are commonplace in Zola's novel where, for example in chapter one, the protagonist, Florent, encounters unpleasant odours: 'l'odeur fade de la boucherie, l'odeur âcre de la triperie l'exaspéraient'. Émile Zola, *Le Ventre de Paris*, Les Œuvres complètes, 4 (Paris, 1927), p. 37.

49 See Stockenström, 1972, p. 68.

50 Swedenborg, *Om himlen och dess underbara ting och om helvetet. På grund av vad som blivit hört och sett*, translated from the Latin by Gustaf Bæckström (Stockholm, 1944), p. 341.

51 'Nous ne sçavons plus quelles sont les choses sens, etc'. Montaigne, *Essais*. Texte établi et annoté par Albert Thibaudet. Bibliothèque de la Pléiade 14 (Paris, 1933), p. 584.

52 'La première consideration que j'ai sur le sujet, c'est que je mets en doubte que l'homme soit prouveu de tous sens naturel. [. . .] qui sçait si en nous assui il ne manque pas encore un, deux, trois et pluseues autre sens? Car s'il en manque quelqu'un, nostre discours n'en peut découvrir le defaut'. Montaigne, *Essais*, p. 572.

53 Jean Starobinski, *Montaigne en mouvement* (Paris, 1982), p. 12.

54 'La leçon du scepticisme pour lui, c'est précisément le retour aux apparances. Les apparances sont indépassables: voilà qui, loin de nous détourner d'elles, nous délivre du souci de chercher une réalité cachée au nom de laquelle nous les mépriserons. [. . .] Alors même que nos aurions découvert qu'elle ne livre pas accés à l'essence mesme de la verité, cette expérience gard *pour nous* sa valeut de plénitude vecue.' Montaigne, *Essais*, pp. 104–5.

55 Hellquist, *Ton och tystnad. Tankar, iakttagelser och samtal om musik* (Stockholm, 1992), p. 89 and 'Aufschwung. Melodram för en pianist', *Artes*, 20:1 (1994), 16–24. Illus.

56 The note – or part of it – may have been written at a later date.

57 Schumann's 'Aufschwung' made a strong impact on Strindberg. He connected it with the idea that he was being subjected to death threats; the reason seems to have been that the Polish writer Stanislaw Przybyszewski, had played the piece for him during the period they spent together in Berlin, and that because of their mutual relationship with the Norwegian writer and pianist Dagny Juel, Strindberg thought he had reason to fear the Pole. Behind Strindberg's reaction lies a complex range of feelings of guilt and fear which I have not sought to analyse here. See Brandell, [1950] 1974, pp. 79–84 and Cullberg, 1992, pp. 48–51.

58 For example, Bååth's collection *Dikter* (1879) contains the poems 'Skåne'(Scania) and 'Sydskånsk sommarnatt' (Summer Night in South Scania). In Ola Hansson's more extensive volumes of poetry devoted to Skåne (*Dikter*, 1884, *Notturno*, 1885), the social aspects are given greater prominence than the idyllic, in the manner of the 1880s. Hansson himself wrote of Bååth's Scanian lyricism: 'Nature was not perceived religiously or metaphysically or historically; it was depicted as nature, possessing a beauty of its own'. Ola Hansson, *Samlade skrifter* II (Stockholm, 1920), p. 161.

2 The Return

1 The Lady's sudden departure from the chapel is preceded by a change on stage, which is audible and visible to the audience as well, and which does not necessarily imply supernatural elements: '*The sound of bells from the church tower; the sun breaks through and lights up the stained-glass window above the church door, which opens and reveals the interior of the church; organ music is heard, and the Ave Maris Stella*' (p. 35). The fact that the door opens – seemingly of its own accord – can of course be interpreted as supernatural.

2 Egil Törnqvist, *Strindbergian Drama. Themes and Structure*, Svenska Litteratursällskapets skrifter, vol. 37 (Uppsala, 1982), p. 88.

3 This was expressed in the preface to *Miss Julie*: 'the theatre has always been an elementary school for the young, the semi-educated and women, who still retain the primitive capacity for deceiving themselves or allowing themselves to be deceived, that is to say, for succumbing to illusions and to the hypnotic suggestions of the author' (SV 27, p. 101). Strindberg sometimes alludes to this by using the expression 'altered vision'. A person who attracts an audience can under certain circumstances be accused of 'altering their vision'. The expression is found in *Open Letters to the Intimate Theatre* and refers to actors who appear coquettish on stage (SV 64, p. 31). On such occasions the performance is like a 'hypnotic seance' and 'is reminiscent of altering someone's vision, of practising magic' (p. 32). In *Gustav III*, Anckarström passes similar comments about the actor king: 'Don't you see that he is playing Mirabeau and alters our vision; he plays at making the French Revolution, he, the King. It is as perverse as the entire man' (SV 48, p. 240). In *Black Banners* there is a similar commentary about damaging suggestions: 'you have been under the influence of the lecturer, the speaker, the artist. You have applauded stupidity as if it were pure wit, you have admired the ugly as if it were beauty, you have worshipped evil as if it were good. It is called altering vision, and you have been under its influence' (SV 57, p. 150).

4 The director Ralf Långbacka has commented interestingly on different ways of solving these acoustic elements in his book *Möten med Tjechov* (Stockholm, 1986), pp. 283–6. See also Maurice Valency, *The Breaking String. The Plays of Anton Chekhov* (New York, 1966), pp. 284–7, and David Magarshack, *Chekhov the Dramatist* (New York, 1960), p. 286.

5 Cf. *Crimes and Crimes*, Act II, scene 1: '(*The third glass stands at the fourth side of the table facing the back of the stage, where a third chair seems to be waiting for the missing "third party"*.) MAURICE: [. . .] If he isn't here within five minutes, he won't come. – Shall we perhaps drink to his

spirit. (*Clinks his glass against the unused third one*)' (SV 40, p. 167). Also Act I, scene 2: 'I didn't see her, for it was as if she suddenly flew into my arms, came so close to me that I couldn't focus. And she left a trace of herself in the air; I can still see her as if she were standing there – *he goes towards the door and makes a gesture as if he had just pricked his finger*' (p. 152).

6   Regarding this type of conversion, caused by fear or angst, see Hans-Göran Ekman, 'Death angst, death wish: aspects of death in Strindberg's post-Inferno plays', *Strindberg's Post-Inferno Plays. Lectures given at the 11th International Strindberg Conference*, ed. Kela Kvam (Copenhagen, 1994), p. 35.

7   Act I, scene 2, 'At the Doctor's'.

8   See Ekman's comments in SV 40, p. 254.

9   In this presentation, 'monologue' is defined structurally and not from its context – i.e. by monologue I do not mean 'soliloquy' – a definition used for an extended speech by a person who is alone on stage. I use Pfister's definition of the structural criterion, which refers to the length and degree of autonomy of a particular speech' (Pfister, 1977, p. 127). The Judge's monologue begins and ends with the following stage directions: '*looks in front of himself as if in a dream*', respectively '*wakes up*' (p. 112), which isolates it from the context sufficiently for it to be classified as a 'monologue' in this structural sense.

10 Martin, Lamm *Strindbergs dramer* II (Stockholm, 1926), p. 116.

11 See Ollén's explanation of the telephone wires in *Ensam*, SV 52, p. 303: 'At this time it was possible to hear, inside a house, a singing tone in the telephone wires, which were attached to chimneys or roof tops; the sound was caused by the wind amongst the wires or by a change in voltage as the result of fluctuations in temperature.'

12 Cf. a letter about *Easter* addressed to Richard Bergh, dated 30 January 1901: 'What does Maeterlinck say, 1896, in Le Réveil de l'âme? "A time comes . . . when our souls will see each other without the intermediary of the senses."'

13 *The Dance of Death* was written at the end of October 1900. *Easter* was written earlier that month.

14 See Margareta Wirmark, *Kampen med döden. En studie över Strindbergs Dödsdansen*, (Uppsala, 1989), p. 76.

15 'Welche Bedeuting die Beobachtungsgabe der Gestalten hat, zeigt sich daran, dass das häufigste Verbum "se där" (sieh da), und dass das Demonstrativpronomen "denna" (dieser) rund fünfzigmal vertreten ist.' Helmut Müssener, *August Strindberg, 'Ein Traumspiel' Struktur- und Stilstudien*. (Meisenheim am Glan, 1965), p. 139–40.

16 'Elis (*on the telephone*): Hello! – – – No answer! – – – Hello! – – – It answers me with my own voice! – – – Who's there? – – – How

strange! I can hear my own words like an echo!' (SV 43, p. 298). For some interesting observations on the way telephone conversations are represented in *The Father* see Barry Jacobs, 'Bland amerikanska läsare och kritiker: Strindberg i översättning' *August Strindberg och hans översättare*, ed. Björn Meidal and Nils Åke Nilsson, Kungl. Vitterhets Historie och Antikvitets Akademien. Konferenser 33 (Stockholm, 1995), p. 83. Jacobs comments on the same topic in English in 'Strindberg's *Fadren* (The Father) in English Translation' *Yearbook of Comparative and General Literature*, 35 (1986), pp. 112–21.

17   Cf. Strindberg's description in 'Deranged Sensations' of the marble passageway and the wings of the main bulding at Versailles as 'a large ear' (above, p. 26).

18   The same theme is presented in volume three of *A Blue Book* (1908): 'Man grasps sensuality with the brain's intestine-like mush, all that can be seen, heard, smelt, tasted. Only with the heart one can feel heaven and know divine truth' (SS 48, p. 824).

19   Pfister, 1977, p. 117.

3 The Chamber Plays

1   See Gunnar Ollén, *Strindbergs 1900-talslyrik* (Stockholm, 1941), p. 171–3.

2   Quoted from the commentary in SV 51, p. 308.

3   The commentary in SV 51, pp. 253–6.

4   See Peter Hallberg, 'Strindbergs kammarspel', *Edda* 1958, p. 4 and Egil Törnqvist, 'Hamlet och Spöksonaten', *Meddelanden från Strindbergssällskapet*, 37 (1965), pp. 1–17, and '*Hamlet* and *The Ghost Sonata*', *Drama Survey* (Minneapolis), 7:1–2 (1969), 25–41.

5   *Shakspers Dramatiska arbeten* translated by Carl August Hagberg, 1 (Lund, 1892), p. 3.

6   Shakespeare, *Hamlet*, edited by Harold Jenkins, The Arden Shakespeare (London and New York, 1993), pp. 166–7.

7   Martin Lamm, 1926, p. 374.

8   Lamm, 1926, p. 374.

9   See *Samlade Otryckta Skrifter*, II (Stockholm, 1918).

10   See Maurice Maeterlinck, *Théâtre* II (Brussels and Paris, 1902), p. 175.

11   Maeterlinck, 1902, pp. 176–7.

12   Maeterlinck, 1902, p. 176.

13   Maeterlinck, 1902, pp. 183, 186.

14   Maeterlinck, 1902, p. 187. Cf. Lamm, *Det moderna dramat* (Stockholm, 1948), p. 168.

15   In a letter to his German translator Schering on 27 March 1907, which included the manuscript to *The Ghost Sonata*, Strindberg

remarked somewhat condescendingly of *Storm*: 'When you've given me your impression of The Ghost Sonata, I'll send you Opus I of The Chamber Plays, an excellent piece for philistines, which may "work".'

16   In the prose piece 'Lethe' in *A Blue Book I* there is a description of 'The World of the Senses': 'All this web of lies, mistakes, misunderstandings which form the background of our lives changes life itself into something dreamlike and ought to disperse when we pass on to the other life' (SV 65:166). What the passage describes is how in death the memory of every miscalculation vanishes while every elusive hope becomes reality: 'children who have abandoned him, are now seen in their heyday, and "the tiny steps" on the chamber floor, so characteristic of a happy home, he now hears with a sunny smile'.

17   Such pessimistic reactions in anticipation of messages are not unusual in Strindberg's texts. Knowledge is sometimes shunned because it is feared as potentially destructive. See, e.g., the first scene of *To Damascus I* where the Stranger decides not to collect a letter since he believes it has to do with legal proceedings against him and how, in the final scene, he discovers that it contains the money that he has been in need of all along.

18   This connection inspired Sven Delblanc to write the important essay 'Kärlekens föda', *Stormhatten* (Stockholm, 1979).

19   See Barbro Ståhle Sjönell, *Strindbergs Taklagsöl – Ett prosaexperiment* (Stockholm, 1986), p. 123 and p. 185, notes 88 and 89. Cf. Birgitta Ottosson-Pinna, 'Strindbergs levande hus', *Strindbergiana*, 5 (Stockholm, 1990) and Birgitta Steene, 'The house as setting and metaphor in Strindberg's chamber plays', *Nordic Theatre Studies*, 6:1–2 (1993), pp. 37–41.

20   Gunnar Brandell, 'Byggmästaren Ibsen', in *Nordiskt drama – studier och belysningar*, p. 42.

21   'Tobakslådans hemligheter', *Sagor*, SV 52, p. 159.

22   See SgNM 4:5, 1–2.

23   Gaston Bachelard, *La psychanalyse du feu* (Paris, 1995 [1949]), p. 36.

24   Bachelard, *La flamme d'une chandelle* (Paris, 1986 [1961]), p. 12.

25   Bachelard, 1961, p. 16. Cf. the Gentleman's penultimate line: 'It's beginning to grow dark, but then comes understanding and shines its blind lamp, so that one doesn't go down false pathways' (p. 82). 'Blind lamp' is defined in SV as 'A lamp whose light can be dimmed, so that it concentrates the light while at the same time leaving the bearer unilluminated' (p. 447). It is worth noting that in his *La flamme d'une chandelle* Bachelard refers to Strindberg's *Inferno*. Unfortunately he agrees with Jaspers's view that Strindberg suffered from schizophrenia (p. 46) but, in the passage he quotes from *Inferno* in which

Strindberg describes his lamp and his stove, Bachelard notes that rather than affording him contemplative peace, the lamp torments him, 'singing, moaning and whining' as the coal crumbles. Nevertheless, according to Bachelard, this is merely an accident with a certain dignity: 'Mais le désastre est à la fois le plus fin et le plus grand quand il vient de la lumière' (p. 46).

26 In his dissertation on Strindberg's imagery Karl-Åke Kärnell's discussion of the significance of words designating colour focuses primarily on the early writings and concludes that Strindberg – who was also a painter – 'had produced a highly differentiated vocabulary of colours', Kärnell, 1962, p. 99.

27 Anders Fryxell, *Berättelser ur svenska historien* 27 (Stockholm, 1858), p. 118.

28 See Barbro Ståhle Sjönell, 1986, p. 185, note 89. The parallels in *Charles XII* might appear to point in the same direction, but in this drama Strindberg has been bound by historical facts. When it comes to the Gentleman in *Storm* he was free to create a happy ending.

29 Cf. the entry in the Occult Diary for 20 March 1903 and his letter to Bosse of 16 October 1905.

30 Lamm, *August Strindberg*, translated by by Harry G. Carlson (New York, 1971), p. 195.

31 Ibsen, *The Wild Duck*, translated by James McFarlane, *The Oxford Ibsen* vol VI (Oxford, 1960), p. 211.

32 Ibsen, *The Wild Duck*, p. 214.

33 Ibsen, *The Wild Duck*, p. 216.

34 Ibsen, *The Wild Duck*, p. 218.

35 Ibsen, *The Wild Duck*, p. 151.

36 See Ollén, 1982, pp. 499–502. In OD Strindberg writes on 9 January 1907: 'Now I think the darkness comes from her, and I want to free myself. At our last meeting I found her dumber than before, just as snobbish and evil! Black and poisonous!'

37 See Rune Helleday's commentary to the edition in SV 57: 'En blå bok som kommentar till Svarta fanor' (A Blue Book as a Commentary to Black Banners), pp. 334 ff.

38 See, for example, the passage 'Projections' in *A Blue Book I*, p. 203: 'But there are also projections that I cannot explain. Possibly it is so that poets and artists alone possess the ability in everyday life to project their inner images onto a sort of half-reality. It is after all very common for dying people to reveal their spectre to others who are absent, and the living can also appear in visible shape but only to those who bear them in their thoughts.'

39 SgNM 4:7, 4.

40 In his essay '*Sein* und *Schein* in *The Ghost Sonata*', Egil Törnqvist

has underlined this theme in Strindberg's third chamber play. See *Strindbergian Drama* (Uppsala, 1982).

41 Göran Lindström, 'Strindbergs Brända tomten', *Diktaren och hans formvärld*, ed. Rolf Arvidsson, Bernt Olsson and Louise Vinge (Lund, 1975), pp. 99–118.

42 See, for example, the story 'Odlad frukt' (Cultivated Fruit) in *Svenska öden och äventyr I*, SV 10, p. 10.

43 See, Ekman, 'Death angst, death wish: aspects of death in Strindberg's post-Inferno plays', pp. 43 ff.

44 'As you can see from my Chamber plays I have returned to *long* lines and monologues, this from a reading of Clavigo, Stella, etc.'

45 The idea is not a new one for Strindberg; he had already developed it in the foreword to *Miss Julie*, 1888.

46 In different drafts Strindberg uses the word 'mirage' (*hägring*) synonymously with the word 'illusion' (*villa*). It is also used about the false notion of a constant character: 'Mirages. (how when being observed, characters go up in smoke, fall apart, appear to be illusions, only exist in other people's fantasies.)' (SgNM 3:I,13, watermark 1900).

47 See Ollén's (1982) commentary, pp. 395 ff.

48 Ollén, 1982, pp. 411 ff.

49 Cf. Törnqvist, 1982, pp. 186–206.

50 'the world of *The Ghost Sonata* is a charnel-house of guilt, obsessions, madness, and absurdity.' Martin Esslin, *The Theatre of the Absurd*, 3rd ed. (London, 1991 [1961]), p. 353.

51 See Sprinchorn, *Strindberg as Dramatist* (New Haven and London, 1982), p. 266 and Törnqvist, 1982, p. 187.

52 Brandell, 'Frågor utan svar. Något om Strindbergs dialog – och Ibsens', *Nordiskt drama – Studier och belysningar* (Uppsala, 1993).

53 Even in an analysis of the dialogue, it is of interest to note how physical barriers undermine listening. In the opening scene the Woman in Black speaks to the Concierge: '*The Old Man listens, but the audience hears nothing*' (171). At another point Johansson speaks '*inaudibly*' (181) with Hummel, whose answer we overhear in a 'half dialogue': 'So, not at home? You're an idiot! – And the telegraph? – Nothing? — Go on! — Six o'clock tonight? That's good! – The extra number?' (181).

54 In a comprehensive draft of the play (SgNM 4:4:1) Strindberg has written the word 'Pantomimes' (i.e. mimed action) at the head of the page. Törnqvist has carefully registered the presence of action without words in the completed play: 'no less than ten of the forty-nine sequences depend on action without words' (Törnqvist, 1982, p. 184).

55 Törnqvist has highlighted several of the drama's metaphors based on sight. See *Bergman och Strindberg. Spöksonaten – drama och iscensättning, Dramaten 1973* (Stockholm, 1973) pp. 72ff.

56 Müssener, 1965, p. 134.

57 When Strindberg refers to the song in the Third Act (225), he uses 'So it appeared to me' instead of the original 'So it seemed to me'.

58 Lamm is of the opinion that for all its originality, the opening of the Second Act of *The Ghost Sonata* is an example of old-fashioned dramaturgy: 'Despite the fact that he has used a whole Act for the exposition, Strindberg has not succeeded in familiarizing the audience with the situation, and so – much against his normal practice he has to begin the next Act with a conversation between the two servants, who through their gossip inform the audience about the circumstances, just as in the French comedy'. See Lamm, 1926, p. 397. I prefer to see this scene, not as an exposition but as a parody of one. I would argue that *The Ghost Sonata* contains a number of parodied elements directed against certain theatrical conventions. 'The Death Screen' appears as a variation of the screens in, for example, Molière's comedies; a hero's death on stage is parodied in Hummel's exit into the cupboard, and the Second Act's parodied servants – who turn out not to be who they appear to be – complement the Third Act's ravaging Cook. A seasoned theatregoer may well recognize a number of conventional elements only to find them rapidly undermined.

59 SV 64:70. See Hallberg, 1958, pp. 5, 16.

60 *The Works of Shakespeare*, under the editorship of John Dover Wilson (Cambridge, 1957), p. 18.

61 Leif Leifer, 'Den lutrende ild. En studie i symbolikken i Strindbergs kammarspil', *Samlaren* 1960, p. 179.

62 Törnqvist, 1973, p. 82.

63 Törnqvist, 1973, p. 85.

64 Sprinchorn, 1982, p. 268.

65 Hans Lindström, 'Mosaiken i Spöksonaten', *Svensk litteraturtidskrift* 1979:3, p. 31.

66 See 'Evil's Musical Representative' in *En blå bok I*, SV 65, p. 230, and 'Bayreuth' in *En blå bok II*, SV 66, p. 911.

67 Claës Lundin, *Oxygen och Aromasia. Bilder från år 2378 efter en främmande idé* (Stockholm, 1847) p. 7.

68 *Samlade Otryckta Skrifter II* (Stockholm, 1918), p. 128.

69 Peter Szondi, *Theorie des modernen Dramas* (Frankfurt am Main, 1956), p. 56.

70 Esslin, 1991, p. 253.

71 See Ollén, 1982, p. 528.

72 Törnqvist, 1973, p. 78; Sprinchorn, 1982, pp. 269–70.

73 In *The Occult Diary* hallucinations related to scent play a major role in Strindberg's erotic long-distance relationship with Harriet Bosse. On 4 February 1901 he presents an interpretation of this scent: '(Incense = The prayers of the blessed ones)'. The phrase 'witchcraft and madness' from *The Gothic Rooms* is repeated in an entry dated 16 February the same year: 'The strange smell of incense appeared today, more intensely than before. Then the idea struck me that it was (β). I sniffed her letter, and it smelt of incense! – So it is she, in other words! But the smell had become nauseous. At first it was good, uplifting; then it smelt of madness and witchcraft. Finally, nauseous and terrifying.' Similar descriptions are numerous in 1901 and 1902, after which their use diminishes, only to reach a new climax in 1908. The pattern of these diary entries is that 'celery' stands for lechery and 'incense' for purity. His experiences of this absent woman are 'translated' by Strindberg via the scents that he consciously describes as scent hallucinations in *The Gothic Rooms*.

74 '*Faust* and *The Ghost Sonata*', in Wilhelm Friese, ed., *Strindberg und die Deutschsprachigen Länder, Internationale Beiträge zum Tübinger Strindberg-Symposion 1977* (Basel and Stuttgart, 1979), p. 77.

75 Törnqvist, 1979, p. 353.

76 Wolfgang von Goethe, *Faust*. Herausgegeben und erläutert von Erich Trunz, Band III, vierte Auflage (Hamburg, 1959), p. 352.

77 Goethe, 1959, p. 353.

78 Goethe, 1959, p. 354.

79 Goethe, 1959, p. 353.

80 Strindberg himself points out the source. See SV 57, p. 203. Cf. Lamm, [1948] 1961, p. 366.

81 See Ollén's commentary, SV 58, p. 409. Ruben G:son Berg also points to Hoffmann as an inspiration in 'August Strindberg', *Ord och Bild*, 1912:6, p. 304.

82 SV 58, p. 408.

83 August Strindberg, *Spöksonaten* (Lund, 1988 [1964]), p. 97.

84 Strindberg, *Spöksonaten*, 1988.

85 Hans Lindström, *Strindberg och böckerna* I. Skrifter utgivna av Svenska Litteratursällskapet 36 (Uppsala, 1977), p. 137.

86 However, I find Lindström's association with the spiritualist Johan Arckenholtz (1997, p. 8) very noteworthy. Hans Lindström, 'Mosaiken i Spöksonaten' *Svensk litteraturtidskrift*, 1979:3.

87 E. T. A. Hoffmann, *Sämtliche Werke*, ed. Eduard Griesbach, Erster Band (Leipzig, 1900), p. 180.

88 Hoffmann, 1900, p. 209.

89 Hoffmann, 1900, p. 240.

90 See, for example, Lamm, *Strindbergs dramer II*, p. 400. Cf. an entry in
The Occult Diary for 21 April 1907 in which Strindberg elevates the
problem of his 'watered down' food out of its everyday context
through references to the Book of Job and Ezekiel.

91 In a letter following the première to the actor Helge Wahlgren,
dated 2 February 1908, Strindberg emphasizes the importance of
the scent scene: 'And mark the poisonous influence of the flowers
which drives him mad like his father and accounts for his eruption.'
In this note to an actor, Strindberg naturally falls back on arguments
that are psychologically plausible. There is a similar example of
disorientation prompted by outward stimuli in the novella *The Roofing Feast* where a morphine injection causes the protagonist to
embark on a series of capricious associations.

92 Ollén's (1982) commentary, p. 403. SgNM 25 (22): 7, 38.

93 This work was in all three of Strindberg's book collections. See
Hans Lindström, *Strindberg och böckerna I*, pp. 34, 67, 162. One can
read about *tydor* in R. Hylten-Cavallius, chapter III and 73 ff. It is
clear, however, from Strindberg's notes in his last copy of this work
(1864–8) that in this case he used the work mostly for his linguistic
studies.

94 Cf. Axel Herrlin, *Från sekelslutets Lund* (Lund, 1936), p. 148.

95 Szondi, *Theorie des modernen Dramas*, p. 46.

96 Szondi, 1956, p. 47.

97 Cf. Pfister, 1977, p. 182.

98 The student first speaks of his father who had been over-
whelmed by a similar outburst of truth-telling: 'he was tired after
working all day and from the effort of keeping quiet, or talking crap
with the guests [. . .] Then the muzzle slipped, and he spoke on and
on, stripping the entire company bare, one after the other, told every
one of them just how false they were. Then, exhausted, he sat down
on the table and told them to go to hell!' (223)

99 SgNM 4:4, 4.

100 In Strindberg's plays a statue also serves the function of a memorial.
This is again the case in the Second Act of *The Ghost Sonata* where
the white statue represents the Colonel's wife in her younger days.
Strindberg was apparently inspired by a postcard replica of a statue
representing a lifesize woman. He was sent the postcard by his relatives in Austria. On 27 April 1907 he writes to his German translator Emil Schering: 'On a postcard from Mondsee (Salzkammergut)
there's a statue, full size, of Maria Weyerbrunnen. It represents my
deceased sister-in-law, née Uhl. Question 1: Who is the sculptor? 2.
Was she such a famous author or how did she get a statue in marble

in a public place?' The card is now in the Sulzbach collection in the Royal Library in Stockholm. To the letter may be added two texts from *A Blue Book III*: 'A Statue of His Own' and 'His Ideal'. 'A Statue of His Own' records how 'A postcard recently arrived in my hands. It represented a monumental fountain with a woman above it, in white marble, natural size [. . .]. But I remember her in situations that did her no honour. [. . .]. And now, after her death, he raises a marble statue in a public place. Is it to himself? I might ask. Yes, he has raised it to himself, to the memory of the beautiful things he put into her soul, which I never saw' (SS 48, p. 851). See Ekman, 'Death angst, death wish: aspects of death in Strindberg's post–Inferno plays'. p. 46 and *passim*.

101   Göran Lindström's edition of *The Ghost Sonata* contains a thorough study of Strindberg's borrowings. See pp. 84–6.

102   See Sprinchorn, 1982, p. 254.

103   Cf. *Storm*: 'The four shades look like theatre curtains behind which bloody dramas are being rehearsed' (p. 15).

104   In a letter to Schering, 30 April 1907, he mentions the doctrine of reminiscence in passing.

105   Added notation on page 201 B.

106   Plato, *Phaido*, Loeb Classical Library, ed. H. N. Fowler (Cambridge, Mass., 1966), pp. 227 and 289.

107   Plato, *Valda skrifter* IV, transl. Magnus Dalsjö (Stockholm, 1896). See Lindström, *Strindberg och böckerna* I, p. 109. The book is numbered 5373 in the Strindberg library.

108   Plato, *Timaeus*, Loeb Classical Library, ed. R. G. Bury (Cambridge, Mass., 1966), p. 101.

109   *Timaeus* (1966), p. 137.

110   Plato, Dalsjö's commentary to the *Timaeus* (1896), p. 298.

111   *Timaeus* (1896), p. 298.

112   *Timaeus* (1966), p. 121.

113   Emanuel Swedenborg, *Om himlen och dess underbara ting och om helvetet. På grund av vad som blivit hört och sett*, translated by Gustaf Bæckström (Stockholm, 1944) p. 341.

114   Swedenborg, 1944, p. 341.

115   Swedenborg, 1944, p. 380.

116   For an English version of *Toten-Insel* with commentary, see *The Pelican and The Isle of the Dead*, Studies in Drama and Dance, edited and translated by Michael Robinson (Birmingham, 1994).

117   *Rig-Veda*. Übersetzt und mit kritischen und erläuternden Abmerkungen versehen von Hermann Grassman. Zweiter Theil (Leipzig, 1877), p. 400. Nr. 2288 in the Strindberg library. See *The Occult Diary*, for example, 5 June, 18 June and 29 August 1904,

7 April and 5 May 1907. The notes indicate that Strindberg often viewed rainbows as augurs of something good. It is probable that he associated them with a passage in Genesis 9:13, where the rainbow is a sign that there will be no second flood.

118 *Kâthaka-Upanishad*, translated from the Sanskrit by Andrea Butenschön (Stockholm, 1902), p. 40. Nr. 1174 in the Strindberg library.

119 *Kâthaka-Upanishad* (1902), p. 60.

120 Nathan Söderblom, *Främmande religionsurkunder*, I (Stockholm, 1907) p. 96.

121 *Främmande religionsurkunder*, I (1907), p. 27.

122 *Främmande religionsurkunder*, II, section one (Stockholm, 1908), pp. 230 and 626.

123 See Strindberg's letter to Schering, 26 April 1907.

124 See Strindberg's letter to Schering, 19 June 1907.

125 Until the very end of the play the Gentleman in *Storm* believes he is tied to the apartment but is not locked up in it: 'I've become immobile, I'm bound to this apartment by memories . . . only in there can I find peace and protection' (p. 17).

126 See above, p. 117.

127 Gösta M. Bergman, 1966, p. 286.

128 Leif Leifer analyses the motif in his essay 'Den lutrende ild' (*Samlaren* 1960): 'Fire is the great mystic symbol of the chamber plays, harbouring the polarities in life – uniting annihilation, purification, and rebirth. As a symbol of purification, it replaces water, which appears in *To Damascus II*, Act 4, In the Ravine. In *A Dream Play* fire is emphasized at the expense of water; fire is the total destroyer' (p. 193). I would add that the water in *A Dream Play* as well as in *The Ghost Sonata* symbolizes a passive form of purity. See, Ekman, *Klädernas magi. En Strindbergsstudie*, p. 118. I do not interpret the fire in a biographical-psychological way but see it rather as a symbol in interplay with other symbols.

129 'Their constantly feeling cold is caused less by the lack of proper heating than by Elise's icy nature', Törnqvist, 1982, p. 211.

130 *Strindbergs dramer* II, p. 400. In his review in *Svenska Dagbladet* following the première on 27 November 1907, August Brunius writes of an 'eternal squabble regarding food and fuel' (SV 58, p. 429).

131 Törnqvist, 1982, p. 211. Törnqvist convincingly rejects Lamm's simplistic explanation for the presence of all these references to food: 'We can now see that the frequent references to food, far from being a testimony to Strindberg's failure to keep household problems outside the play, form an integral part of a larger thematic pattern, which structurally helps to keep the play together. Taking

these references at their face value means misunderstanding their true metaphorical function. [. . .] In these metaphors Strindberg has seen a possibility to express inner processes in a theatrically effective way. Theatre, we must remember, is a physical medium asking for stageable imagery' (p. 211). I share Törnqvist's view that Strindberg sees the theatre as something physical, but the fact is that food is visible on only one occasion in *The Pelican* (p. 289). I would argue that the references to food, which are almost all entirely verbal, are used to illustrate a form of deception, illusion, which is rather the opposite of the concreteness that Törnqvist finds.

132   In *Hamlet* the association of foul smell with moral decrepitude is a frequent one. In *Leka med elden* the Friend blurts out the line: 'And I think myself that the source of the whole of the rotten smell that pervades this house is you!' (SV 33, p. 270). That even a pleasant smell can be deceptive, as in the Third Act of *The Ghost Sonata*, is something that Strindberg has learned from Swedenborg: 'She only cares about a moral life on the exterior and in that way becomes a dual person, a sheep on the exterior, a wolf on the interior. She's like a gold box that contains poison. Or someone with bad breath who chews on fine-smelling spices so that those nearby won't notice anything. Or she's like a perfumed rat's skin.' Swedenborg, *Vera Christiana Religio*, § 568.

133   See Ollén's (1983) comment, p. 463.

134   See Leifer, (1960), p. 191.

135   Among the merits of Peter Hallberg's essay 'Strindbergs kammarspel' (*Edda* 1958, pp. 1–21) is the emphasis he places on Shakespearian influences. Regarding *The Pelican* he thus concludes: 'The Pelican is a Hamlet drama in a confined bourgeois milieu' (p. 17). Cf. Törnqvist, '*Hamlet* and *The Ghost Sonata*', *Meddelanden från Strindbergssällskapet*, 37 (1965) pp. 1–17. For an English version of this essay see '*Hamlet* and *The Ghost Sonata*', *Drama Survey* (Minneapolis), 7:1–2 (1969), 25–44.

136   It is the Mother who is alluded to in the play's ironic title. Strindberg may also have derived this idea from *Hamlet*. In Act IV, scene 5 Laertes says: 'To his good friends thus wide I'll ope my arms,/And, like the kind life-rendering pelican,/Repast them with my blood.'

137   See, Ekman, 'Death angst, death wish: aspects of death in Strindberg's post-Inferno plays', p. 35.

138   Act II, scene 2, 56–7.

139   Act V, scene 1, 72–3.

140   Towards the end of the last Act the three knocks are heard again, only this time they are also audible to the audience (292).

141   It is worth remarking here that in *Miss Julie* Jean also describes how

he once picked elderberry flowers and then laid down among them in an oat–bin (SV 27, p. 142).

142 Pfister, 1977, p. 136.

143 'By putting the language of a scene in contrast to the action, by reducing it to meaningless patter, or by abandoning discursive logic for the poetic logic of association or assonance, the Theatre of the Absurd has opened up a new dimension of the stage,' Esslin, 1991, p. 406.

144 SV 51, p. 24.

145 Kerstin Dahlbäck calls the letter 'a nineteenth–century dramatic plot element *par préférence*'. '"Det stängda rummet" några reflektioner kring postkontor och brev i Till Damaskus I', *Poesi och vetande*, ed. Urpu–Liisa Karahka and Anders Olsson (Stockholm, 1979), p. 96.

146 In a letter dated 14 October 1884.

147 She herself calls it a 'window' (p. 295). The expression 'balcony door' is therefore only apparent to a reader of the text, not to the theatre audience.

148 Pfister, 1977, p. 126–7.

Select Bibliography

UNPUBLISHED MATERIAL

Royal Library, Stockholm

The Nordic Museum's Strindberg Collection (SgNM), 3:1,6, 3:1,10, 3:1,11, 3:1,13, 3:1,16, 31I,17,2, 3:22,62, 4:4,1, 4:4,2, 4:4,4, 4:5, 1–2, 4:7,4, 4:19,1–9, 4:23,1, 9:2,3, 24(22):7,38.
The Occult Diary (SgNM 72).
Three notebooks with notations regarding Swedish nature (SgNM, unsign.).
Typewritten copy of 'The Fifth Letter' (I:SgNM:17).
Des Arts Nouveaux! Où Le Hasard dans la production artistique (manuscript, SgNM 6:17,12).
Letter from Hjalmar Öhrvall 13 December 1890.

Uppsala University Library, Uppsala

Manuscript of Études Funèbres, part 1 (Söderblom Collection).

Royal Library, Copenhagen

Manuscript of 'Sensations détraquées' (Ny Kgl. Saml. 2943.40).

PUBLISHED MATERIAL

Abbé de l'Epée, *Institution des sourdes et muets par la voie des signes méthodiques* (Paris, 1776).
Ahlström, Stellan, *Strindbergs erövring av Paris. Strindberg och Frankrike 1884–1895.* Diss. Stockholm (Stockholm, 1956).
Bachelard, Gaston, *La flamme d'une chandelle* [1961], 8e édition (Paris, 1986).
Bachelard, Gaston, *La psychanalyse du feu* [1949] (Paris 1995).
Berg, Ruben G:son, 'August Strindberg', *Ord och Bild* 1912 nr 6.
Bergman, Gösta M., *Den moderna teaterns genombrott 1890–1925* (Stockholm, 1966).
Bergquist, Lars, *Swedenborgs drömbok. Glädjen och det stora kvalet* (Stockholm, 1989).

Brandes, George, *Wolfgang Goethe* II, tredie Utgave (Köpenhamn, 1920).

Brandell, Gunnar, 'Byggmästare Ibsen', *Nordiskt drama – studier och belysningar*. Skrifter utgivna av Svenska Litteratursällskapet 43 (Uppsala, 1993).

Brandell, Gunnar, 'Forskning om drama', *Nordiskt drama – studier och belysningar*. Skrifter utgivna av Svenska Litteratursällskapet 43 (Uppsala, 1993).

Brandell, Gunnar, 'Frågor utan svar. Något om Strindbergs dialog – och Ibsens', *Nordiskt drama — Studier och belysningar*. Skrifter utgivna av Svenska Litteratursällskapet 43 (Uppsala, 1993).

Brandell, Gunnar, *Strindberg – Ett författarliv* 1–4 (Stockholm, 1987, 1985, 1983, 1989).

Brandell, Gunnar, *Strindberg in Inferno* [1950]. Trans. Barry Jacobs (Cambridge, Massachusetts, 1974).

Bååth, Albert Ulrich, *Dikter* (Stockholm, 1879).

Carlsson, Harry G., *Genom Inferno, Bildens magi och Strindbergs förnyelse*. Övers. Gun R. Bengtsson (Stockholm, 1995).

Cullberg, Johan, *Skaparkriser. Strindbergs inferno – och Dagermans* (Stockholm, 1992).

Dahlbäck, Kerstin, ' "Det stängda rummet", några reflexioner kring postkontor och brev i Till Damaskus I. *Poesi och vetande*, red. Urpu-Liisa Karahka och Anders Olsson (Stockholm, 1979).

Delblanc, Sven, 'Kärlekens föda', *Stormhatten* (Stockholm, 1979).

Ekman, Hans-Göran, 'Death angst, death wish: aspects of death in Strindberg's post-Inferno plays', *Strindberg's Post-Inferno Plays. Lectures Given at The 11th International Strindberg Conference*, ed. Kela Kvam (Copenhagen, 1994).

Ekman, Hans-Göran, *Klädernas magi. En Strindbergstudie* (Stockholm, 1991).

Ekman, Hans-Göran, 'Pröva på – vattnet är icke farligt!' *Parnass* 1995 nr 1.

Ekman, Hans-Göran, 'Strindberg's senses, symbols and synesthesia'. *The Moscow Papers*, ed. Michael Robinson (Stockholm, 1998).

Erlande-Brandenburg, Alain, *The Lady and the Unicorn: Sight, Hearing, Taste, Smell, A mon Seul Désir* (Paris, 1989).

Esslin, Martin, *The Theatre of the Absurd* [1961] 3rd ed. (London, 1991).

Floridor (sign.), *Recension sv Fröken Julie. Dagens Nyheter* 19/12 1906.

Fryxell, Anders, *Berättelser ur svenska historien* 27 (Stockholm, 1858).

Gierow, Carl-Olof, *Documentation – évocation. Le Climat Littéraire et théâtral en France des années 1880 et 'Mademoiselle Julie' de Strindberg*. Acta Universitatis Stockholmiensis. Romanica Stockholmiensia 3. Diss Stockholm (Stockholm, 1967).

Girard, Gilles, Oullet, Réal, Rigault, Claude, *L'univers du théâtre*. 3e édition revue et corrigée (Paris, 1995).

Goethe, Wolfgang von, *Faust*. Herausgegeben und erläutert von Erich Trunz, Band III, vierte Auflage (Hamburg, 1959).

Hallberg, Peter, 'Strindbergs kammarspel', *Edda* 1958 (Oslo, 1958).

Hansson, Ola, *Dikter* (Stockholm, 1884).

Hansson, Ola, *Samlade skrifter* II (Stockholm, 1920).

Hellqvist, Per Anders, 'Aufschwung. Melodram för en pianist'. *Artes* 1994, nr 1.

Hellqvist, Per Anders, *Ton och tystnad. Tankar, iakttagelser och samtal om musik* (Stockholm, 1992).

Hemmingsson, Per, *August Strindberg som fotograf*, 2:a uppl. (Stockholm, 1989).

Herrlin, Axel, *Från sekelslutets Lund* (Lund, 1936).

Hoffmann, E.T.A., 'Der goldene Topf'. Sämtliche Werke in fünfzehn Bänden. 1 (Leipzig, 1900).

Hyltén-Cavallius, Gunnar Olof, *Wärend och Wirdarne* I (Stockholm, 1921).

Jacobs, Barry, 'Bland amerikanska läsare och kritiker: Strindberg i översättning', *August Strindberg och hans översättare. Föredrag vid symposium i Vitterhetsakademien 8 september 1994*, red. Björn Meidal och Nils Åke Nilsson, Kungl. Vitterhets Historie och Antikvitets Akademien. Konferenser 33 (Stockholm, 1995).

Kâthaka-Upanishad, öfvers. från sanskrit af Andrea Butenschön (Stockholm, 1902).

Kärnell, Karl-Åke, *Strindbergs bildspråk. En studie i prosastil*. Diss. Stockholm (Stockholm, 1962).

Lamm, Martin, *August Strindberg* [1948]. Transl. and ed. by Harry G. Carlson (New York, 1971).

Lamm, Martin, *Det moderna dramat* (Stockholm, 1948).

Lamm, Martin, *Strindbergs dramer* II (Stockholm, 1926).

Laurin, Carl, Recension av Fröken Julie i *Ord och Bild* 1907.

Leifer, Leif, 'Den lutrende ild. En studie i symbolikken i Strindbergs kammerspil', *Samlaren* 1960.

Lindström, Göran, 'Strindbergs Brända tomten', *Diktaren och hans formvärld*, red. Rolf Arvidsson, Bernt Olsson och Louise Vinge (Lund, 1975).

Lindström, Hans, 'Mosaiken i Spöksonaten', *Svensk litteraturtidskrift* 1979, nr 3.

Lindström, Hans, *Strindberg och böckerna*. Skrifter utgivna av Svenska Litteratursällskapet 36 (Uppsala, 1977).

Linné, Carl von *Linnæi Skånska Resa förrätttad år 1749*. Red. Carl-Otto von Sydow (Stockholm, 1982).

Lundin, Claës, *Oxygen och Aromasia. Bilder från år 2378 efter en främmande idé.* (Stockholm, 1847).

Långbacka, Ralf, *Möten med Tjechov* (Stockholm, 1986).

Maeterlinck, Maurice, *Théâtre* II (Bruxelles och Paris, 1902).

Magarshack, David, *Chekhov the Dramatist* (New York, 1960).

Montaigne, *Essais*. Texte établi et annoté par Albert Thibaudet. Bibliothèque de la Pléiade 14 (Paris, 1933).

Müssener, Helmut, *August Strindberg, 'Ein Traumspiel'. Struktur- und Stilstudien*. Diss. Mainz (Meisenheim am Glan, 1965).

Ollén, Gunnar, *Strindbergs dramatik*, 4:e uppl. (Stockholm, 1982).

Ollén, Gunnar, *Strindbergs 1900-talslyrik*. Diss. Stockholm (Stockholm, 1941).

Ottosson-Pinna, Birgitta, 'Strindbergs levande hus', *Strindbergiana*, femte samlingen (Stockholm, 1990).

Paul, Adolf, *Min Strindbergsbok* (Stockholm, 1930).

Pfister, Manfred, *Das Drama. Theorie und Analüse* (München, 1977).

Platon, *Valda skrifter* I, övers. Magnus Dalsjö (Stockholm, 1896).

Rig-Veda. Übersetzt und mit kritischen und erläuternden Anmerkungen versehen von Hermann Grassman. Zweiter Theil (Leipzig, 1877).

Robinson, Michael, *The Pelican and The Isle of the Dead*. Studies in Drama and Dance (Birmingham, 1994).

Schleich, Carl Ludwig, *Hågkomster om Strindberg*. Övers. Gustaf Lindelöf (Stockholm, 1917).

Shakespeare, *The Works of Shakespeare* under the editorship of John Dover Wilson (Cambridge, 1957).

Shakespeare, *Hamlet*, edited by Harold Jenkins. The Arden Shakespeare (London and New York, 1993).

Shakspers Dramatiska arbeten öfversatta af Carl August Hagberg 1, 7, 9 (Lund, 1892–1899).

Sprinchorn, Evert, *Strindberg as Dramatist* (New Haven and London, 1982).

Starobinski, Jean, *Montaigne en mouvement* (Paris, 1982).

Steene, Birgitta, 'The house as setting and metaphor in Strindberg's chamber plays', *Nordic Theatre Studies*, Vol 6/1–2 (Oxford, 1993).

Stockenström, Göran, *Ismael i öknen, Strindberg som mystiker*. Acta Universitatis Upsaliensis. Historia litterarum 5. Diss. Uppsala (Uppsala, 1972).

Strindberg, August, *Brev 1–15*. Utgivna av Torsten Eklund (Stockholm, 1948–1976).

Strindberg, August, *Brev 16–20*. Utgivna av Björn Meidal (Stockholm, 1989–1996).

Strindberg, August, *Dikter på vers och prosa. Sömngångarnätter och strödda tidiga dikter*, SV 15, red. James Spens (Stockholm, 1995).

Strindberg, August, *Dödsdansen*, SV 44, red. Hans Lindström (Stockholm, 1988).

Strindberg, August, *En blå bok I*, SV 65, red. Gunnar Ollén. (Stockholm 1997).

Strindberg, August, *En blå bok II*, SV 66, red. Gunnar Ollén (Stockholm 1998).

Strindberg, August, *En blå bok III*, SS 48 (Stockholm, 1918).

Strindberg, August, *Ensam, Sagor*, SV 52, red. Ola Östin (Stockholm, 1994).

Strindberg, August, *Ett drömspel*, SV 46, red. Gunnar Ollén (Stockholm, 1988).

Strindberg, August, *'Études funèbres'*, La Revue des Revues 1896 vol. XVII (Paris, 1896).

Strindberg, August, *Fadren, Fröken Julie, Fordringsägare*, SV 27, red. Gunnar Ollén (Stockholm, 1984).

Strindberg, August, *Folkungasagan, Gustav Vasa, Erik XIV*, SV 41, red. Gunnar Ollén (Stockholm, 1992).

Strindberg, August, *Götiska rummen*, SS 40 (Stockholm, 1916).

Strindberg, August, *Hövdingaminnen*, SS 43 (Stockholm, 1921).

Strindberg, August, *I havsbandet*, SV 31, red. Hans Lindström (Stockholm, 1982).

Strindberg, August, *Inferno och Legender*, SS 28 (Stockholm, 1919).

Strindberg, August, *Inferno*, SV 37, red. Ann-Charlotte Gavel Adams (Stockholm, 1994).

Strindberg, August, *I Vårbrytningen*, SV 2, red. Carl Reinhold Smedmark (Stockholm, 1981).

Strindberg, August, *Kammarspel*. (Oväder, Brända tomten, Spök-sonaten, Pelikanen, Svarta handsken), SV 58, red. Gunnar Ollén (Stockholm, 1991).

Strindberg, August, *Karl XII, Engelbrekt*, SV 47, red. Gunnar Ollén (Stockholm, 1993).

Strindberg, August, *Klostret, Fagervik och Skamsund*, SV 50, red. Barbro Ståhle Sjönell (Stockholm, 1994).

Strindberg, August, *Kristina, Gustav III*, SV 48, red. Gunnar Ollén (Stockholm, 1988).

Strindberg, August, *Likt och olikt* II, SS 17 (Stockholm, 1913).

Strindberg, August, *Midsommar, Kaspers fet-tisdag, Påsk*, SV 443, red. Gunnar Ollén (Stockholm, 1992).

Strindberg, August, *Nio enaktare 1888–1892*, SV 33, red. Gunnar Ollén (Stockholm, 1989).

Strindberg, August, *Ordalek och småkonst*, SV 51, red. Gunnar Ollén (Stockholm, 1989).

Strindberg, August, *Le Playdoyer d'un fou*. Ed. Lars Dahlbäck och Göran

Rossholm. Svenska författare utgivna av Svenska vitterhetssamfundet XXIII (Stockholm, 1978).

Strindberg, August, *Prosabitar från 1880-talet*, SS 22 (Stockholm, 1914).

Strindberg, August, *Prosabitar från 1890-talet*, SS 27 (Stockholm, 1917).

Strindberg, August, *Röda rummet*, SV 6, red. Carl Reinhold Smedmark (Stockholm, 1981).

Strindberg, August, *Samlade Otryckta Skrifter* II (Stockholm, 1918).

Strindberg, August, 'Sensations détraquées', *Le Figaro littéraire*, november 1894, januari 1895 (Paris 1894–1895).

Strindberg, August, *Spöksonaten*, 'Klassiker'. Förord och kommentarer av Göran Lindström (Lund 1988).

Strindberg, August, *Svarta fanor*, SV 57, red. Rune Helleday (Stockholm, 1995).

Strindberg, August, *Svenska öden och äventyr* I, SV 10, red. Bengt Landgren (Stockholm, 1981).

Strindberg, August, *Till Damaskus*, SV 39, red. Gunnar Ollén (Stockholm, 1991).

Strindberg, August, *Ungdomsdramer II*, SV 3, red. Birger Liljestrand (Stockholm 1991).

Strindberg, August, 'Un regard vers le Ciel et les 23 degrés', *L'Initiation* Avril 1896 (Paris, 1896).

Strindberg, August, *Utopier i verkligheten*, SV 19, red. Sven-Gustaf Edqvist (Stockholm, 1990).

Strindberg, August, *Vid högre rätt (Advent, Brott och brott)* SV 40, red. Hans-Göran Ekman (Stockholm, 1983).

Strindberg, August, *Vivisektioner, Blomstermålningar och djurstycken, Skildringar av naturen, Silverträsket*, SV 29, red. Hans Lindström (Stockholm, 1985).

Strindberg, August, *Teater och Intima Teatern*. SV 64, red. Per Stam (Stockholm, 1999).

Ståhle Sjönell, Barbro, *Strindbergs Taklagsöl–Ett prosaexperiment*. Diss. Stockholm (Stockholm, 1986).

Swedenborg, Emanuel, *Memorabilier. Minnesanteckningar från himlar och helveten*. Urval och övers. Carl-Göran Ekerwald (Stockholm, 1988).

Swedenborg, Emanuel, *Om himlen och dess underbara ting och om helvetet. På grund av vad som blivit hört och sett*. Översatt från latin av Gustaf Bæckström (Stockholm, 1944).

Swedenborg, Emanuel, *The Five Senses*. Transl. from the Latin by Enoch S. Price (Philadelphia, 1914).

Szondi, Peter, *Theorie des modernen Dramas* (Frankfurt am Main, 1956).

Söderblom, Nathan, *Främmande religionsurkunder*. I–II (Stockholm, 1907–1908).

Törnqvist, Egil, *Bergman och Strindberg, Spöksonaten – drama och iscensättning. Dramaten 1973* (Stockholm, 1973).

Törnqvist, Egil, '*Faust* and *The Ghost Sonata*', *Strindberg und die deutschsprachigen Länder, Internationale Beiträge zum Tübinger Strindberg-Symposion 1977.* Beiträge zur nordischen Philologie 8, ed. Wilhelm Friese (Basel und Stuttgart, 1979).

Törnqvist, Egil, 'Hamlet och Spöksonaten', *Meddelanden från Strindbergssällskapet* 1965 nr 37.

Törnqvist, Egil, *Strindbergian Drama. Themes and Structure.* Svenska Litteratursällskapets skrifter 37 (Uppsala, 1982).

Valency, Maurice, *The Breaking String. The Plays of Anton Chekhov* (New York, 1966).

Vinge, Louise, *The Five Senses. Studies in a Literary Tradition.* Skrifter utgivna av Kungliga Humanistiska Vetenskapssamfundet i Lund. LXXII (Lund, 1975).

Wirmark, Margareta, *Kampen med döden. En studie över Strindbergs Dödsdansen*, Skrifter utgivna av Svenska Litteratursällskapet 41 (Uppsala, 1989).

Zola, Émile, *Le Ventre de Paris*, Les Œuvres complètes 4 (Paris, 1927).

Ögonvittnen. August Strindberg. Mannahår och ålderdom. Red. Stellan Ahlström och Torsten Eklund (Stockhom, 1961).

Öhrvall, Hjalmar, *Om sinnesvillor.* Verdandi småskrifter 250–251 (Stockholm, 1921).

Name and Title Index